CULTIVATING SOCIAL JUSTICE TEACHERS

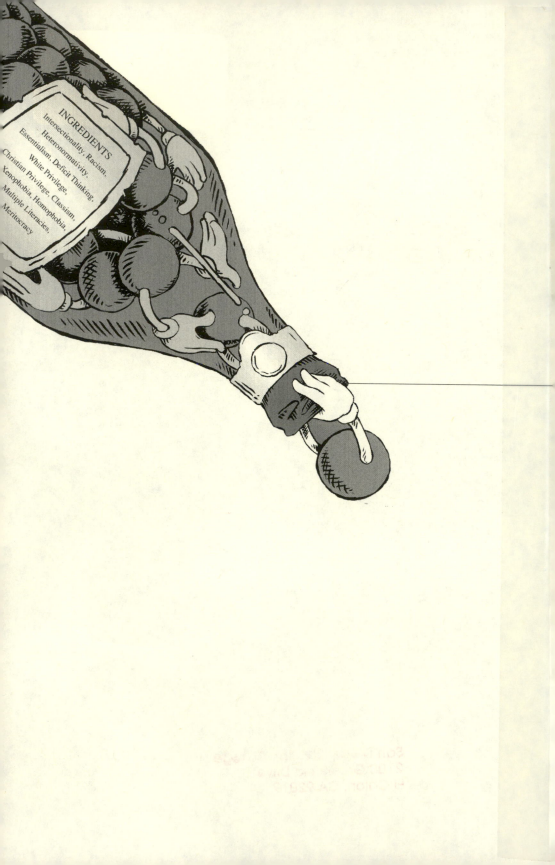

INGREDIENTS

Intersectionality, Racism,
Heteronormativity,
Essentialism, Deficit Thinking,
White Privilege,
Christian Privilege, Classism,
Xenophobia, Homophobia,
Multiple Literacies,
Meritocracy

CULTIVATING SOCIAL JUSTICE TEACHERS

How Teacher Educators Have Helped Students
Overcome Cognitive Bottlenecks and Learn
Critical Social Justice Concepts

EDITED BY

Paul C. Gorski, Kristien Zenkov,
Nana Osei-Kofi, and Jeff Sapp

Foreword by David Stovall

STERLING, VIRGINIA

COPYRIGHT © 2013 BY
STYLUS PUBLISHING, LLC.

Published by Stylus Publishing, LLC
22883 Quicksilver Drive
Sterling, Virginia 20166-2102

Library of Congress Cataloging-in-Publication Data
Cultivating social justice teachers : how teacher educators
have helped students overcome cognitive bottlenecks and
learn critical social justice concepts / edited by Paul C.
Gorski . . . [et al.] ; foreword by David Stovall.—1st ed.
   p. cm.
Includes bibliographical references and index.
ISBN 978-1-57922-887-3 (cloth : alk. paper)
ISBN 978-1-57922-888-0 (pbk. : alk. paper)
ISBN 978-1-57922-889-7 (library networkable e-edition)
ISBN 978-1-57922-890-3 (consumer e-edition)
1. Teachers—Training of—United States.   2. Social
justice—Study and teaching (Graduate)—United States.
3. Critical pedagogy—United States.   I. Gorski, Paul.
LB1715.C83   2013
370.71'10973—dc23   2012029622

13-digit ISBN: 978-1-57922-887-3 (cloth)
13-digit ISBN: 978-1-57922-888-0 (paper)
13-digit ISBN: 978-1-57922-889-7 (library networkable
e-edition)
13-digit ISBN: 978-1-57922-890-3 (consumer e-edition)

Printed in the United States of America

All first editions printed on acid-free paper
that meets the American National Standards Institute
Z39-48 Standard.

Bulk Purchases

Quantity discounts are available for use in workshops
and for staff development.
Call 1-800-232-0223

First Edition, 2013

10   9   8   7   6   5   4   3   2   1

From Paul C. Gorski

For Walter Enloe, Vivian Johnson, Carol Mayer, and Barbara Swanson,
with love, respect, and a million thanks, for making me want to be
a better and more collaborative teacher and for modeling for me
just exactly how to do it.

From Kristien Zenkov

For my Mom and Dad, who continue to share the everyday principles
and practices of social justice with your kids and the world through
your work and your words and your art.

From Nana Osei-Kofi

Till minne av Agneta Osei-Kofi (1944–2006).
[In memory of Agneta Osei-Kofi (1944–2006).]

From Jeff Sapp

For my Mother and Father, Helen and Bill, who truly have taught me what
it means to be a dynamic and authentic Christian.

CONTENTS

Into the Messiness: Struggle, Defeat, and the Victory Condition in Troubling Times

The institution of marriage is not under attack as a result of the President's words. Marriage was under attack years ago by men who viewed women as property and children as trophies of sexual prowess. Marriage is under attack by low wages, high incarceration, unfair tax policy, unemployment, and lack of education. Marriage is under attack by clergy who proclaim monogamy yet think nothing of stepping outside the bonds of marriage to have multiple affairs with "preaching groupies." Same-gender couples did not cause the high divorce rate, but our adolescent views of relationships and our inability as a community to come to grips with the ethic of love and commitment did. We still confuse sex with love and romance with commitment.

—Rev. Otis Moss III, pastor,
Trinity United Church of Christ

P aul C. Gorski, Nana Osei-Kofi, Kristien Zenkov, and Jeff Sapp have dedicated time, space, and will to create a timely edited volume on the complex realities of teaching for social justice in teacher education programs. In light of their efforts, I find the foregoing epigraph necessary and challenging. Although not the topic of their volume, the most recent same-sex marriage debate provides a relevant parallel to the current state of teacher education. For some, Rev. Moss's words speak what many feel should never be spoken given the myriad of concerns in many African American communities. His comments represent the proverbial airing of "dirty laundry" that should be discussed only in the company of family or extremely close friends. To this day, for a number of African American Christian congregations, Rev. Moss's words represent blasphemy. Any discussion of same-sex relationships is considered an affront to the "values" of good, God-fearing folks. However, on the opposite end of the spectrum a culture of silence has plagued the Black church while a considerable portion of its membership spend their lives living in fear of persecution and removal.

In teacher education, we have lived in a silence of ineptitude while capable teachers of color have been refused admission to colleges of education in the name of "academic excellence." Simultaneously, the vast majority of White women who graduate from teacher preparation programs and populate the majority of the teaching force remain underprepared to engage the realities of marginalization, racialization, and criminalization in schools. As Moss sheds light on the necessity of equity, he also poses a challenge for his colleagues and congregation to come to grips with the pain of silence and denial. *We need to do the same in teacher preparation programs.*

The editors of this volume present us with chapters by comrade authors who openly discuss the difficulties encountered by those who have made a conscious attempt to break the silence in teacher preparation programs. Through their realities we are reminded of the ever-present mantra in any discussion of social justice in K–20 education: *Good teaching is hard work.* Just think for a moment about the times we're living in: The state of Texas has banned the word "capitalism" in textbooks, Raza Studies in Tucson public schools has been declared illegal resulting in a banned-books campaign, collective bargaining has all but ended in the state of Wisconsin, several urban centers are developing merit-based pay programs for teachers while operating under mayoral control, and the media corporate baron Rupert Murdock has recently become a vendor for Chicago Public Schools by way of assessment evaluation. Yes, for critically conscious, justice-minded teacher educators, this is enough to make us pull our hair out and run screaming from wherever we're sitting. In my quiet time I'm fearful that, if I close my eyes for too long, I might wake up to find that someone has decided to test how kindergarteners go to the bathroom and will make that part of the assessment for graduating to first grade. Understanding this as a strange possibility, we have to ask another question: How do we in good faith train K–12 teachers to go out into this madness if we're not willing to stand in solidarity with them? To my delight, the editors have taken this task head-on.

Despite the fact that the newly crowned educational "reformers" know very little about education, they make our efforts as social justice educators even more difficult with their framing of the problem. It's very difficult to argue a "golden age" of education for historically marginalized and disinvested communities. Education management organizations (EMOs) swoop down like vultures and play on the desperation of disaffected families with rhetoric that suggests, "Anything is better than what you currently have." I find this sentiment emblematic of the larger colonial project as Western European states in the mid-twentieth century would exacerbate conflicts between ethnic and regional groups, while convincing the group in power that things would be best if there were continual contact with the colonial power. In the current instance, some EMOs present themselves as "true" reformers by providing families with the façade of quality education. Often going unspoken is the reality that these "new" schools engage draconian discipline practices and test-score schemes to raise scores. Unmentioned is the fact that many schools run by EMOs (most notably charters) have policies that dismiss low-performing students while claiming high graduation rates and "rising" test scores. Further impacting this space is that charter and contract schools are the few spaces where teachers of color who went through alternative certification programs are provided with teaching positions. Oddly, teacher education programs largely are silent about these conditions, failing to prepare future teachers for the mess they're about to step in. These are the kinds of issues faced head-on in *Cultivating Social Justice Teachers*, where authors discuss how they have come to find and enact strategies to prepare teachers to see these conditions and to teach for social justice.

In this way, the editors have embarked on a journey on which few teacher educators have been willing, or have known how, to go. The "messiness" we talk about in doing educational justice work cannot be dismissed as "touchy-feely" attempts to bond with our students. Instead of race, class, gender, sexuality, ability, disinvestment, and marginalization as add-ons for teacher education programs, they must be the focal points through which we engage the possibilities of justice. To their credit, the editors engage the fact that the larger justice project in education requires relationship building beyond the walls of our classrooms. In these spaces our hearts and souls are challenged to face what sometimes appear to be insurmountable odds. These are the spaces where tenure is not guaranteed. You will not be liked by the masses for supporting educational justice initiatives at the grassroots level. You will not be the first choice for "faculty of the year." Instead, your commitment will live in the words and actions of your students. In these spaces the larger justice project is actualized.

I commend my comrades for taking on such a task. I am thankful for their willingness to fight. Stirring up trouble is something that many are unwilling to do in such troubling times. Through this edited volume their struggle continues the legacy of activist, community-based, justice-minded scholars who have come before them. I hope that you, as a reader, are encouraged by this book to research, reflect, act, and raise hell with a purpose. We will not achieve justice if we sit idly by and watch the neoliberal avalanche ravage public education, including teacher education.

As always, I am humbled by Paul, Nana, Kristien, and Jeff's willingness to allow me to contribute to their endeavor. For these reasons, I stand with them eternally in solidarity.

David Stovall
June 28, 2012

INTRODUCTION

Paul C. Gorski, Nana Osei-Kofi, Kristien Zenkov, and Jeff Sapp

Consider the challenge of introducing the concept of "heteronormativity" to a classroom predominantly comprised of heterosexual teacher candidates who are relatively new to conversations about homophobia and heterosexism. Imagine you are teaching a course on social justice or multicultural education, perhaps the only class your students will take that will broach these topics explicitly. You are charged with facilitating experiences that will prepare future teachers to understand, both conceptually and pragmatically, what it means to create an equitable and just learning environment for every student and family. Given your experience and expertise, however limited you acknowledge them to be, you believe that, for your students to grasp concepts like heterosexism or to strengthen their abilities to recognize subtle forms of heterosexual privilege in their pedagogies, in school policies, or in curricular materials, you first must help cultivate in them a deep understanding of "heteronormativity"—a formidable task.

Failure to guide your students successfully toward a nuanced awareness of this concept could result in a learning "bottleneck," a sort of collective comprehension backup that occurs when educators struggle to facilitate effective learning around a foundational concept or competency—what Meyer and Land (2003) have called "threshold concepts." When this happens, the learning process literally becomes cluttered or clogged. As a result, progress toward bigger learning goals and understandings may stall or fizzle.

Making matters all the more challenging, every semester some of your students resist outright any conversation suggesting that lesbian, gay, bisexual, transgender, or queer people experience bias or oppression at all, or that their experiences belong in a conversation about "diversity," "multiculturalism," or "social justice." Others argue on misinformed scientific or even religious grounds that heterosexuality *is* normal, so it only makes sense that anything other than heterosexuality would be deemed abnormal, if not deviant. And every week you fight the temptation to interpret these responses as hostile or judgmental. You have turned to colleagues in search of pedagogical strategies only to learn that the challenge you face is a common one; you turn to the research literature and find, in fact, that the challenge is well documented there (Blackburn & Smith, 2010; Garcia & Slesaransky-Poe, 2010).

In fact, you remember some of your earliest exposures to conversations about social justice, perhaps in a college class very much like the one you now are teaching, when it seemed as though what you were learning conflicted with many of the other messages you were hearing about *what* and *how* you ought to think. This reminiscing is comforting for a moment, but the difficult truth remains: you must find a way to help your students understand and examine this thing called "heteronormativity." If you fail to do so, you limit the extent to which they will grasp the complexity of a variety of other concepts and competencies. In other words, if you fail to do so, you might leave your students stuck in that learning bottleneck.

We, the coeditors of this book, have been there, if not specifically in regard to our students' struggles to understand "heteronormativity," then in our attempts to find effective pedagogical strategies for teaching about Christian hegemony or patriarchy or *something* as deeply as we would have liked. From *hegemony* and *deficit ideology* to *White privilege* and *essentialism*, we have tried and failed and tried again to puzzle through many of the common bottlenecks that crop up in social justice and multicultural teacher education contexts. We have struggled, tripped, reformulated our pedagogies, read incessantly, interviewed our students, and engaged in action research. We have attempted, in most every conceivable way, to ensure that our students appreciate the foundational concepts and competencies—the *threshold* concepts and competencies—that will bolster their development as equity- and justice-minded educators. And, like you, perhaps, we sometimes have felt as though we may never quite get there.

Partially out of frustration with these challenges, we started to think and talk about what might help us, as teacher educators, do a better job teaching social justice threshold concepts and avoiding, or at least more effectively mitigating, common social justice learning bottlenecks. What we did too rarely, we came to believe, was to share with each other the sorts of pedagogical challenges and student (as well as colleague) resistance that make our work unique from teaching, say, mainstream history or biology. The social justice and multicultural teacher education literatures increasingly are exploring these and other challenges: the implications of student resistance to learning about topics like systemic racism, xenophobia, and Christian privilege (de Courcy, 2007; Gayle-Evans & Michael, 2006; Thomas & Vanderhaar, 2008); the larger sociopolitical context in which today's teacher education programs are situated (Grant, 2004; Hursh, 2005; Sleeter, 2008); and the general messiness of feeling like we are teaching, at times, against virtually every other influence in some of our students' lives (Bruna, 2007; Gorski, 2010; Reed & Black, 2006). Similarly, there is an increasingly robust literature on concepts and theoretical frameworks related to, say, *patriarchy* and its implications on schooling. There is a growing body of scholarship defining contemporary forms of patriarchy, examining intersectionalities around patriarchy, using patriarchy as a conceptual lens for critically analyzing all sorts of educational phenomena, and even documenting student resistance to discussions of patriarchy or feminist pedagogy. However, there is very little on exploring how to teach these concepts in teacher education contexts. The result is that we, the collective "we" of social justice teacher educators, seem to spend considerably more of our scholarly and pedagogical energies examining resistance to the notion of patriarchy and explicating the significance of patriarchy than considering how we might improve the ways we help future educators understand its influence on schooling.

Exceptions exist, of course. Although the social justice and multicultural education literatures addressing the bottleneck phenomenon and identifying "threshold concepts" are thin, they do include some attention to teacher educators' and others' challenges with helping students understand and apply concepts like deficit ideology, Christian hegemony, and White privilege, among others (e.g., Aveling, 2006; Bannick & van Dam, 2007; Case & Hemmings, 2005; Cho & DeCastro-Ambrosetti, 2005; Mueller & O'Connor, 2007; Sleeter, 2001; Solomona, Portelli, Daniel, & Campbell, 2005). A more limited subset of this scholarship identifies pedagogical responses to these challenges (Gorski, 2009; Klug, Luckey, Wilkins, & Whitfield, 2006; Lucas, 2005; Moss, 2008; Pennington, 2007). However, in most of these cases, attention to the challenge of teaching complex and critical concepts is tangential.

What remain nearly invisible in both of these literatures and, in our own experiences, at the few conferences and workshops meant to strengthen social justice teacher educators' practice, are concerted and sustained conversations among social justice teacher educators about common content- and pedagogy-related challenges we face in our work. Particularly for those of us doing this work in relative or literal isolation, where collegial understanding cannot be found down the hall or around the corner, we feel, as social justice teacher educators, that a more thoughtful attempt to engage in a collaborative exploration of these challenges could bolster our individual practice in the short run. More important, if sustained, such efforts might strengthen social justice teacher education more systemically in the long run.

A Primer on Threshold Concepts and Learning Bottlenecks

Every discipline, field, and movement has its threshold concepts and its common cognitive bottlenecks. For example, Middendorf, Pace, Shopkow, and Díaz (2007), drawing on in-depth interviews of history professors, identified seven common bottlenecks of college- and university-level history education. History students, they found, tended to struggle to identify with people from another time and place, interpret primary sources, and understand the role and nature of "facts" from a historical perspective. These were the concepts and competencies the interviewees considered to be among the cognitive building blocks, or *threshold concepts*, for learners of history. They knew that their students needed these skills to mature as historical thinkers, but they overwhelmingly agreed that, semester after semester, their students continued to struggle to understand them. And their instructors were not much help. In fact, Middendorf et al. found that professors regularly struggled to help their students make progress learning these and other concepts or competencies. As a result, the students often were left cognitively stuck.

When the professors were asked how much time and energy they had spent reflecting on *how* they were facilitating student learning around these threshold concepts—how much energy they were putting into strengthening their pedagogical strategies, their curricular materials, and the levels of student engagement they were encountering—they revealed that they had spent very little time and energy doing so. Similarly, we, the editors of this volume, recognize our own lack of effort exploring how to teach threshold concepts related to social justice.

Threshold concepts are critical to social justice teacher education because, if students are unable to grasp them in deep and integrated ways, they have little chance of developing complex understandings of a whole network of other social justice–related concepts (Meyer, Land, & Davies, 2006). For example, if I struggle to grasp the connection between corporate capitalism and the test-score-centric framing of the "achievement gap" discourse in the United States, it will be difficult for me to understand why deficit ideological approaches to mitigating the socioeconomic achievement gap—approaches focused on fixing economically disadvantaged people rather than the conditions that disadvantage them—are problematic. Failure to understand what is problematic about deficit ideology likely will hamper my ability to reverse, or even to recognize, how symptoms of class inequity are playing out in my classroom or school.

Equally important about threshold concepts is the fact that, as research has shown, once an individual develops a deep understanding of one of them—once she or he *crosses* a cognitive threshold—the likelihood of reverting to previous ways of knowing is extremely slim (Meyer & Land, 2003). Timmermans (2010) explains,

> Thus, on a path of development from one way of knowing and meaning-making, one epistemic stage or stance to the next, there seems to exist a point in our journey when we cross a threshold and our old way of knowing is no longer "tenable." There is an irreversible shift in the way in which "essence" is coordinated. There emerges a new space from which to observe and analyze the world. (p. 13)

Many of us have observed students at various times leaping, sprinting, or, with every ounce of their energy, crawling across that point in their journeys, shifting from a "colorblind" perspective to a racial justice perspective or from a view that interprets poverty as a "culture" to one that interprets it as an unjust social condition. And, of course, many of us have felt what it is like to cross one of those thresholds; to realize that what we thought we knew was more ideology than reality. Imagine how much more effective we, as social justice teacher educators, could be if we understood those moments better, if we knew how to help our students approach them more consciously. Imagine how your students' experiences might be different if you strengthened your ability to take full advantage of what Meyer and Land (2005) call the "reconstitutive effect of threshold concepts" (p. 375). How might our teacher education classrooms be different if we had better strategies for helping students manage what Cousin (2006) describes as the "liminal state," when learners are caught in dissonance as they grapple with the possibilities of new ways of seeing in light of old ways of knowing.

Critical to understanding the nature of threshold concepts and learning bottlenecks, particularly those related to social justice, is this: It's not that most students in teacher education do not *want* to learn these concepts and competencies, or that they do not *want* to create and sustain equitable and just learning environments—not for the most part, at least. Bottlenecks form for a wide variety of interrelated reasons. In the social justice education context, one complexity lies in the fact that the most well-meaning teacher educators and students alike have much to *unlearn* before transformational social justice learning can commence. Another complexity is the challenge inherent in the very process of attempting to facilitate learning experiences around a discipline or movement like social justice or multicultural education. In many ways, this task requires each of us to be a sort of social justice generalist, as pedagogically competent teaching about economic injustice as about heteronormativity, systemic racism, patriarchy, and intersectionalities, and attempting to do all of this in what inevitably turns out to be too little time.

The scarcity of time itself ratchets up the pressure to do all we can do to facilitate in our students an understanding of foundational concepts and competencies while we do have access to them, if only to help provide building blocks for their ongoing development as social justice–minded teachers. Plus, as Timmermans (2010) explains in her exploration of the transformational nature of threshold concepts, "there may exist highly individual reasons determining responses to threshold concepts, reasons such as alternative [cognitive] commitments and readiness for change" (p. 11). Inevitably, this combination of conditions, in addition to all sorts of other contextual factors such as where we teach, who our students are, and our own biases and dispositions, collude to ensure that we will not always do as good a job as we would like to do helping students learn and apply all of the concepts and competencies that are essential to social justice teaching and learning. In light of this reality, we believe it is crucial that we prepare ourselves as well as we can to provide all students with the best possible chance of developing deep and complex comprehensions and applications of social justice–related threshold concepts and to avoid the sorts of learning bottlenecks that may hinder their chances of doing so.

Cultivating Social Justice Teachers: How Teacher Educators Have Helped Students Overcome Cognitive Bottlenecks and Learn Critical Social Justice Concepts represents one collaborative attempt to hasten this exploration. We invited social justice teacher educators to share their trials, their tribulations, and, of course, their triumphs teaching threshold concepts related to multicultural and social justice education. We asked our contributors to identify a learning bottleneck related to one or two specific threshold concepts that they, at times, struggled to help their students overcome. Rather than simply providing a theoretical exploration of these concepts or pontificating on likely cognitive or sociopolitical sources of the bottlenecks, contributors agreed to tell how they came to find strategies for facilitating through them, despite the challenges they faced doing so. Each chapter, then, is, among other things, a narrative about individual efforts toward sometimes profound pedagogical adjustment, about ambiguity and cognitive dissonance and resistance, about trial and error and trial, and about a radical determination on the part of social justice teacher educators to find ways to facilitate foundational social justice learning among a diversity of education students. Although this is not intended to be a how-to manual or to provide *five easy steps for teaching every heterosexual man about heteronormative patriarchy*, each chapter does describe practical strategies that you might adapt as part of your own teacher education practice.

Introduction to Remaining Chapters

We begin with "The Art of Teaching Intersectionality" (chapter 2), in which Nana Osei-Kofi describes the arts-based pedagogies she has developed to help her students understand and apply intersectionality theory.

Stephanie Jones and James F. Woglom collaborate on "Overcoming Nomos" (chapter 3), a graphic novel–style exploration of strategies for helping students dissect hegemonic thinking about what is and is not "normal."

Mollie V. Blackburn details how she has come to use and sequence feature films to teach about the complexities of gender expression and heteronormativity in "Learning to Tell a Pedagogical Story About Heteronormativity" (chapter 4).

In "Overcoming Deficit Thinking Through Interpretive Discussion" (chapter 5), Curt Dudley-Marling describes how he has helped teachers shift from a deficit approach to a social constructivist perspective through interpretive question-posing and deep, reflective, discussion.

Paul C. Gorski shares the struggles he has experienced and the strategies he has developed while engaging his students in critical examinations of dominant discourses about poverty and schooling in "Teaching Against Essentialism and the 'Culture of Poverty'" (chapter 6).

In "Disrupting Denial and White Privilege in Teacher Education" (chapter 7), Darren E. Lund and Paul R. Carr offer exercises and insights for teaching through denial and toward racial equity in predominantly White contexts.

Warren J. Blumenfeld discusses how he engages even the most hostile students in explorations of Christian privilege in "Teaching About Christian Privilege in the Teacher Education Classroom" (chapter 8).

"From Literacy to 'Literacies': Using Photography to Help Teachers See What Youth Can Do" (chapter 9), by Kristien Zenkov, Athene Bell, Marriam Ewaida, Megan R. Lynch, and James Harmon, documents how a group of educators has worked to expand conceptions of "literacy" by equipping students with cameras and asking them to document their educational experiences.

Edward M. Olivos discusses how he helps his students become better advocates for immigrant students by developing a deeper, more contextualized understanding of immigration in "Teaching and Learning About Immigration as a Humanitarian Issue: The Sociopolitical Context Bottleneck" (chapter 10).

In "'You're Going to Hell!': When Critical Multicultural Queer Affirmation Meets Christian Homophobia" (chapter 11), Jeff Sapp highlights how he uses an affirming queer pedagogy and a deep knowledge of the biblical passages people cite to justify homophobia in an attempt to engage even the most reluctant of his students at the intersections of sexual orientation and religion.

Finally, Jody Cohen and Alice Lesnick share a strategy they call "overlaying," in which various social or classroom conditions are understood in relation to one another, as a way to uncover the myth of meritocracy in "Beyond Open-Mindedness: How 'Overlaying' Can Help Foster Impactful Discussions of Meritocracy in Teacher Education Classrooms" (chapter 12).

References

Aveling, N. (2006). "Hacking at our very roots": Rearticulating white racial identity within the context of teacher education. *Race, Ethnicity & Education, 9*(3), 261–274.

Bannick, A., & van Dam, J. (2007). Bootstrapping reflection on classroom interactions: Discourse contexts of novice teachers' thinking. *Evaluation & Research in Education, 20*(2), 81–99.

Blackburn, M. V., & Smith, J. M. (2010). Moving beyond the inclusion of LGBT-themed literature in English Language Arts classrooms: Interrogating heteronormativity and exploring intersectionality. *Journal of Adolescent and Adult Literacy, 53*(8), 625–634.

Bruna, K. (2007). Finding new words: How I use critical literacy in my multicultural teacher education classroom. *Journal of Education for Teaching, 33*(1), 115–118.

Case, K., & Hemmings, A. (2005). Distancing strategies: White women preservice teachers and antiracist curriculum. *Urban Education, 40*(6), 606–626.

Cho, G., & DeCastro-Ambrosetti, D. (2005). Is ignorance bliss?: Pre-service teachers' attitudes toward multicultural education. *The High School Journal, 89*(2), 24–28.

de Courcy, M. (2007). Disrupting preconceptions: Challenges to pre-service teachers' beliefs about ESL children. *Journal of Multilingual and Multicultural Development, 28*(3), 188–216.

Cousin, G. (2006). Threshold concepts, troublesome knowledge, and emotional capital: An exploration into learning about others. In J. H. F. Meyer & R. Land (Eds.), *Overcoming barriers to student understanding: Threshold concepts and troublesome knowledge* (pp. 134–147). New York: Routledge.

Garcia, A., & Slesaransky-Poe, G. (2010). The heteronormative classroom: Questioning and liberating practices. *The Teacher Educator, 45*(4), 244–256.

Gayle-Evans, G., & Michael, D. (2006). A study of pre-service teachers' awareness of multicultural issues. *Multicultural Perspectives, 8*(1), 45–50.

Gorski, P. (2009). Cognitive dissonance as a strategy in social justice teaching. *Multicultural Education, 17*(1), 54–57.

Gorski, P. (2010). The scholarship informing the practice: Multicultural teacher education philosophy and practice in the United States. *International Journal of Multicultural Education, 12*(2), 1–22.

Grant, C. (2004). Oppression, privilege, and high-stakes testing. *Multicultural Perspectives, 6*(1), 3–11.

Hursh, D. (2005). The growth of high-stakes testing in the USA: Accountability, markets, and the decline of educational equality. *British Educational Research Journal, 31*(5), 605–622.

Klug, B. J., Luckey, A. S., Wilkins, S., & Whitfield, P. T. (2006). Stepping out of our own skins: Overcoming resistance of isolated preservice teacher populations to embracing diversity in educational settings. *Multicultural Perspectives, 8*(3), 30–37.

Lucas, T. (2005). Fostering a commitment to social justice through service learning in a teacher education course. In N. M. Michelli & D. L. Keiser (Eds.), *Teacher education for democracy and social justice* (pp. 167–188). New York: Routledge.

Meyer, J. H. F., & Land, R. (2003). Threshold concepts and troublesome knowledge: Linkages to ways of thinking and practicing. In C. Rust (Ed.), *Improving student learning: Ten years on*. Oxford, UK: Oxford Centre for Staff and Learning Development.

Meyer, J. H. F., & Land, R. (2005). Threshold concepts and troublesome knowledge: Epistemological considerations and a conceptual framework for teaching and learning. *Higher Education, 49*(3), 373–388.

Meyer, J. H. F., Land, R., & Davies, P. (2006). Implications of threshold concepts for course design and evaluation. In J. H. F. Meyer & R. Land (Eds.), *Overcoming barriers to student understanding: Threshold concepts and troublesome knowledge* (pp. 195–206). New York: Routledge.

Middendorf, J., Pace, D., Shopkow, L., & Díaz, A. (2007). Making thinking explicit: Decoding history teaching. *National Teaching & Learning Forum, 16*(2).

Moss, G. (2008). Diversity study circles in teacher education practice: An experiential learning process. *Teaching & Teacher Education, 24*(1), 216–224.

Mueller, J., & O'Connor, C. (2007). Telling and retelling about self and "others": How pre-service teachers (re)interpret privilege and disadvantage in one college classroom. *Teaching & Teacher Education, 23*(6), 840–856.

Pennington, J. (2007). Silence in the classroom/whispers in the halls: Autoethnography as pedagogy in white pre-service teacher education. *Race, Ethnicity & Education, 10*(1), 93–113.

Reed, J., & Black, D. J. (2006). Toward a pedagogy of transformative teacher education: world educational links. *Multicultural Education, 14*(2), 34–39.

Sleeter, C. (2001). Preparing teachers for culturally diverse schools: Research and the overwhelming presence of whiteness. *Journal of Teacher Education, 52*(2), 94–106.

Sleeter, C. (2008). Equity, democracy, and neoliberal assaults on teacher education. *Teaching and Teacher Education, 24*(8), 1947–1957.

Solomona, R., Portelli, J., Daniel, B., & Campbell, A. (2005). The discourse of denial: How white teacher candidates construct race, racism, and "white privilege." *Race, Ethnicity & Education, 8*(2), 147–169.

Thomas, S., & Vanderhaar, J. (2008). Negotiating resistance to multiculturalism in a teacher education curriculum: A case study. *The Teacher Educator, 43*(3), 173–197.

Timmermans, J. A. (2010). Changing our minds: The developmental potential for threshold concepts. In R. Land, J. H. F. Meyer, & C. Ballie (Eds.), *Threshold concepts and transformational learning* (pp. 3–19). Rotterdam, Netherlands: Sense Publishers.

THE ART OF TEACHING INTERSECTIONALITY

Nana Osei-Kofi

"Being a Black woman you basically have to choose whether you are going to be a part of the women's movement or part of the Black movement, basically you have to choose whether you are a woman or Black."

"Even though we talk a lot about race, it is really all about class."

Each fall semester I teach a graduate-level introductory social justice research, theory, and practice course. The majority of students who take the class are beginning their studies in graduate education programs such as curriculum studies, multicultural education, foundations, higher education, and student affairs. Additionally, I typically have a few students in the class from sociology, sustainable agriculture, interdisciplinary graduate studies, and English. This chapter's opening quotations exemplify the types of comments students in my class often make about social injustice. Frequently, they see complex conditions of social injustice as the result of singular structural forces, such as racism or sexism. I believe some recognize the ways in which multiple forces shape particular social realities; however, they often believe that to work successfully for change necessitates a straightforward and clear focus on one aspect of oppression at a time. These perspectives exemplify what is probably the greatest challenge I face in my efforts to teach intersectionality.

Intersectionality represents a threshold concept in social justice studies in that it plays an important role in understanding oppression and domination. Jan Meyer and Ray Land (2003) describe "threshold concept[s] . . . as akin to a portal, opening up a new and previously inaccessible way of think-ing about something. It represents a transformed way of understanding, interpreting, or viewing something without which the learner cannot progress" (p. 412). Accordingly, the effect of not understanding intersec-tional theories, nor being able to apply them to critical issues of social justice, creates what we describe in this book as a learning bottleneck, with multiple consequences. Hence, the focus of this chapter is on the bottleneck that results when students are unable to make connections among different social, political, and economic issues; identity categories; and structural realities.

To address this issue, I first provide a brief theoretical overview of some of the different ways in which intersectionality is understood in the litera-ture. Following this overview, I discuss a number of the challenges I have faced teaching intersectionality and how they have shaped my current approach to the subject matter. This is followed by a discussion of the ways in which I now teach intersectionality using arts-based pedagogy.

Mapping Theories of Intersectionality

Intersectionality has a complex history. Although scholars and practitioners concerned with social change agree about its importance as a concept, the tensions surrounding the meaning of intersectionality are many. By and large, they center on the "what" and the "how" of intersectionality. What is it that intersects, how does it intersect, and through what approaches to research and practice can we best understand this complexity and address the issues this concept makes salient? Additionally, intersectionality has become a buzzword, which means that it is also often used without much clarity or depth (Davis, 2008; Nath, 2009). In an effort to capture the broad-ness and the complexity of the many varied approaches to intersectionality, Nina Lykke (2010) describes intersectionality as,

> A theoretical and methodological tool to analyze how historically specific kinds of power differentials and/or constraining normativities, based on discursively, institutionally and/or structurally constructed socio-cultural categorizations such as gender, ethnicity, race, class, sexuality, age/genera-tion, dis/ability, nationality, mother tongue and so on, interact, and in so doing produce different kinds of societal inequities and social relations. (p. 50)

Grappling with the many ways in which intersectionality is conceptual-ized, several scholars have attempted to map and, in different ways, cluster the various perspectives (e.g., Lykke, 2010; McCall, 2005; Prins, 2006). In an advanced class focused specifically on intersectionality, I see delving deeply into these perspectives while simultaneously engaging with the critiques of these approaches to intersectionality (e.g., Alexander-Floyd, 2012; May, 2011) as being of great value. However, I teach intersectionality as part of a class that covers a number of other concepts and ideas, which limits the opportunity for comprehensive comparative analysis. Hence, I have identified three key issues as most helpful in providing students with a foundational understanding of intersectionality: (1) differentiating intersectionality as a descriptor from intersectionality as an idea; (2) identifying varied levels and categories of analysis in the study of intersectionality; and (3) distinguishing intersectionality from interlocking systems of oppression.

Intersectionality as a Descriptor and as a Paradigm

One way to distinguish among different approaches to intersectionality is by considering the difference between intersectionality as a descriptor and intersectionality as an idea or paradigm (Alexander-Floyd, 2012; McGee, 1980; Salter, 2002). When intersectionality is used as a descriptor, it seeks to describe how different social categories intersect in determining a particular social reality. When intersectionality is used as a paradigm, it represents a host of ideas that are informed by specific ideological perspectives and aims (Alexander-Floyd, 2012). There is value in both of these ways of understanding intersectionality; however, from a social justice perspective, I suggest that there is reason to be cautious about the use of intersectionality simply as a descriptor. Too often what happens with this use of the concept is that the social justice framework that is part and parcel of understanding intersectionality as a paradigm is absent. Therefore, in my own teaching I view it as crucial to advance an understanding of intersectionality as a paradigm.

Intersectionality and Categories of Analysis

Much of the scholarly discussion of intersectionality as a paradigm concerns questions about what represent "appropriate" categories of analysis. Do we look at intersectionality at the individual level, the group level, or the structural level? What social categories should be used in the study of intersectionality? From my perspective, intersectionality can be a useful paradigm for understanding social conditions at multiple levels. There is value in identifying and exploring how oppression functions at different societal levels, including the personal, community, and systemic (Hill-Collins, 1990). What I see as critical is that, from a social justice perspective, an analysis of systemic inequities (i.e., an analysis of the social structure) must always be at the center of the work. This means that in looking at the United States, it is necessary to recognize capitalism as the overarching structural force in society and to consider capitalist formations in relation to how multiple forms of inequity manifest and intersect.

Intersectionality and Interlocking Systems of Oppression

Distinguishing the difference between intersecting and interlocking systems of oppression, which are both discussed under the umbrella of theories of intersectionality, is not always easy. At the most basic level, in making a distinction, intersectionality is often explained as referring to discrete forms of oppression, such as racism, sexism, and classism, that intersect—and through intersecting—shift the character of individual forms of oppression (Carastathis, 2008). Meanwhile, interlocking systems of oppression cannot be separated as the term refers to simultaneous factors that are interdependent (Razack, 1998). An example of this would be to look at race, class, and gender as inseparable structural factors shaping the experiences of women of color. The challenge in thinking through these distinctions is that they are not consistent across the literature, so students must understand how these terms are used in the literature rather than simply relying on singular fixed definitions. Moreover, from my own perspective, I argue that understanding intersectional categories of analysis as interlocking is essential to any engagement that seeks to advance substantive social change in the interest of social justice.

One might argue that these divergent conceptualizations represent the most challenging aspect of teaching intersectionality. There is *some* truth in this perspective. However, what I see as even more challenging are habits of thought that dominate the academy, and society at large, that encourage and reward the fragmentation of knowledge. Although all who see themselves as doing social justice work probably agree with Audre Lorde's (1984) assertion that "there is no such thing as a single-issue struggle because we do not live single issue lives" (p. 138), a single-issue approach remains dominant when it comes to how we engage with issues of oppression and domination in the United States today. Addressing this issue, Kimberle Crenshaw (1991), who is credited with coining the term *intersectionality* (being very careful to acknowledge that what she was suggesting was not necessarily a new idea or a totalizing theory of identity), used the example of battered women of color to illustrate the need to consider multiple factors, including poverty, racism, sexism, and gendered violence, when trying to understand the realities women of color face when seeking services at women's shelters.

What this makes evident to me in thinking about how we teach social justice is that if students are unable to understand the ways complex social, economic, and political realities interact to create particular realities, the solutions they are able to envision most likely will be responsive to symptoms of injustice rather than its root causes. I believe failures to recognize intersectional realities often make elements of social injustice invisible, as we overly focus on a single aspect of a condition of social inequity. An example of this focus on symptoms and single issues that comes to mind is after-school tutoring programs. While these programs are helpful to the academic achievement of students who have the opportunity to participate, they are only responsive to a single symptom of injustice rather than the root causes of inequitable educational outcomes that result from structural factors such as racism, sexism, and classism.

Teaching Intersectionality

So how do I teach intersectionality? I believe it is important to begin by recognizing that intersectionality does not represent a unified approach or perspective. To the contrary, as I have attempted to outline, it represents a wide spectrum of ways to understand different social realities. In my efforts to teach theories of intersectionality over the years, I have tried different readings, class projects using published case studies, discussion groups, and guest speakers, to name a few approaches.

In fact, one of my worst attempts at teaching intersectionality was when I attempted to use published case studies. It was something I was very excited about trying and that I thought would work very well. Students worked in groups, each group choosing a different case study to analyze. Each case represented a real-life scenario in which race, class, gender, and sexuality issues were present. The task for students was to analyze each case from an intersectional perspective and identify multiple ways in which to best address the issues at hand. The case studies also included specific questions for students to answer. When students presented their analyses, I found that their focus typically centered on one of the main issues in each case; they struggled to consider the implications of intersecting forms of oppression, often pointing out that there were too many unknowns for them to make a judgment about the situation they were asked to analyze.

The reason this exercise did not turn out the way I had hoped may have had something to do with some students not having understood the concept of intersectionality thoroughly enough before participating. More than that, though, I think it related to what C. Wright Mills (1959) would describe as a lack of sociological imagination. Students struggled with taking what they had read and discussed in class and applying it to real-life situations; they struggled to make connections among the actions of individuals, the social context in which these actions occurred, and structural factors. Although I have had some success with some of the approaches I have attempted, I never found these successes to be consistent over the years, until I decided to try arts-based approaches to teaching intersectionality.

Because I use arts-based inquiry in my own research, I have included arts-based pedagogical projects in my courses for many years. As a result, what I realized as I took stock of my courses and teaching materials about two years ago was that arts-based assignments were having a strong positive effect on helping students understand social justice in more complex ways. I am in no way claiming that arts-based work in the classroom is a panacea, but I do believe it is of great value in building understanding of threshold concepts related to a critical understanding of social and economic injustice. To engage with art is itself a connective experience, so it is interesting to think about the ways it facilitates an understanding of connections among different concepts, theories, and ideas, beyond the act of engaging in the practice that brings it into being.

Intersectional Theories and Arts-Based Pedagogies

> *At the heart of arts-based inquiry is a radical, politically grounded statement about social justice and the control over the production and dissemination of knowledge.*
>
> —Susan Finley, 2008, p. 72

Ardra Cole and Gary Knowles (2008) describe arts-informed approaches to scholarship as aimed at "enhanc[ing] [our] understanding of the human condition through alternative (to conventional) processes and representational forms of inquiry, and to reach multiple audiences by making scholarship more accessible" (p. 59). Arts-based inquiry explicitly challenges logical positivism and technical rationality as the only ways in which we can come to understand human experience (Cole & Knowles, 2008). As such, I believe arts-based work has unique potential to address social injustice through new and innovative approaches to inquiry (Finley, 2008). It is an approach that recognizes the many dimensions and complexity of lived experience, while at the same time acknowledging that there are many different ways we can engage the world (Cole & Knowles, 2008). Based on these characteristics, in my experience, arts-based pedagogies encourage students to think in new ways, to grapple more effectively with complexity as they make meaning of issues of social injustice, and to come to knowledge in a more holistic way than what is possible through more traditional pedagogical approaches (Butler-Kisber, 2008; Leavy, 2009). In what follows, I outline three different arts-informed approaches I use to teach intersectional theories.

Poetry/Short Story

Dorthe Staunæs (2003), in a discussion of the ways in which categories of difference interlock, notes that "the way the categories intermingle, their concrete dominance and elaboration must be studied in concrete situations" (p. 105). She goes on to suggest that "categories do not intermingle equally. In principle, there is not a predetermined or pre-hierarchical pattern between the categories. . . . [However,] in lived experiences there may be a hierarchy in which certain categories overrule, capture, differentiate and transgress others" (p. 105). Living intersectionality, or doing intersectionality as Staunæs describes it, highlights how different people are situated in relation to the dominant or that which is considered the norm.

To help students understand intersectionality at the individual level as Staunæs and others discuss it, I use a poetry/short story assignment early in the process of teaching intersectionality to encourage students to reflect on how the ways they experience the world are constructed through "discourses that weave together narratives of gender, race, ethnicity, sexuality, nationality, age and so on" (Lykke, 2010, p. 73). I am interested in students considering how they experience the social categories to which they view themselves as belonging, with an emphasis how their experiences are constructed through intersections of multiple categories. Through this process, I also am concerned with developing students' understanding of how structural forces shape the ways they construct their own identities and how processes of socialization (re)produce a particular hegemony. To achieve this, I ask students to draw on their own life experiences as a way to grapple with intersectionality, their understanding of themselves as individuals, the relationship between structural forces and their individual experiences, and the function of hegemony in their lives.

To do this, I assign Jamaica Kincaid's (1978) poem/short story, "Girl." In "Girl," Kincaid, who grew up in Antigua, West Indies, writes about the relationship between a mother and daughter. It is a story about the mother instructing her daughter on how to act, how to be a woman. It is a story about the mother warning the daughter about the consequences of not meeting social expectations and demanding that she conform.

> This is how you set a table for lunch, this is how you set a table for break-fast; this is how you behave in the presence of men who don't know you very well, and this is the way they won't recognize immediately the slut I have warned you against becoming; be sure to wash every day, even if it is with your own spit; don't squat down to play marbles—you are not a boy, you know; don't pick people's flowers—you might catch something. . . .
> (p. 29)

I use "Girl" because, in addition to being about a mother-daughter relation-ship, it is about intersections of gender, sexuality, class, religion, and colo-nialism, and highlights what Patricia Hill-Collins (1990) describes as the ways in which matrixes of domination operate on the personal, community, and structural level.

In class, I begin by asking one or two students to read the poem/short story aloud. I provide students with some background on Jamaica Kincaid's work and ask them about their interpretations of the story, which we discuss as a group. As students begin to identify the messages that are being commu-nicated to the girl, I ask them to grapple with how intersectionality may be playing out in the narrative. After discussing the work at some length, I ask students to write their own poem or short story using Kincaid's work as a guide to reflect on the messages and directives they received growing up and to consider the ways these messages are tied to different intersectional catego-ries of analysis. I do not give directions in terms of any specific length for their writing or what intersectional categories they should focus on. I want this to be a reflective process in which students identify for themselves what is most salient in their own lives and what they want to say about it. Students have a week to complete the assignment. When the class meets again, they share their work with the group. In giving direction for the assignment, I make it very clear that students will never be required to read any part of their poem or short story they are not comfortable sharing publicly. I believe this level of confidentiality gives students the freedom to look more deeply at their own lived experience, to write more candidly, and thus to come to understand more effectively the concepts tied to intersectionality.

While "Girl" may speak to what Staunæs (2003) would describe as individuals who, as a function of power and hegemony, are seen as being at the margins, the work students produce shows that they grasp the essence of the assignment. The poems and short stories they produce illustrate intersectional identities that represent both dominant identities, such as being White and male, which is seen as the norm, as well as marginalized identities, such as being a lesbian and of color, which is viewed as divergent from the norm. Despite my insistence that students can limit what they share in class, I find that some students, with great courage, are willing to share deeply personal experiences. When one or two students do this, a level of trust begins to develop in the classroom, whereby others who initially had not planned to share certain parts of their work, do so. Through this exercise, intersectionality comes to life; if these theories were abstract to students prior to this assignment, they begin to understand them in concrete ways through their own experiences and those of their classmates. As one might suspect, most students find it easiest to identify and come to understand intersections at the personal level. I can remember a student sharing how, until the point she worked on this assignment, she had always thought of herself only in terms of her racialized identity. In completing the assignment, she started to realize how many of her experiences with some of her science teachers in high school were not only a function of how she was positioned in relation to race but also to her gender. She came to see that her experiences were situated at the intersection of race and gender, and she was able to articulate this reality to the class.

One way students develop a better grasp of the idea of intersections, functioning on the group and structural level, is by listening to each other's work. As they listen, I ask them about recurring themes, and by looking across the multiple poems and short stories, those who previously might not have done so begin to make the links between individual experiences and structural factors, such as patriarchy, racism, heterosexism, and classism. As an example, for one student, her relationship with her father growing up was no longer just about their interpersonal relationship; through the assignment and our classroom discussion, she spoke of seeing how both patriarchy and classism also shaped their relationship. Articulating the power of poetry to foster understanding, which very much informs the intention behind this assignment, Patricia Leavy (2009) suggests that "more than a window onto an aspect of social life, poetry places a *magnifying glass* in front of that reality, where the experience is even bolder than in everyday life. . . . creat[ing] *a vivid and sensory scene* that *compels* . . . [and] teach[es] . . . something about a particular aspect of social experience" (p. 68). Poetry also has the ability to illustrate connections between different issues on both the micro and macro level (Leavy), as the students' assignments demonstrate.

Alongside the strictly conceptually educative aspect of this project, there is also a deeply reflective element that causes students to look more critically at their own social location in relation to a range of social justice issues, which is why I am very intentional about assigning this project early in the semester. Additionally, through this exercise I get to know students in ways that help me in my role as an instructor. By knowing something about what people bring to the classroom, I can better determine how to best teach a wide range of content.

Photography

Another project I assign when I teach intersectional theories is a visual analysis project for which students, working collaboratively in groups, conduct photographic surveys of our campus. The purpose of this project is to demonstrate how intersectional categories such as race, class, gender, and sexuality "operate in the structuring and use of space" (Willis, 2010, p. 82). As space can mean many different things, for the sake of clarity, the analysis students carry out is not simply about architecture; rather it is about the sum of the built environment. That is to say, in addition to buildings, their projects capture the physical environment holistically, how it is organized, what artifacts it contains, and what surrounds it (Costello, 2001; Lemecha, 2000; Sutton, 1996). Students look at, for instance, where different types of campus buildings and services are located in relation to one another, what is found on the walls of different campus spaces, what is included in the campus public art collection, what spaces are designated for different groups on campus, and the type of furniture used in different campus offices and classrooms and how that furniture is organized.

To carry out this project, I organize students in groups of four or five. I try to make the groups as diverse as possible to capture a diversity of perspectives in the surveys each group conducts. Many times, students will read space differently based on how they are located socially, based on their identities, which allows for rich conversations within each group and with the class as a whole. Equipped with cameras, the groups survey the campus, paying close attention to architecture, hallways, entryways, classrooms, artwork, meeting places, food outlets, offices, student housing, social gathering spots, and the overall layout of the campus. As students document these spaces, I ask them to reflect on a number of things, such as "how the space is used, by whom, under what conditions, and with what results" (Willis, 2010, p. 81). I also ask them to think about what messages the space conveys; who belongs; what knowledge is privileged; and what the space says symbolically about history, power, and privilege. Drawing on their readings, students consider how race, class, gender, sexuality, national identity, and other intersectional categories both mediate, and are mediated by, the spaces they survey.

When students have completed their information-gathering, they review the materials they have collected and do close readings of their photography, creating a visual presentation that they share with the entire class. The finished work becomes "a visual resource for examining power relations . . . [providing] structural information about social, cultural . . . [and political] relations" (Willis, 2010, p. 81). Their analyses reveal the assumptions that inform the physical organization of space and the ways in which social and cultural values and beliefs inform these assumptions. As students view the presentations and listen to each group's analysis, it allows for a very rich discussion about a space with which we are all familiar and of which we are all a part.

Engaging with space expands many contemporary conceptions of intersectionality. It acknowledges the ways experience is mediated through power-laden spaces (Valentine, 2007). At the same time, as Sherene Razack (2002) suggests, working with space is particularly well suited for analysis of intersectionality: "The lure of the spatial approach is precisely the possibility of charting the simultaneous operation of multiple systems of domination" (p. 6). For students, this is a particularly powerful exercise because the analysis concerns their everyday, yet it is an element of their environment of which they are often unconscious and which they have never questioned (Schein, 1997). Razack (2002) explains, "To question how spaces come to be, and to trace what they produce as well as what produces them is to unsettle familiar everyday notions" (p. 7). It is a process that Razack has described as "unmapping," as denaturalizing a space. This exercise aids students in understanding some of the complexities of intersectional theories in very concrete, personal, and material ways.

Collage

The third project I use to teach intersectionality is based on using collage as a form of inquiry. For this assignment students pick a topic with which we have engaged in class and design a collage that represents their analysis of the ways intersectionality functions in relation to that topic. If at all possible, I refrain from showing the class examples of how previous students have completed this project. I find that, much like the way in which beautiful pictures in recipe books set up expectations for how dishes should look, examples of earlier work can stifle creativity and create limiting expectations that shape how students approach the assignment. However, although most people remember cutting and pasting from elementary school, my students typically are not used to engaging with art in a graduate education class that has nothing to do with preparing art teachers. Therefore, their levels of anxiety can be high. As a result, in some cases, I decide to share some examples of previous work to lower anxieties and allow students to focus on the essence of the project.

One of the reasons I use collage to help students grasp the essence of intersectional theories is because of the multivocal, nonlinear, contextualized, diverse, and reflexive forms of representation this art form makes possible (Butler-Kisber, 2008; Vaughan, 2005). Collage has the potential to reveal new and different ways of thinking about a subject and of lifting forth elements of everyday life of which the creator might not be fully conscious (Butler-Kisber, 2008). Therefore, when students engage in collage-making, they are not only representing knowledge, they are also constructing and generating it (Vaughan, 2005).

The process through which students create their collages in many ways mirrors the process involved in a research study. They begin by gathering materials. They then have to make choices about what they are going to use from the materials they have gathered, analyze these materials, synthesize them, and finally put them together in some form of presentation (Vaughan, 2005). If time allows I ask students to share their works-in-progress in class to get feedback midway on how the class understands their work and to help stimulate their thinking further as they finalize their collages.

When we think of collage, most people probably think of different materials such as photographs and magazine clippings that are cut up, organized, and pasted onto a large poster board. This understanding of collage reflects the original conception in fine arts and the translation from the French, meaning glued work (Butler-Kisber, 2008; Vaughan, 2005). However, as the art form has evolved, various artists have modified it. As a result, students' work is not only one-dimensional, sometimes it is two- and three-dimensional. In addition to more traditional visual elements, students produce collages in the form of music, sculpture, video, web-based work, and other digital platforms. Accompanying their collages, students are required to write brief artist statements about their work. These statements give me additional insight into their thought processes for creating their collages.

Once students complete the assignment, it is exhibited on campus. We host an opening reception for the exhibit to which the campus community is invited. At the event, each student discusses her or his work and has the opportunity to engage in a large-group discussion as well as one-on-one conversations with attendees about the work. Discussions typically focus on the social justice issues that are the subject of the different works as well as the role of art in social justice work. By discussing their collages and responding to questions from others in attendance, students continue to learn from the work they have created. Each time they discuss it, their language and articulation of the concepts and theories with which they engaged become more clear and concise. They are learning by teaching. Additionally, they become very cognizant of the ways in which collage makes academic concepts more accessible to a wider audience.

Even though some students initially experience discomfort with the idea of creating art, at the end of this assignment they display a sense of pride and accomplishment in their work; many describe it as their favorite activity in the class. Not only have they constructed a creative representation of complex theories of intersectionality, they have been able to articulate these theories through their art to members of the campus community, for many of whom these concepts are new.

Conclusion

Teaching intersectionality using arts-based pedagogies necessitates addressing larger issues of the production of knowledge and art as a form of knowing. Therefore, when I introduce intersectionality to students through arts-based projects, I make a point of grounding it in a conversation about multiple ways of knowing and emphasizing that my classroom is a space where multiple knowledges are valued and recognized. I make it clear to students that arts-based assignments are as important as more traditional written assignments, and that I expect them to give the same amount of effort and attention to these projects. I do this because I have found that although students theoretically may understand issues of ontology, epistemology, power, and hegemony in the process of knowledge production, in practice they do not always give equal weight to alternative ways of knowing until they have experienced some of these approaches.

In my experience, once students are engaged, arts-based pedagogies provide creative, imaginative, participatory, and action-oriented approaches to examining a range of issues related to social and economic justice, from questions regarding how knowledge is defined, to relations of power, to social inequities, to modes of resistance to oppression, and to possibilities for radical praxis. In the examples I have outlined in this chapter, art functions as a powerful tool to teach intersectionality. I know that students "get it" when they start making references to intersectionality when sharing experiences from their everyday lives or discussing the role of intersectionality in scholarly literature where this is not explicitly addressed. Of course there is never a *perfect* pedagogical approach to anything. As with any other approach to teaching, using arts-based pedagogies requires understanding the context in which one is teaching and recognizing where students are and what modifications may be required to maximize student learning, while at the same time finding ways to challenge students to engage critically with their own assumptions, values, and beliefs.

In some ways introducing both intersectional theories for understanding social injustice and arts-based pedagogies at the same time may seem potentially overwhelming for students. I have not found this to be the case. Once students recognize that they can bring more than one part of their beings to their work, that they can be artistic, creative, and emotive and still be "academic," still produce "legitimate" knowledge that is not limited to the written word, freedom and excitement become more evident in their work, and their understanding of intersectionality is deepened. I firmly believe that as we develop new and promising forms of pedagogical engagement that are based on social justice aims, arts-based approaches to teaching, research, and practice create new possibilities for coming to know, for discovery of self and others, for creativity and embodiment of our work, for consciousness-raising, for questioning, for community engagement, for action, and, ultimately, for social change.

References

Alexander-Floyd, N. (2012). Disappearing acts: Reclaiming intersectionality in the social sciences in a post-Black feminist era. *Feminist Formations, 24*(1), 1–25.

Butler-Kisber, L. (2008). Collage as inquiry. In G. Knowles & C. Cole (Eds.), *Handbook of the arts in qualitative research: Perspectives, methodologies, examples and issues* (pp. 265–276). Thousand Oaks, CA: Sage.

Carastathis, A. (2008). The invisibility of privilege: A critique of intersectional models of identity. *Les Ateliers de L'Éthique, 3*(2), 23–38.

Cole, A., & Knowles, G. (2008). Arts-informed research. In G. Knowles & C. Cole (Eds.), *Handbook of the arts in qualitative research: Perspectives, methodologies, examples and issues* (pp. 55–70). Thousand Oaks, CA: Sage.

Costello, C. (2001). Schooled by the classroom: The (re)production of social stratification in professional school settings. In E. Margolis (Ed.), *The hidden curriculum in higher education* (pp. 43–59). New York: Routledge.

Crenshaw, K. (1991). Mapping the margins: Intersectionality, identity politics, and violence against women of color. *Stanford Law Review, 43*, 1241–1299.

Davis, K. (2008). Intersectionality as buzzword. *Feminist Theory, 9*(1), 67–85.

Finley, S. (2008). Arts-based research. In G. Knowles (Ed.), *Handbook of the arts in qualitative research* (pp. 71–81). Thousand Oaks, CA: Sage Publications.

Hill-Collins, P. (1990). *Black feminist thought: Knowledge, consciousness and the politics of empowerment.* London, UK: HarperCollins.

Kincaid, J. (1978, June 26). Girl. *The New Yorker*, 29.

Leavy, P. (2009). *Method meets art: Arts-based research practice.* New York: Guildford.

Lemecha, V. (2000). The feminist reconstruction of space: An introduction. In W. May (Ed.), *The feminist reconstruction of space* (pp. 7–13). Manitoba, Canada: St. Norbert Arts and Cultural Centre.

Lorde, A. (1984). *Sister outsider.* Freedom, CA: The Crossing Press.

Lykke, N. (2010). *Feminist studies: A guide to intersectional theory, methodology and writing.* New York: Routledge.

May, V. (2011, November). *Instrumentalizing intersectionality: examining the problem of nominal use.* Paper presented at the meeting of the National Women's Studies Association, Atlanta, GA.

McCall, L. (2005). The complexity of intersectionality. *Signs: Journal of Women and Culture and Society, 30*(3), 1771–1800.

McGee, M. (1980). The "ideograph": A link between rhetoric and ideology. *The Quarterly Journal of Speech, 66*(1), 1–16.

Meyer, J., & Land, R. (2003). Threshold concepts and troublesome knowledge: Linkages to ways of thinking and practising. In C. Rust (Ed.), *Improving student learning: Ten years on* (pp. 412–424). Oxford, UK: Oxford Center for Staff and Learning Development.

Mills, C.W. (1959). *The sociological imagination.* London, UK: Oxford University Press.

Nath, N. (2009, May). *Rediscovering the potential of feminist theories of intersectionality.* Paper presented at the meeting of the Canadian Political Science Association, Ottawa, Ontario.

Prins, B. (2006). Narrative accounts of origins: A blind spot in the intersectional approach? *European Journal of Women's Studies, 13*(3), 277–290.

Razack, S. (1998). *Looking White people in the eye: Gender, race, and culture in courtrooms and classrooms.* Toronto, Canada: University of Toronto Press.

Razack, S. (2002). *Race, space, and the law: Unmapping a White settler society.* Toronto, Ontario: Between the Lines.

Salter, L. (2002). Challenging orthodoxy. In R. Mansell, R. Samarajiva & A. Mahan (Eds.), *Networking knowledge for information societies* (pp. 60–67). Netherlands: Delft University Press.

Schein, E. (1997). *Organizational culture and leadership.* London, UK: Jossey-Bass.

Staunæs, D. (2003). Where have all the subjects gone? Bringing together the concepts of intersectionality and subjectification. *NORA, 2*(11), 101–110.

Sutton, S. (1996). *Weaving a tapestry of resistance: The places, power, and poetry of a sustainable society.* Westport, CT: Bergin & Garvey.

Valentine, G. (2007). Theorizing and researching intersectionality: A challenge for feminist geography. *Professional Geographer, 59,* 10–21.

Vaughan, K. (2005). Pieced together: Collage as an artist's method for interdisciplinary research. *International Journal of Qualitative Methods, 4*(1), Article 3. Retrieved October 23, 2010, from http://www.ualberta.ca/~iiqm/backissues/4_1/pdf/vaughan.pdf

Willis, J. (2010). Feminist scholarship and the interrogation of spatial formation. *Transformations: The Journal of Inclusive Scholarship and Pedagogy, 20*(2), 81–96.

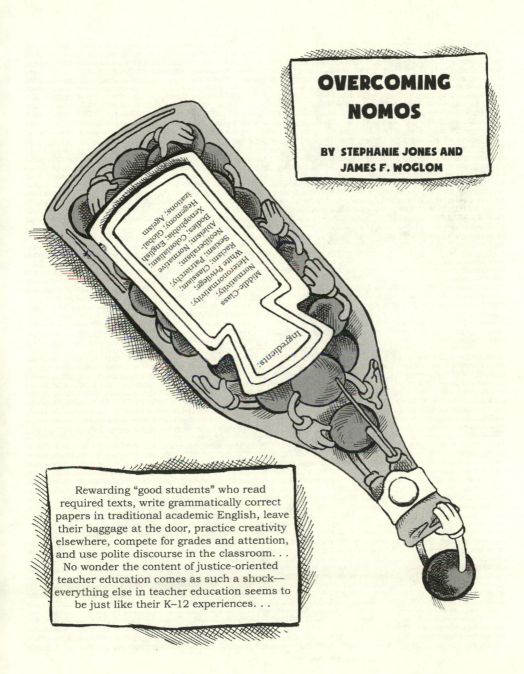

OVERCOMING NOMOS

BY STEPHANIE JONES AND
JAMES F. WOGLOM

Ingredients:
Middle-Class
Normativity;
Heteronormativity;
White Privilege;
Sexism; Patriarchy;
Racism; Normative.
Neoliberalism;
Ableism; Colonialism;
Bodies; Colonialism;
Xenophobia; Global-
Hegemony; Ageism
izations; Ageism

Rewarding "good students" who read
required texts, write grammatically correct
papers in traditional academic English, leave
their baggage at the door, practice creativity
elsewhere, compete for grades and attention,
and use polite discourse in the classroom. . .
No wonder the content of justice-oriented
teacher education comes as such a shock—
everything else in teacher education seems to
be just like their K–12 experiences. . .

31

Early Childhood and Elementary Education is dominated by women, with nearly 90% of all teachers identifying as women. Administrators and policymakers in education are still mostly men. And too many people still stereotype education majors as babysitters looking for a "Mrs. Degree."

Women have persistently been infantilized through schooling and the media, and many young women too often believe they are never good enough. Even "privileged" women are not immune to the messages saying they need to be thinner, whiter, prettier, richer. . .

Bitter Milk

Schoolgirl Fictions

Feminist Theory: From Margin to Center

Telling Women's Lives

Feeling Power

School for Wom...

"Women were expected to be the medium through which the laws, rules, language, and order of the father, the principal, the employer were communicated to the child. Their own passivity was to provide the model of obedience for the young to emulate. And teachers have yet to announce which side of the line we are on." —Grumet

Teacher Education is the ideal space for feminist pedagogies— to encourage strength, courage, social and political critique, activism and solidarity, intellectualism, and nonjudgment of ourselves and others.

I mean, don't we want the most confident, capable, intellectual women and men teaching our young children?

PATRIARCHY

Radical feminism aims to eradicate all forms of domination. It's for women and men.

33

Students pointed out the systemic problem of media and popular culture representations of African Americans as poor, violent, and criminal.

The group questioned why white collar criminals, whose crimes often account for more economic and life loss in a year than street crime, were either invisible or represented as suave.

These movies make us all look like gangsters and criminals.

Could the mass indentification of African American boys in Special Education be related to the criminalized images in our society?

And could the treatment of African American boys in schools lead to their mass incarceration as adults?

RACISM

In 2008, 1 in 9 African American men aged 20–34 were behind bars. A shocking number even for the U.S.—the country with the highest percentage of its population behind bars.

Readers connected, disconnected, and placed their books in a larger social and political context.

My mom was so focused on being skinny. What did she <u>think</u> that would do to me? It's like <u>Moose</u>.

My best friend was bulimic. I hated that she compared herself to me. The media is terrible.

Well, we do it, too. I mean, why don't we stand up when guys say mean things about other girls—like at that party?

Hangin' at a party...

MISOGYNY

Dude, her body is shaped like a ketchup bottle! I don't know how you do that, man.

Yeah! But at least I'm doin' it.

Is it okay to just blame the media or "society" when we see these things happen and don't do anything to challenge them?

42

And they questioned their own limited "education" about the world.

Persepolis was amazing. I never thought I would like a graphic novel—but I was sucked in right away. And I learned so much!

I feel so stupid. Why didn't we learn about these things in school? Is the revolution still happening?

It's like we only get the stereotyped version of the Middle East—if we are taught about it at all. Terror, terror, terror.

CHRISTIAN HEGEMONY

Students even started doing their own research—reading books, searching the Internet, and talking to Muslims about politics in the Middle East.

44

Even the students who rarely spoke in class produced intense, provocative projects from their choice books. Talents were unleashed and teacher education escaped its nomos, if only temporarily.

Pecola Breedlove; so different than me
From your deep brown eyes, I do not see.
I, like all, at some point, struggle to find
my place in the world,
But for you it is different. Immoderate.
Who should be so unloved and outcast?
Such a little girl.
Though I do not have your vision, what
can you make to me clear?
Is it your father who has hurt you,
or those who are not so near?
Shall you teach me to not be like
them; so brutal, judgmental,
unwilling to know you, doing a job
only meant for God?
Teach me to teach my children
so they do not live in fear,
Sure, I have been judged, dismissed,
turned away and withdrew,
But never so much as you.
Never so much that I wanted to change
my identity with a simple shade of blue. . .
The world is relentless. Not to stigmatize
would just not do. Still your
appearance just won't do.
No matter what you do. You quite simply
just will not do.
They want to blame you for what you did
not do.
They want to blame you for what was
done to you. . .
Will you help me separate from this world so
I may clearly see you, you, and you,
and you?
Make me look at them,
unlike those who
will not look at you.
Make me see inside of their hearts,
minds, souls
So that I may love them even without
eyes of blue
So that I may give them their fair
chance as every teacher should do.
Don't let me judge them based on the
prostitutes that live above them,
along with all the other skeletons in
their closets that they don't
even know are there, because it was
us, not them, that put them there.
Teach me, Pecola Breedlove. . .

45

"Testimonial reading pushes us to recognize that a novel or biography reflects not merely a distant other, but analogous social relations in our own environment, in which our economic and social positions are implicated." —Megan Boler

After reading their books and having multiple in-class conversations about them, the students responded to the books in any way they wanted. Most chose the arts to use their out-of-school passions and hobbies to make sense of the individual, social, economic, and political issues raised in the novels and memoirs.

The bottleneck of nomos breaks open, spilling social and political issues important to the students today, and important for their teaching in the future. Not perfect, but a good start.

Back at the research conference...

The carefully cultivated nomos of educational institutions has shaped students' expectations of institutions. Teacher Education is no exception.

Before we ask ourselves which individual "topics" or "issues" become bottlenecked, we should ask ourselves which parts of the institutional nomos create the conditions for a bottleneck to emerge, preventing different things to be thought, spoken, or performed.

Do we continue orienting students' bodies and minds toward an institutional nomos they've incorporated in their bodies since K–12...

Or do we disrupt the nomos by engaging their lived experiences through literature, media, and art?

We can invite students' whole selves into the complex journeys with us by opening up new spaces of creativity and possibility.

Overcoming Nomos: Engaging Bodies and Minds Differently in Justice-Oriented Teacher Education

I wonder if this nomos is impacting my teaching.

I'd like to read those books.

I'm still not sure what it has to do with education.

References

Alexie, S. (2009). The Absolutely True Diary of a Part-time Indian. New York: Little, Brown Books for Young Readers.

Allison, D. (1988). Trash. Ithaca, NY: Firebrand Books.

Boler, M. (1999). Feeling Power: Emotions and Education. New York: Routledge.

Bureau of Justice Statistics. Retrieved from http://bjs.ojp.usdoj.gov/

Diaz, J. (2008). The Brief Wondrous Life of Oscar Wao. New York: Riverhead Books.

Grumet, M. (1988). Bitter Milk: Women and Teaching. Amherst: University of Massachusetts Press.

Hadjii (2008). Don't Let My Mama Read This: A Southern-Fried Memoir. New York: Broadway Books.

hooks, b. (2000). Feminist Theory: From Margin to Center. Cambridge, MA: South End Press.

International Centre for Prison Studies. http://www.prisonstudies.org

Klein, S. (2008). Moose: A Memoir of Fat Camp. New York: William Morrow.

Lyon, G. E. (1999). "Where I'm From" In Where I'm From: Where Poems Come From. Spring, TX: Absey & Co.

Miller, J. (1996). School for Women. London, UK: Virago.

Morrison, T. (1994). The Bluest Eye. New York: Penguin Books.

Pew Center on the States. http://www.pewcenteronthestates.org

Satrapi, M. (2007). The Complete Persepolis. New York: Pantheon Books.

Smith, D. (1987). The Everyday World as Problematic: A Feminist Sociology. Boston: Northeastern University Press.

Walkerdine, V. (1990). Schoolgirl Fictions. London, UK: Verso.

Weedon, C. (1997). Feminist Practice and Poststructuralist Theory. Malden, MA: Blackwell Publishers.

Weiler, K. (1999). Telling Women's Lives: Narrative Inquiries in the History of Women's Education. Philadelphia: Open University Press.

**The authors would like to acknowledge their production manager, Jenny Mary Brown, for her commitment to the project.

4

LEARNING TO TELL A PEDAGOGICAL STORY ABOUT HETERONORMATIVITY

Mollie V. Blackburn

I came to teach graduate education students at a large, public, land-grant university in the Midwest having taught middle- and high-school English language arts for six years, having come out as a lesbian four years earlier, and having worked in a youth-run center for lesbian, gay, bisexual, transgender, and questioning (LGBTQ) youth for three years. Therefore, I was committed to literacy education, but I also was deeply dedicated to working on behalf of lesbian, gay, bisexual, transgender, queer, and questioning (LGBTQQ)[1] people. These commitments shaped my pedagogy and curriculum. Sometimes in my teaching, I encountered explicit resistance from some students who claimed it was wrong to convey to them that being anything other than straight was a viable and valuable option. Other times I experienced more discreet forms of resistance, like having some students tell me that teachers should not be teaching values on such controversial issues. There were also, though, students who shared my commitments.

I struggled with how to engage students with such a wide range of perspectives on issues that mattered so much to me. My struggle in part defines the bottleneck that is the focus of this chapter. I'm thinking less of the neck of a literal bottle, where you can simply tip the bottle and let gravity do the work of getting the wine through the neck, over the lip, and into your glass, and more of a bottleneck you'd encounter in, say, kayaking, which requires great focus and effort to navigate along a river around rocks and other obstacles. In other words, this bottleneck took some work to get through. This work is particularly evident in my designing, teaching, revising, and re-teaching, again and again, a course entitled "Reading Gender," an elective, one-week, intensive summer course. In this course, student perspectives ranged from rather stereotypical notions of what it means to be boys and girls and men and women to notions of gender that include the suspension of classifications of such identifications.

Heteronormativity

An important distinction among these understandings of gender is related to the concept of heteronormativity, which I have come to see as my thresh-old concept in navigating through the aforementioned bottleneck. Hetero-normativity is based on the ideas that it is right or "normal" for males to be boys and men who are attracted to women, and for females to be girls and women who are attracted to men. *Male* and *female* refer to one's sex, which is defined biologically and anatomically. *Boys*, *men*, *girls*, and *women* refer to one's gender, which is constructed socially, culturally, and politically. Sex and gender are directly correlated within heteronormativity. Moreover, sex and gender prescribe and proscribe attraction and desire; that is, boys and men are attracted to or desirous of girls and women, and women are attracted to or desirous of men. Such embodiments of sex, gender, and sexuality are, within the realm of heteronormativity, considered to be normal. Sex, gender, and sexuality experienced in any other way is considered wrong or "abnormal."

Sometimes these messages of what is normal and abnormal are explicit. Consider, for example, the tradition of a homecoming or prom king and queen. Other times they are more implicit, like when a straight teacher doesn't think twice about referencing her spouse or even bringing her husband or his wife to school events, but a gay teacher in the same school worries about whether to put a rainbow sticker on her or his car bumper. She or he knows, after all, that she or he will drive the car to school and park it in the school lot and some student at some time will see this teacher get out of that car and that student might make an assumption—an accurate one—that makes the teacher more vulnerable in any number of ways, rang-ing from a discreet homophobic comment in the hallway to losing his or her job. It is currently legal, remember, to fire gay employees, including teachers—*just* because they are gay—in 29 states ("Sexual discrimination: Your rights," 2012).

Whether explicit or implicit, whether comparatively innocuous or insidious, heteronormativity constrains everyone, not just women and men, not just those who are queer or those who are straight. Those most vulnerable within heteronormative power dynamics are those who experience their gender in ways that do not conform to the gender they were assigned at birth: people who identify as transgender. Lesbians, gay men, and bisexual people, even those who otherwise conform to gender norms, are not recognized as gender normative because of their same-sex desire. People who actively resist classification in terms of gender or sexuality, and even those who merely question their gender or sexuality, are also vulnerable. This dynamic is ubiquitous. A woman whom others interpret as masculine is treated as a threat when she enters a public restroom. A man whom others interpret as feminine is also a target of abuse. A recent survey found:

> Those who expressed a transgender identity or gender non-conformity while in grades K–12 reported alarming rates of harassment (78%), physical assault (35%) and sexual violence (12%); harassment was so severe that it led almost one-sixth (15%) to leave a school in K–12 settings or in higher education. (Grant, Mottet, Tanis, Harrison, Herman, & Keisling, 2011)

Moreover, it is legal in 34 states to fire transgender employees just because they are trans (Weiss, 2011).

Understanding heteronormativity requires thinking of *sexual* identities in relation to *gender* identities, among others; thinking of them in the context of a world filled with power dynamics defined, in part, by heterosexism and sexism; and coming to terms with the fact that these power dynamics both impact and implicate all of us. Once one understands heteronormativity, one can no longer grapple with what it means to be a woman, for example, without thinking about her romantic and sexual desires and the way those desires shape her experiences in the world. Understanding heteronormativity means knowing that sexual and gender identity performances are not just about desire. Women are not only expected to desire men, they are also expected to appear feminine, marked by things such as clothing, accessories, and hairstyles. Within the realm of heteronormativity, men can be easily recognized as men and women as women. In a seemingly infinite number of ways, gender rules and regulations put and keep people in place. Not only LGBTQQ people are boxed in by socially constructed notions of what counts as appropriate behavior for women and men, and not only straight men and women enforce gender rules and regulations.

Understanding heteronormativity as a type of hegemony that constrains all of us in terms of sexual and gender identity performances is a threshold concept that allows students to navigate the bottleneck characterized by contentious topics related to LGBTQQ people. Students who fail to understand heteronormativity are less likely to understand why it might be useful to present and discuss gender and sexuality in nondichotomous terms. Adhering to dichotomous notions of gender and disentangling them from sexuality entirely is a sensible approach *if one fails to understand heteronormativity*, for a couple of reasons. One is that so many people, including many students, parents, colleagues, and administrators, are deeply invested in heteronormative dynamics and are even profoundly threatened by any effort to destabilize these dynamics. Another reason is that if gender and sexuality are disentangled from each other, then we can avoid talking about sexuality with people, particularly young people, whom many apparently need to believe are asexual and thus innocent beings. Given these reasons, rejecting the idea of heteronormativity is entirely reasonable. It's just so much easier to be a teacher and a student without messing with this system of oppression. It is easy to divide our classes into lines of boys and girls and lead them into separate bathrooms and locker rooms, not even questioning whether the labels they were assigned at birth align with how they experience the world, not even considering the fact that some people experience desires most intensely within the group that is designed to interrupt such desire, that is, gay boys desire boys (and lesbians desire girls), so putting them in boys' (or girls') bathrooms and locker rooms does not achieve the intended effect of eliminating sexual tension from those contexts. It is easy, unless, of course, you are the one whose assigned gender label doesn't align with your experience of the world or you are the one who experiences same-sex desire. This is why we must bother to navigate the bottleneck, for those who suffer the most under heteronormativity, and with an understanding that, really, we all suffer under it to varying degrees.

LGBT-Inclusivity and Queering

An understanding of the differences between two pedagogical approaches—LGBT-inclusivity and queering—can facilitate an understanding of heteronormativity. An LGBT-inclusive approach comes out of positivist, essentialist, even assimilationist paradigms. That is, undergirding the LGBT-inclusive approach is the belief that there is a set body of knowledge in the world about people who essentially are (or are not) lesbian, gay, bisexual, and/or transgender that, when accessed, would solve the problem of LGBT people being rejected by the straight mainstream. This approach suggests a false dichotomy between those who are and are not LGBT, which is dangerous for those positioned on the LGBT end of this false dichotomy because they are labeled as "the Other" and thus understood as vulnerable (Foucault, 1982). People who identify as bisexual and transgender are in even more danger in that they are positioned along with lesbians and gay men but often excluded from those groups' collective efforts toward seeking equal protections and rights. But this dichotomy is also dangerous for those it excludes, such as those who are questioning their sexual and/or gender identities as well as those who experience their sexual and/or gender identities more fluidly than such a dichotomy allows. Still, this approach effectively acknowledges, and attends to, in some important ways, the material realities of a population that traditionally has been ignored or maligned, such as the physical, verbal, and emotional abuse experienced by LGBT students, and those perceived to be LGBT students, in schools (Kosciw, Greytak, Diaz, & Bartkiewicz, 2010).

An alternative approach to pedagogy is *queering*, which comes from poststructural and critical paradigms in which beliefs of any set body of knowledge and essentialized identities are called into question. Scholars coming from a queering perspective believe that knowledge and identities are constructed in social, cultural, and political contexts and, therefore, are always changing. They reject the notion that being outside of the mainstream is a problem and instead argue that being pigeonholed by the mainstream into categories, such as L, G, B, and T, is the problem (e.g., Martino, 2009; Quinliven & Town, 1999; Sumara & Davis, 1999; Winans, 2006). According to Foucault (1982), when people can be labeled or named, they can be controlled. He asserts that oppressed people need to reject such naming. He states that "taking the forms of resistance against different forms of power [is] a starting point" (p. 780), but that oppressed people need to "promote new forms of subjectivity through the refusal of this kind of individuality which has been imposed on us" (p. 785) to free ourselves from oppression. Therefore, scholars coming from this perspective value suspending such classifications. Alternatively, queer theorists focus on related power dynamics, such as Rubin's (2004) "sex/gender system," Rich's (1980) "compulsory heterosexuality," Warner's (1991) "heteronormativity," which I described previously, and Butler's (1999/1990) "heterosexual matrix." As such, a queering approach can effectively evade the debate over whether to include

LGBTQ themes by engaging instead in discussions of power dynamics influenced by sexual and gender identities conceptualized more fluidly and perhaps more abstractly.

So, in retrospect, I see these two pedagogical approaches as characterizing my bottleneck journey of engaging topics pertinent to LGBTQQ people. That is, I see my early use of the LGBT-inclusive pedagogical approach as trapping my students in the metaphorical bottle, and my later use of the queering pedagogical approach as facilitating their move through the bottleneck and across the threshold concept of heteronormativity.

Storytelling

Shifting from an LGBT-inclusive to a queering approach, however, did not come easily to me. It was my struggle to tell a pedagogical story that provoked the shift. Adichie (2009) talks about the "danger of a single story"; that is, by reading, hearing, or witnessing only one story, one might generalize those experiences across all people who share some characteristic with the author, speaker, or person who lived those experiences. So, for example, recall *Philadelphia* (Demme & Saxon, 1993), a movie about a lawyer who sued his law firm for wrongful dismissal based on his having HIV/AIDS. If this were the only movie you ever saw about gay men, as it was for many people when this film came out, you might have come to believe that all gay men were rich, White, and suffering from HIV/AIDS. Indeed, this is the danger of a single story, and it cautions us to draw on the accounts of many to understand any given phenomenon.

As I analyzed my teaching of Reading Gender, I came to see that there is not only the danger of a single story, there is also the danger of a collection of stories. Which stories get told and how their telling influences one another matters. Gilbert and Kline (2006), in the introduction to their collection of interviews, write that they "wanted to ensure that each person had a distinctive story to tell—and that when read in the context of a larger collection of stories, each narrative would follow a common thread" (p. 19). Such an approach might benefit pedagogy as well. Whatever the course, whatever the context, the stories a teacher selects and the ways that she or he organizes them have consequences, often unintended, for the messages the teacher ultimately conveys to his or her students. Not one of the stories included in a curriculum stands alone; they all come together to tell yet another story. Here, I examine the messages I conveyed as I selected and positioned stories in the form of films, revising over and over again over the course I have taught for several years.

Reading Gender

Initially I struggled with the need for students to read scholarship in the field of education, literacy, and gender and the need for them to be exposed to theories of gender that challenged that body of literature, all in a one-week time frame. There simply was not enough time to read it all, and many students were not prepared to do the sort of theoretical reading needed in the course. I decided to use films to tell stories that might challenge traditional notions of gender and provoke exploration of gender in relationship to sexuality. I knew this approach would not provide the theoretical clarity that a text explicitly created to articulate theoretical ideas of gender might, but I believed it could give my students a feel for some theories of gender. I believed films could help me tell a story about gender, and, more specifically, a counterstory to those that undergird much of the scholarship they were reading, most of which talked about boys or girls in quite normative terms. I knew I wanted to tell a story about meeting the needs of gender nonconforming youth, but, as you will see, I was not sure how to tell it. Storytelling, like kayaking, requires great focus and effort. I needed to choose the right words, or in this case, films, to tell the story, but I also needed to place the words carefully. After a couple of mistellings, I came closer and closer to telling the story I wanted to tell.

Year 1: Being trans is bad but not bad enough to be punished by death.

The first time I taught the course I selected five films, but I focus here on one of them, the one that is at the crux of my evolving understanding of telling a pedagogical story about heteronormativity: *The Brandon Teena Story* (Muska & Olafsdóttir, 1998). I had started with *Osama* (Fraser, LeBrocquy, & Barmak, 2003), a 2003 film set (and made) in Afghanistan under the Taliban regime, because I wanted to expose gender rules and regulations by looking at a context in which they are intensely pronounced relative to how most people in the class experienced them every day. Then I showed *Thirteen* (Levy-Hinte, London, & Hardwicke, 2003) and *Hoop Dreams* (James, Gilbert, & Marx, 1994), both set in the United States, the former an autobiographical film about a White middle-school girl using her gender and sexuality to gain power in a heteronormative context, and the latter a documentary about two African American boys who dream of becoming professional basketball players. Having shown a film focused on girls and another focused on boys, I wanted to show a film focused on a transgender person. I wanted to include a broader range of gender, and this seemed like one way to do so. *The Brandon Teena Story* focuses on a White trans man, and, like the previous two films, is set in the United States. Brandon Teena, you might recall, was murdered in 1993 when the discrepancy between his assigned gender and his experienced and lived gender was discovered.

The effect of this film, in my experience, was disastrous. One student in particular passionately expressed her opinion that transgender identities were invalid, so Brandon Teena was essentially a lesbian deceiving an innocent straight girl into sleeping with her (Brandon), which, even if it had been consensual, was still sinful. Her expression of these troubling opinions, however, was essentially excused when she followed it with a statement about how it still was not okay to murder her (Brandon). There were two lesbian students who had, by this time in the class, come out to me. One of these two was also one of the two African Americans in the class, and the other lesbian was the only biracial student in the class. Whether there were other LGBTQQ people in the room, I do not know, but no one offered a clear rebuttal to the passionate student's comments. It was certainly not the lesbians' right or responsibility to speak for all LGBTQQ people, and considering how their classmates had evaded their recent contributions around race, I could appreciate their reluctance to speak again from their unique positionalities. Still, I had expected that someone would respond to the student who articulated such explicit transphobia. It has been my experience that I can respond to such a comment, but when it comes from me, it comes across as heavy-handed and essentially ends the conversation. However, when a student offers a response, the conversation continues, opening more opportunities for people to share their thoughts on what is, for some, a difficult conversation. This often is a very positive experience, but in this case no one spoke up. I had not created a classroom context in which anyone, even students who identified with LGBTQQ communities, could communicate support for trans people.

The student's comment about Brandon Teena undid much of what I was hoping to accomplish. I was hoping that the film would provoke more understanding of and empathy for trans people. Instead, students with negative beliefs and values regarding trans people were never challenged, and students who might have had positive beliefs and values around trans people never articulated those beliefs and values. The class's attention had shifted to the issue of murder and away from the biases and hatred that provoked the murder of Brandon Teena. I responded to the comment, but more out of passion than intellect, not that the two are mutually exclusive, just that the former eclipsed the latter in my response. For me, this film and the related *Boys Don't Cry* (Vachon, Kolodner, & Peire, 1999) leave me raw and thus vulnerable, feelings that clearly shaped my response in our class. This is perfectly sensible since the dominating tone suggested that, although such beliefs and values are not worthy of capital punishment, they are worthy of punishment just short of that. As a result of this incident I realized that, to accomplish what I was hoping, I needed to show a film that focused on trans life rather than trans death, both for myself as a discussion facilitator, so I might feel less raw and vulnerable and more capable of responding with both passion and intellect, and for the students, many of whom had much to learn about trans people.

I had hit a rock in the river. I had unintentionally posed the question of whether trans people should be included in discussions of gender, reading, and education—a question that essentially was grounded in an LGBT-approach—and the answer was *no*.

Year 2: Being trans is so, so sad.

I didn't teach the course again for three years. I knew, though, that when I had the chance to teach it again, I would have to revise the film selections significantly, not because there was some right set of films that I had just not figured out yet, but because I had told a story through a collection of films that was understood quite differently from the one I had intended to tell. This time, I wanted to tell a story about people who break gender rules and regulations, why they do it, and the consequences they face. I wanted students to reflect on reasons why some people might break gender rules and regulations that so many people value and even celebrate. Moreover, I wanted students to recognize which, if any, gender rules and regulations they followed, honored, and even enforced. I wanted them to think about the consequences of enforced gender rules and regulations and the roles they wanted to play, or did not want to play, in the case of such consequences. I wanted students to think about gender in relationship to other identities, including, but not limited to, sexual identities. And I wanted them to understand gender and sexual dynamics as systemic and, therefore, as impacting and implicating them. In short, I wanted them to understand heteronormativity.

Another change I made in this second year was to provide background information on each of the films prior to viewing by distributing information sheets I created to describe a bit about the making of the films, the time periods in which they were set, and the cultures they represented. This seemed to help students hear the story more like I was trying to tell it. This was a practice I continued throughout my teaching of this course.

In this version of the course, I started with *Whale Rider* (Barnett, Hübner, Sanders, & Caro, 2002). This New Zealand film focuses on Pai, a 12-year-old girl who, in all ways except cultural expectations, seems destined to follow her grandfather as chief of their tribe. Cultural expectations dictate that this role is reserved for men. Again and again, Pai excels at what only boys in her tribe even attempt. For example, Pai's grandfather designs a challenge to identify the next chief by taking a small group of boys to the sea and throwing his whale tooth necklace, which symbolizes the values of the tribe, in the water. Several of the boys dive in the water, but none is able to bring the tooth back to Pai's grandfather. Later, Pai asks her uncle to take her back to the spot where her grandfather threw the necklace. She dives, searches, finds, and returns the tooth, but because her grandfather is not yet ready to admit that a woman might follow him as chief, she gives the tooth to her grandmother, who holds on to it until he can admit it. Ultimately, Pai is accepted and celebrated as chief of the tribe. Overall, this is a story about a girl breaking gender rules and regulations in ways that are ultimately, if not immediately, celebrated.

I followed *Whale Rider* with *Billy Elliot* (Brenman, Finn, & Daldry, 2000), a British film from 2000 about an 11-year-old boy who loves and excels at ballet. Although his grandmother was a dancer, his father and brother are coal miners. The film is set during the 1984–1985 miners' strike, so the family does not have the money or inclination to nurture Billy's growing interest in dance. Billy eventually, and unintentionally, performs for his father, who becomes convinced of Billy's gift for dancing. Billy's father then commits to supporting Billy's new craft. At the end of the film, Billy's father and brother are shown attending a performance starring the adult Billy in *Swan Lake*. It concludes with a cut of Billy's incredibly muscular back. It is as if Billy can break gender rules and regulations by engaging in the stereotypically feminine activity of ballet and be tolerated for doing so as long as he excels; he might even be celebrated if he does so with great strength and masculinity.

These two films worked as a starting point. Students mostly enjoyed them, and they engaged in discussions about gender rules and regulations. In Pai and Billy, students were able to see both a girl and a boy who broke gender rules and regulations in ways that they valued, and they questioned the efforts of characters who tried to enforce gender rules and regulations on them. In short, they were on Pai and Billy's sides. I worried, however, that students' unequivocal support relied, in part, on the asexualization of Pai and Billy. Pai never seems to experience any sexual desire at all in *Whale Rider*. Billy experiences sexual advances from both a girl friend and a boy friend, but he rejects each of their advances and is thus, like Pai, not understood in terms of his desire. I wondered what might have happened, in terms of students' understandings of and receptiveness to gender diversity, had Billy accepted the advances made by the boy but not the girl, for example.

I knew that the next film we watched needed to show characters, not just engaging in behaviors stereotypically associated with those of the "opposite" gender, as Pai and Billy did, but also actually performing the "opposite" gender, as Brandon Teena did, to push students' thinking about gender diversity. I use the word *opposite*, here, and put it in quotation marks, to recognize common conceptualizations of male and female, man and woman, boy and girl as opposites but also to call such conceptualizations into question, or to disrupt or queer them, a distinction I articulated to my students toward the middle of our week together, when I showed this third film. This recognition and disruption of dichotomized notions of gender seem to me to be important work in the queering of heteronormativity.

I selected *Baran* (Majidi & Nahas, 2001), an Iranian film focused on Afghan refugees in Tehran in contemporary times. The central characters are Lateef, a 17-year-old boy who works in building construction, and Rahmat, an Afghan coworker. Lateef discovers Rahmat is actually Baran, a girl disguised as a boy, and falls in love with her. Even after they are fired from their jobs because they are Afghan, Lateef seeks Baran, eventually witnessing and trying to free her from her desperate circumstances, which include grueling work reserved for women in the community.

I wanted to build on the notion of people performing genders "opposite" those assigned at birth, but I wanted to call into question what sociocultural circumstances made this acceptable or unacceptable. In other words, Baran's need to become Rahmat for economic survival seemed indisputably acceptable to students, as had the girl's performance of Osama in the film I showed previously. In the earlier version of the course, I tried to expand students' notions of "acceptable" with *The Brandon Teena Story*, but this time I tried *Paris Is Burning* (Livingston, 1991), a 1990 documentary about drag balls in New York City. In this film, racially diverse gay men and trans women are interviewed about their experiences performing gender both in competitions or balls and in their lives beyond these events. The film appeals to me, in part, because of its focus on intersectionality; that is, it effectively explores issues of race, class, gender, and sexuality in relationship to one another.

The combination of *Baran* and *Paris Is Burning*, however, seemed to undo the work that *Whale Rider* and *Billy Elliot*, together, had done. Students tended to judge the people in *Paris Is Burning* for cross-dressing, a behavior that had dire consequences, as evidenced when one of the girls interviewed in the film was killed before production wrapped. It was as if *Baran* was tolerable and maybe even pitiable because she had to cross-dress for economic survival, but the youth in *Paris Is Burning* were scorned because their cross-dressing was about things less tangible, such as identity expression. This was the third U.S. film that seemed to provoke my students' judgment of the featured young person or people (*Thirteen*, *The Brandon Teena Story*, and *Paris Is Burning*). Students raised rhetorical questions about why the people documented in *Paris Is Burning* did not just adhere to gender norms to make life easier for themselves. Much like the one student's response to *The Brandon Teena Story* three years earlier, my students in this version of the course disapproved of the murder, but they also seemed to disapprove of the person or people breaking gender rules and regulations. This was in direct conflict with my intention.

The final film of this version of the course was *Ma Vie en Rose* (Scotta, Berliner, & Stappen, 1997). This 1997 Belgian and French film focuses on Ludovic, a seven-year-old child who was assigned the gender of boy at birth and was raised accordingly but knows herself to be female and, more specifically, a female who is attracted to males. Ludo's family struggles to understand her and to negotiate the homophobia and transphobia they all endure as a result of who Ludo knows herself to be. My erroneous thinking in placing this film last in the progression was that it pushes notions of gender diversity more intensely than the other films I showed. Ludo did not just perform the "opposite" gender because she had to do so for economic survival, for example; in fact, her performances actually jeopardized her family's financial stability. Nor did Ludo perform the "opposite" gender for particular events, like a ball. Ludo knew with all of her being that she was a girl. Rather than allowing for or even celebrating Ludo's girlhood, students pitied Ludo and her family. Again, this was not my intent.

Upon reflection, I interpret my earlier efforts at Reading Gender as coming from an LGBT-inclusive approach. I was very focused on what I could and could not include in terms of my commitment to LGBTQQ people. I worried about being accused of making everything about LGBTQQ people because I was a lesbian and had worked with LGBTQQ youth.

Within the parameters of an LGBT-inclusive approach, and thus without a commitment to the notion of heteronormativity, I felt as though I was allowed to include issues pertinent to trans people, since those identities were about gender, which was in the title of the course, and not allowed to include issues pertinent to LGB people, since those identities were about sexuality, not gender. As a result of my efforts to disentangle sexuality from gender, I could not move students to understanding heteronormativity, and my LGBT-inclusive approach fell apart, leaving only a T-inclusive approach. And the transgender person represented was ultimately murdered because of his trans identity. The overall story the collection of films seemed to tell was that being trans is bad but not so bad as to be deserving of murder. This is not to say that all students in this class heard this particular story, but one could have heard it that way, indeed at least one did, and I crafted the story in a way that allowed for such an interpretation. Even with films such as *Paris Is Burning* and *Ma Vie en Rose*, the story of the films seemed to suggest that being trans was pitiable. This was certainly not what I was trying to accomplish.

This account points to a pitfall to watch out for when exploring the lives of any marginalized people. It is not unusual for marginalized people to be treated poorly, and for people, including teachers, with good intentions to use those stories to motivate other people, like their students, to change things for those who are marginalized. An unintended consequence, though, can be to reify marginalization. That is, in trying to advocate on behalf of transgender people, I underscored their victimhood and elicited pity instead of understanding. I needed to take more care in choosing the films.

Years 3 and 4: Learning to meet the needs of gender-nonconforming youth.

Based on the previous year, I believed that starting with *Whale Rider* and *Billy Elliot* allowed students to discuss youth breaking gender rules and regulations in ways that positioned them as advocates for young people, so I planned to start there again. I also thought that moving from characters engaging in behaviors stereotypically associated with those of the "opposite" gender to those performing "opposite" genders would be effective in terms of pushing students' thinking about gender diversity, so I considered both *Osama* and *Baran* again. I selected *Osama* mostly because students seemed to follow it better, since *Baran* is an almost silent film. Rather than juxtaposing *Osama* with *Paris Is Burning*, though, which I thought, like the combination of *Baran* and *Paris Is Burning*, would foster a blaming response toward the characters in *Paris Is Burning*, I moved *Ma Vie en Rose* to day 4 and *Paris Is Burning* to day 5. I wanted to tell a story about meeting the needs of young people oppressed by gender rules and regulations, and this switch in the order of films, this careful placing of words, had a significant impact on achieving my goal.

When students met Ludo after meeting Pai, Billy, and Osama, they seemed to pull for her much as they did the other films' central characters. It seemed to me that, because Ludo was so young, people were less inclined to say that something happened in her life experiences that made her transgender, in contrast to the young adults in *Paris Is Burning*, in which one might argue that Venus Xtravaganza, for example, was born male but became female because she wanted to be supported by men or, in her words, "a spoiled, rich, White girl living in the suburbs." Further, Ludo's White middle-class family discouraged students from blaming her family, as troubling as this is. Some students might have understood Ludo's attraction to and desire for boys and men as inappropriate, given her age, or as "homosexual," given her assigned gender, and thus rejected her. However, Ludo's sexuality did not seem to have either effect in the years I taught this course with the films in this order. Rather, it seemed to me that Ludo gave the class a productive way of discussing the relationship between gender and sexuality by acknowledging her gender assignment as boy and her gender identity as girl and her attraction to and desire for boys. We could talk about how, whether people understood her as a boy or a girl, they understood her attraction to boys and men. People's understandings of whether her attraction was "homosexual" or "heterosexual" depended on their understandings of her gender. In other words, if people, either characters in the movie or students in the class, understood Ludo on her terms, they had to understand her as heterosexual. Otherwise, they had to understand her as gay. There was no way of avoiding the discussion of oppression, whether in the shape of transphobia or homophobia, within the heterosexual matrix. Students made a clumsy but explicit effort to reference Ludo in her preferred gender pronouns. They talked about the dynamics in the film with empathy rather than judgment. They seemed to approach the end of the class with an understanding that, while some people perform the "opposite" gender for economic reasons, others do so for deeply personal reasons, and both of these kinds of reasons were valid.

With this foundation, it felt imperative to bring the discussion of gender rules and regulations back home again, so I ended the course with *Paris Is*

Burning. This film was still challenging to students, but I wanted to challenge them. This film, more than any of the others, queers dichotomous notions of gender by representing real people who experience and embody gender in a full range of ways, and sexuality is one of those ways. That I had reached students with a wide range of perspectives on understandings of and receptiveness to gender diversity was evident in two of the anonymous comments I received on my teaching evaluations for the course. A student who was more receptive to the work I was trying to accomplish simply said, "Great professor, knows her material well, excellent selection of material." Even more inspiring, though, was this:

> Although some of the content was unexpected, I felt the progression of the class had been carefully constructed as to prepare us for more intense and controversial issues to be discussed as the week progressed. I did not agree with some of the content based on my religious beliefs. Despite my disagreement with some of the content, Mollie presented the material [and] structured the course in such a way that I could evaluate my own learning and utilize the knowledge gained in order to meet the needs of my students without compromising my faith.

This, to me, was the point of the class. I wanted to tell a story, via the films, about people who break gender rules and regulations, why they do it, and with what consequences. I wanted those who heard the story to advocate on behalf of all of their students, but particularly those students who do not conform to gender rules and regulations. It seems to me that this course got closer and closer to accomplishing this goal.

Advocacy Through Queering Heteronormativity

Over time, as I worked more to tell a story about gender diversity and raise questions about who breaks gender rules and regulations, why, with what consequences, and how we might advocate on behalf of gender nonconforming youth, my approach shifted from LGBT-inclusive to queering. By raising questions about people engaging in behaviors that are not stereotypically associated with their genders, with Pai and Billy; people performing genders in ways that are the "opposite" of the genders they were assigned at birth, with Osama and Ludo; and people who experience and embody gender less dichotomously, as many of the people in *Paris Is Burning*, and further, by coming to think about these things in relationship to sexuality, particularly

Ludo's and that of many of the people in *Paris Is Burning*, the course worked to queer heteronormative notions of gender.

An ironic result was that, when moving through the bottleneck, that is, away from an LGBT-inclusive approach, which admittedly fell apart, over the threshold of heteronormativity, and toward a queer-inclusive approach, more LGBTQQ people were represented in the course, including Billy's childhood friend, Michael, and Ludo's childhood friend, Chris, and many of the people in *Paris Is Burning*. More important, in response to the queering approach, more students seemed to position themselves as advocates of gender nonconforming youth. They applauded Pai's uncle for teaching her skills typically reserved for boys. They praised Billy's ballet teacher for her faith and persistence. They talked about how they wished Ludo's teacher and therapist might have acted, how they would have acted had they been Ludo's teacher or counselor. They also talked about how they, as teachers, might better serve young people like those in *Paris Is Burning* when they were in school so that they might choose to stay in school. By coming to understand heteronormativity as being about integrated identities, particularly gender and sexuality, and as about systemic oppressions, such as sexism and heterosexism, students were less likely to worry about whether, say, trans people were included or not, and more likely to position themselves as workers of change against these oppressions. They were, in short, more prepared to queer heteronormativity.

I learned several skills to help me navigate the bottleneck. I learned the importance of offering background information about a film so students could attend to the gender dynamics that caused me to select the film in the first place. I also realized that clearly articulating why I selected films helped students look for and examine the aspects that connect the films to the topic of the class. I was reminded of the importance of selecting films that show marginalized people not merely as victims but as both victims and agents. I came to understand the importance of selecting films that I could discuss with both intellect and passion, as lacking only one of the two could prevent me from effectively facilitating discussions. I also learned that, for my students, the heterosexual matrix set in communities most like their own was the most challenging to see. Therefore, students were better able to comprehend the threshold concept of heteronormativity when it was made visible in contexts quite different from their own before being challenged to see it closer to home. This was yet another way in which the collection and arrangement of stories mattered in that they produced yet another, overarching story.

With this in mind, I challenge all of us as social justice educators to reflect on the stories we have collected for our classrooms, whether these are films or books, fiction or fact, but to reflect on the collection of them and consider the stories we are telling. Are these the stories we want to be telling—the stories we want the future teachers in our classes to be telling *their* students? Are they stories that say there are no LGBTQQ people? Or that there is one way to be LGBTQQ? Or that only White people are LGBTQQ? Or that all LGBTQQ people are victims? Let us reflect, too, on the consequences of the stories we are telling. What might it mean for a lesbian in your class to believe she is the only one? Or for a young gay man of color to believe that all gay people are White? Or for a White gay youth to hear and read only stories of queer youth suicides? Let us reflect on the ways we might revise the stories we tell to make life more bearable for these young people. Are we telling stories that put individuals in isolation from society so that they are alone to receive either praise or blame? Or are they stories that explain how the world functions in constructing who they are so they can still assume agency but with an understanding of why they do what they do in relation to what others do? Let us reflect on what it might mean for LGBTQQ youth to understand heteronormativity, and for their classmates to understand it as well.

Understanding heteronormativity prohibits an understanding of LGBTQQ people as victims in need of rescue by altruistic allies or by agents fighting against big, bad bullies, interpretations that, while well intended, simplify and degrade all involved. Instead, understanding heteronormativity challenges one to consider the many ways we all might benefit by working together to disrupt this oppressive social dynamic. And what might this mean for LGBTQQ youth? Truly, it might mean the difference between life and death.

In the end, I figured how to sequence the films to allow students to move conceptually through the bottleneck characterized by contentious topics related to LGBTQQ people. The early films provided the groundwork by helping students interrogate gender rules and regulations as they were imposed on a girl, Pai, and a boy, Billy. I was able to push this interrogation a little further by introducing a girl who, due to economic necessity, had to live her life as a boy. Then I could build on students' understandings of such a concrete necessity to help them understand much more abstract necessities, such as conflicting internal and external perceptions of gender. In doing so, students came to understand the complicated relationship among sex, gender, and sexuality and how rules and regulations around these identities—that is, heteronormativity—oppress a range of people.

Note

1. Generally I use the more inclusive acronym, LGBTQQ. When I do not, it is with respect to the people, place, or scholarship I'm referencing. For example, when I reference the youth center, I use *LGBTQ* youth because that was the acronym the center used. When I reference a body of literature, I use LGBT-inclusivity because that most accurately describes the focus of the literature included in this body, as I discuss.

References

Adichie, C. N. (2009). The danger of a single story. http://www.ted.com/talks/chimamanda_adichie_the_danger_of_a_single_story.html

Barnett, J., Hübner, F., & Sanders, T. (Producers), & Caro, N. (Director). (2002). *Whale rider* [Motion picture]. Toronto: Buena Vista International.

Brenman, G., & Finn, J. (Producers), & Daldry, S. (Director). (2000). *Billy Elliot* [Motion picture]. United Kingdom: Universal Focus.

Butler, J. (1999/1990). *Gender trouble: Feminism and the subversion of identity* (2nd ed.). New York: Routledge.

Demme, J. (Producer & Director), & Saxon, E. (Producer). (1993). *Philadelphia* [Motion picture]. United States: TriStar Pictures.

Foucault, M. (1982). The subject and power. *Critical Inquiry, 8*(4), 777–795.

Fraser, J., & LeBrocquy, J. (Producers), & Barmak, S. (Director). (2003). *Osama* [Motion picture]. United Kingdom: United Artists.

Gilbert, A., & Kline, C. B. (2006). *Always too soon: Voices of support for those who have lost both parents.* Berkeley, CA: Seal Press.

Grant, J. M., Mottet, L. A., Tanis, J., Harrison, J., Herman, J. L., & Keisling, M. (2011). Injustice at every turn: A report of the national transgender discrimination survey, executive summary. Washington, DC: National Center for Transgender Equality and National Gay and Lesbian Task Force.

James, S., Gilbert, P., & Marx, F. (Producers), & James, S. (Director). (1994). *Hoop dreams* [Motion picture]. United States: Fine Line Features.

Kosciw, J. G., Greytak, E. A., Diaz, E. M., & Bartkiewicz, M. J. (2010). *The 2009 National School Climate Survey: The experiences of lesbian, gay, bisexual and transgender youth in our nation's schools.* New York: GLSEN.

Levy-Hinte, J., & London, M. (Producers), & Hardwicke, C. (Director). (2003). *Thirteen* [Motion picture]. United States: Fox Searchlight Productions.

Livingston, J. (Producer & Director). (1991). *Paris is burning* [Motion picture]. United States: Miramax Films.

Majidi, M., & Nahas, F. (Producers), & Majidi, M. (Director). (2001). *Baran* [Motion picture]. Miramax Films.

Martino, W. (2009). Literacy issues and GLBTQ youth: Queer interventions in English education. In L. Christenbury, R. Bomer, & P. Smagorinsky (Eds.), *Handbook of adolescent literacy research* (pp. 386–399). New York: Guilford.

Muska, S., & Olafsdóttir, G. (Directors). (1998). *The Brandon Teena story* [Motion picture]. United States: Bless Bless Productions.

Quinlivan, K., & Town, S. (1999). Queer pedagogy, educational practice and lesbian and gay youth. *Qualitative studies in education, 12*(5), 509–524.

Rich, A. (1980). Compulsory heterosexuality and lesbian existence. *Signs, 5*(4), 631–660.

Rubin, G. (2004). The traffic in women. In J. Rivkin & M. Ryan (Eds.) *Literary theory: An anthology* (2nd ed.) (pp. 770–794). Malden, MA: Blackwell.

Scotta, C. (Producer), & Berliner, A., & Stappen, C. V. (Directors). (1997). *Ma vie en rose* [Motion picture]. United States: Sony Pictures Classics.

Sexual discrimination: Your rights. (2012). *NOLO: Law for all.* Retrieved February 15, 2012, from http://www.nolo.com/legal-encyclopedia/sexual-orientation-discrimination-rights-29541.html

Sumara, D., & Davis, B. (1999). Interrupting heteronormativity: Toward queer curriculum theory. *Curriculum Inquiry, 29*(2), 191–208.

Vachon, C. & Kolodner, E. (Producers), & Peire, K. (Director). (1999). *Boys don't cry* [Motion picture]. United States: Fox Searchlight Productions.

Warner, M. (1991). Introduction: Fear of a queer planet. *Social Text, 9*(4), 3–17.

Weiss, J. T. (2011). Transgender political trends. *The Bilerico Project.* Retrieved February 15, 2012, from http://www.bilerico.com/2011/11/transgender_political_trends.php

Winans, A. E. (2006). Queering pedagogy in the English classroom: Engaging with the places where thinking stops. *Pedagogy: Critical Approaches to Teaching Literature, Language, Composition, and Culture, 6*(1), 103–122.

5

OVERCOMING DEFICIT THINKING THROUGH INTERPRETIVE DISCUSSION

Curt Dudley-Marling

A few years ago I collaborated with one of my doctoral students on a project that challenged four novice teachers, all recent graduates of our teacher preparation program at Boston College, to replace the deficit thinking that shaped their work with struggling learners with a social constructivist perspective. Overcoming deficit thinking is, I believe, fundamental to a social justice perspective that acknowledges a range of systemic factors that limit the life chances of many students in American schools. Therefore, instead of situating school failure in the heads of students or their families, language, culture, and communities, we wanted the novice teachers to consider the complex of social, cultural, curricular, and institutional factors that *construct* students as struggling learners—or competent ones. For instance, we showed them videos of fourth-grade students in a high-poverty, underperforming school in the South Bronx participating in Interpretive Discussions (Haroutunian-Gordon, 2009) in which students read and discussed challenging texts, making claims, citing textual evidence, and, occasionally, explicating the link between their claims and the textual evidence. In a context where these fourth-grade students, almost all of whom did poorly on state and district reading assessments, were challenged with the kind of rich, engaging reading curriculum common in affluent, high-achieving schools they were transformed into competent readers. We also talked to these novice teachers about how the skills-focused, dumbed-down curriculum these same children were subjected to during their first years in school had made them poor readers.

Over the course of the year, we asked the novice teachers to read articles, watch videos, listen to presentations, and, above all, talk about their work with students in their classrooms, all in an effort to get them to view struggling learners as "smart," not deficient. But, in the end, we had only mixed success. The four teachers had no difficulty taking up a social constructivist lens to talk about children in the abstract. However, when they discussed specific low-achieving students in their own classes, especially children who had acquired some sort of label like learning disabled or attention deficit disordered (ADD), they readily defaulted to deficit discourses (Paugh & Dudley-Marling, 2011). After several sessions discussing social constructivist perspectives on learning failure, here's how a teacher we call Molly talked about a student in her class.

> [Michael is] a kid whose intelligence is borderline to like retardation. His intelligence is so low that he is not even aware that he is struggling. And for writing, he'll just write x's and g's and r's because he knows that he's writing down letters. But Michael just doesn't have any idea of the concept of print. . . . Not only that Michael is so behind, but he is very learning disabled and it's discouraging because there is only so much [time] you can sit down with them. It's a little struggle with this. I just don't know . . . it's not even modifying . . . you can't even do that . . . Michael doesn't even know how to add 2 + 3. . . . He goes, one, two, and then one, two, three. . . . He has no clue. (Paugh & Dudley-Marling, 2011, pp. 6–7)

Molly's comments, typical of the four novice teachers, indicate that our efforts to move these novice teachers beyond a deficit perspective were relatively powerless in confronting the dominant discourse of schooling that is saturated with deficit thinking.

My experience with the students I teach at Boston College mirrors our work with the novice teachers. Each semester I push my students to replace the deficit thinking that typically shapes their understanding of struggling learners and their families with a more complex, social constructivist perspective on school failure through the use of videos, lectures, and, particularly, discussions of "powerful" texts. I believe it is critical for my BC students to reject deficit thinking if they're going to challenge students disadvantaged by poverty and discrimination with the kind of rich curriculum common in high-achieving, affluent schools. It is also my hope that overcoming deficit thinking will encourage my BC students to challenge students with disabilities with the sort of engaging curriculum used with the most able students. But, like the novice teachers, my students actively engage in critiques of deficit thinking and have little difficulty articulating alternative, social constructivist perspectives on learning and learning problems—at least *in the abstract*. However, when they talk about individual students in discussions and course assignments, like the novice teachers, they often default to deficit discourses to explain low academic achievement. For example, for the final assignment in a reading methods class I teach each fall, I ask my students to analyze their work with an individual child over the course of the semester. Despite my efforts to get them to adopt a social constructivist perspective on student learning, my students tend to write about "missing skills," "low ability," "learning problems," and various "deficiencies" that, for them, *explain* low academic achievement. It pains me to admit it, but I'm often unsuccessful helping my students resist the power of deficit thinking. Lectures and videos generally fail to transform students' thinking, and discussions of "powerful" texts have proved not to be so powerful.

So, for my students, deficit thinking constitutes a "bottleneck," a way of thinking that leads them to resist systemic perspectives on learning that implicate the structures of schooling and society more generally—and not deficiencies in students, their families, culture, or communities—in school failure. More seriously, deficit thinking makes it more likely that students who end up working in poor, urban schools will reproduce the circumscribed curricula that limits children's educational and vocational possibilities. Therefore, I decided to try a different approach to discussing readings in my classes, a rigorous approach to classroom discussion, called "Interpretive Discussion," that seeks to engage students in thoughtful, critical thinking around challenging texts (Haroutunian-Gordon, 2009).

In this chapter I briefly describe Interpretive Discussion before sharing a project I undertook in one of my graduate classes to examine the potential of Interpretive Discussion to engage students in rigorous, thoughtful discussions of difficult texts. I focus here on our discussion of one of the readings I chose to challenge students' deficit thinking: *Culture as Disability* by Ray McDermott and Harvé Varenne (1995).

Interpretive Discussion

The potential of discussions to promote learning and understanding has led many social justice educators to rely on discussions of powerful texts like Peggy MacIntosh's (1989) article, "White Privilege: Unpacking the Invisible Knapsack," to challenge students' thinking about race and other social justice issues. And there is a body of research indicating that well-orchestrated discussions have the power to affect students' engagement with—and understanding of—challenging texts (Dillon, 1994). However, research also indicates that engaging discussions, focused on a topic that is "maintained, extended or developed" (Dillon, 1994, p. 13), are relatively rare in college classrooms. Often "discussions" in college classrooms are merely recitations in which instructors lead students to predetermined answers or free-flowing conversations where talk drifts aimlessly from topic to topic (Hardman & Mroz, 1999).

Discussion in elementary classrooms is a major focus of my research agenda, yet I have been generally disappointed in the quality of discussions in my courses at Boston College. These discussions go beyond recitation but generally lack the focus and engagement of the academically productive discussions I have observed in many elementary classrooms. So in spring 2010, I introduced Interpretive Discussion (Haroutunian-Gordon, 2009) in one of my graduate courses to improve the quality of our discussions.

Preparing for an Interpretive Discussion begins with a careful reading of the text to be discussed, including creation of an overarching, *interpretive question* for which there is more than one reasonable answer (Haroutunian-Gordon, 2009). The basic, interpretive question is augmented by a set of follow-up questions that keep the discussion moving and focused and point students to different places in the text to answer this question. Interpretive Discussion requires that students respond to the basic or follow-up questions by making claims, using textual evidence to support their claims, and, if necessary, making explicit how the textual evidence supports their claims. Instructors facilitate Interpretive Discussion through the use of various *talk moves* (Michaels, O'Connor, Hall, & Resnick, 2002) that affect the shape and quality of interactions among participants in the discussion, including revoicing ("So are you saying . . . ?"); asking students to clarify their reasoning ("How does that relate to the basic question?"); requesting evidence ("Where does the text support your claim?"); restating the (basic) question; inviting participation ("Anyone we haven't heard from?"); and providing wait time to allow students to formulate a response. Interpretive Discussion also demands that instructors avoid any type of direct or indirect evaluation on the assumption that instructor evaluation will transform discussions into recitations in which students compete for the *right* answer. In the context of Interpretive Discussion, students collaborate to make sense of texts by responding to basic and follow-up questions, but there are no *right* answers.

An Action Research Project

To examine the effectiveness of Interpretive Discussion in engaging students in rigorous discussions of challenging readings, I introduced Interpretive Discussion as an action research project. The class was a graduate course, called "Foundations of Language and Literacy," that focused on literacy theory and research. There were 26 students in the class, one male and 25 females. Two students taught at the secondary level; the rest were elementary teachers. Two students, one male and one female, spoke Spanish as their first language, and another was an African American woman. The rest of the students were White women whose primary language was English. Fifteen of the students were experienced classroom teachers; the other 11 were pre-service teachers. One of the stated goals for the course was to challenge the deficit thinking that dominates language and literacy instruction in American schools.

To support the action research component of this project, I made video recordings of five Interpretive Discussions, each approximately one hour in length, and audio recordings of debriefing sessions with my class in the weeks following Interpretive Discussions. I also collected writing my students did at the end of our discussions. Finally, I kept a research journal in which I recorded my reflections about our discussions. Implementing Interpretive Discussion as action research enabled me to evaluate the effectiveness of this model as a means of engaging students in rigorous discussion. The ongoing nature of action research helped me to modify the practice of Interpretive Discussion based on what I was learning.

In the rest of this chapter I examine the effectiveness of our final Interpretive Discussion based on an article, called "Culture as Disability" (McDermott & Varenne, 1995), one of two we discussed that explicitly challenged deficit thinking.

Challenging Deficit Thinking: "Culture as Disability"

The fundamental argument that McDermott and Varenne (1995) make in "Culture as Disability" is that, from an anthropological perspective,

> Disability refers most precisely to inadequate performances only on tasks that are arbitrarily circumscribed from daily life. Disabilities are less the property of persons than they are moments in a cultural focus. Everyone in any culture is subject to being labeled and disabled. (p. 324)

In other words, disabilities don't reside in people's heads as much as they inhabit the relations among people, tasks, institutions, and so on, and the meaning given to these relationships is always cultural. From this perspective, disability is a cultural construct, not the result of individual traits or *deficits*. As McDermott and Varenne (1995) put it, "one cannot be disabled alone" (p. 337), but only within a cultural context.

My hope was that our discussion of this article would trouble students' deficit thinking by suggesting an alternative, social constructivist lens for conceptualizing learning difficulties. It is important to point out, however, that my goal was to push students' thinking, not to lead them to a particular reading of McDermott and Varenne (1995). Another one of my goals across all of our Interpretive Discussions was for students to develop the tools they would need for engaging with other difficult texts, particularly those that focused on social justice issues.

After multiple readings of "Culture as Disability," I offered the following interpretive question to focus our discussion: "According to McDermott and Varenne, how does culture disable?" This question gets to the heart of the McDermott and Varenne (1995) article while challenging students to challenge the argument that the meaning of disabilities—and deficit thinking in general—is always a function of cultural and institutional norms.

As we prepared to discuss "Culture as Disability," I posed the basic question, and then I offered students some time to collect their thoughts before opening the discussion. Although I expected students to do their own careful reading of the text—and the evidence suggests that they typically read texts multiple times to prepare for our Interpretive Discussions—some of them had suggested during an earlier debriefing session that they would like to have some time to consider their responses to the basic question before discussions began. Later in the term, some of them suggested that writing would be a particularly useful way to prepare for discussions. So before we began our discussion of "Culture as Disability," I gave students seven or eight minutes to write something in response to the interpretive question I had posed and, if they wished, to discuss their responses with someone else, another idea that came from our debriefing sessions.

In the rest of this section, I share a few of my conclusions about the efficacy of Interpretive Discussion as a means of engaging my students in thoughtful and rigorous discussion of the text, "Culture as Disability" and, ultimately, challenging students' deficit thinking.

There Was a High Level of Participation in the Discussion

As I noted previously, discussions in many postsecondary classrooms turn out to be recitations in which instructors do most of the talking. A simple count of turns and total number of words spoken indicate that in our discussion of "Culture as Disability," students did most of the talking. My students took approximately two-thirds of the total number of turns in the discussion and, overall, did 85% of the talking in terms of total number of words spoken. On average, most students took relatively long turns (on average 98 words per turn, ranging from seven to 455 words in a single turn), compared to the short turns that characterize recitation formats. And, of the 25 students present during the discussion, 21 took at least one turn and 11 took at least two turns.[1]

Overall, these descriptive statistics indicate a fairly high level of student participation in the discussion of "Culture as Disability." However, this begs the more important question about the quality of student engagement during our discussion and whether the discussion actually challenged students' deficit thinking.

In the rest of this chapter, I argue that, based on an analysis of Interpretive Discussions in my language and literacy course, my students were substantively engaged in making sense of "Culture as Disability" and how it challenges the notion that deficits reside in the minds and bodies of individual students. However, meaning-making was generally a collective effort as students pushed each other's thinking. And, although students worked together to make sense of the text, they didn't all get the same meaning. They started in different places and drew on different lenses as they interpreted the text. Finally, the various moves I made as I orchestrated this discussion created conversational spaces that affected the quality of student engagement and the meanings students made of the text. The degree to which these moves were effective may suggest some strategies for facilitating thoughtful, engaging discussions in other courses with other readings.

Students Made Sense of Texts Collaboratively

Interactions among students indicated a high level of engagement in the Interpretive Discussion of "Culture as Disability." Students didn't just offer a string of responses as they grappled with McDermott and Varenne's (1995) critique of deficit thinking. As they responded to the basic question—"How do cultures disable?"—they constructed a collaborative sense of the text, explicitly building on and challenging each other's interpretations of the article. For instance, students routinely connected what they said to comments by previous speakers. The following sequence was typical.

> Catherine[2]: "On page 337 . . . it says that 'by this last approach, culture refers to an organization of hopes and dreams about how the world should be.' So I think that cultures disable and enable by sort of defining what they think the norm should be . . . and if you don't meet the norm you're disabled."
>
> Anne: "On the same page it says that 'one cannot be disabled alone.' And to kind of piggyback off of what Catherine was saying, yes, culture disables because it defines what normal should be, what the goal should be for everyone and then if you meet that goal . . . you're successful and if you don't meet that goal then you're not successful."

But students didn't merely connect to other students' comments. They built on, extended, and challenged each other's arguments in a way that created a collective sense of McDermott and Varenne's (1995) challenge to deficit thinking, and, in some cases, students' individual positions on the meaning of disabilities shifted as a result. The following sequence illustrates this collaborative sense-making that culminates in Stephanie stating that she had changed her mind about a previous claim she made. In the interest of page length, I excerpt brief quotes from each turn to indicate assertions students made and how these built on previous turns. This segment begins with several students challenging deficit thinking by citing places in the "Culture as Disability" text to argue that the existence of special education is a function of institutional arrangements rather than *deficiencies* in students.

> Millie: "I've thought about why there are so many kids in special ed, and what I've come up with is because it exists."
>
> ⇩
>
> Stephanie: "I'll just play devil's advocate . . . What about the students that really do need special services?"
>
> ⇩
>
> Millie: "Right."
>
> ⇩
>
> Stephanie: "Good lord, half your school is labeled as having a disability" (referring to an earlier comment Catherine made about the high proportion of students identified as "disabled" in her school).

⇩

Catherine: "We're kind of known as the special ed school in the city."

⇩

Stephanie: "It's amazing, but can you get rid of [the institution of special education]?"

⇩

CDM: "What do you think McDermott and Varenne would say?" [Trying to bring them back to the text]

⇩

Jackie: "If society accepted that people had differences, then their training in education would be different and your classroom setup would be different. It would accommodate more of those differences, and, therefore, the labels would not be needed." [She then referenced an example in the text to support her claim.]

⇩

Stephanie: "Would children still be labeled, though?"

⇩

Jackie: "You wouldn't need the label."

⇩

Stephanie: "But would you need to come up with a special plan?"

⇩

Jackie: "You wouldn't need to. You would have been trained to identify the different ways children learn . . ."

⇩

CDM: "What does this tell us about the ways that cultures disable?" [Returning to the basic question]

⇩

Jackie: "If you do accommodate for everyone and allow them opportunities for learning in whatever ways that they are learning, then perhaps you could eliminate some of those social problems."

⇩

Meaghan: "I had a question . . . Can a culture enable without disabling?" [Referring back to a question another student had asked earlier]

⇩

CDM: "So in terms of Varenne and McDermott, is it possible for cultures not to disable?"

⇩

Catherine: "I think that what [McDermott and Varenne] are saying is that this is how we should view how disabilities are created. I don't think they are arguing that there is really a way to make that not happen . . ."

⇩

Anne: "I agree with you, Catherine, and I thought of the deficit view when I read this . . ." [She goes on to talk about how an earlier article critiquing deficit thinking has led her to think differently about the children she works with.]

⇩

CDM: "Folks we haven't heard from?" [Invitation for participation]

⇩

Tricia: "There are so many [potential teachers] who can go in there and pass the [teacher] test. But they're not really trained to be a teacher. They're not trained to differentiate learning . . . to accommodate . . ." [Makes a lengthy argument connecting to Jackie's earlier point that disabilities are constructed, in part, by poorly prepared teachers]

⇩

Janet: "Let me play devil's advocate . . . In addition to the lack of teacher training I think it's workload and the burnout rate that's really getting teachers." [Returns to the argument that it is institutional factors that lead to so many students to being labeled as disabled]

⇩

CDM: [After a series of exchanges about whether teachers work hard enough, I try to get the discussion back on track with a follow-up question I'd prepared in advance.] "One of the questions we're addressing over and over again is the reality of disabilities . . . And there's this question on p. 327, it's the paragraph that begins 'Disabilities, their definition, their ascription.' So they say in that paragraph, 'We claim that disabilities are best approached as a cultural fabrication.' My question is: Do they mean that disabilities aren't real, or do they mean something else?"

⇩

Stephanie: "When I first read that I was very taken aback. I don't know. I definitely think there is some merit to a child having a disability. I don't think that it's something that's fabricated 100% of the time."

⇩

Hillary: "I think they mean they exist, but what they're saying is that culture defines what's real. So we're defining what's real. So it's real because we've defined it as such . . ."

⇩

Stephanie: "I wasn't done. At first reading it I was very taken aback. But after thinking about it, a lot of the disabilities we see in society, a lot of them are more fabricated than I assumed or thought before."

In the end, Stephanie didn't completely reject her previous position on whether disabilities are "real" or "fabricated." However, the discussion did lead her to modify her position significantly, tentatively embracing the notion that disabilities weren't just a matter of deficits inherent in students, their culture, or their communities. Other students also said that the reading and discussion had challenged the deficit thinking that underpinned their thinking about disabilities. For example, after the discussion one student[3] wrote,

> My perceptions [after the discussions] have changed in that this is much more of a global issue that affects all aspects of culture. This issue is ongoing and will not change until perceptions [about disabilities] change. I feel I have to be an advocate and a part of the solution and not just part of the problem.

Most students indicated that the discussion affected their understanding of the "Culture as Disability" article, or at least helped them to clarify or expand their thinking, although two students said that their thinking about disabilities was largely unaffected by the reading and the discussion. But overall, the evidence suggests that our Interpretive Discussion of "Culture as Disability" led my students to engage seriously with a critique of deficit thinking and, in some cases, the reading and discussion led them to reconsider the deficit thinking that shaped their understanding of disabilities.

Students Didn't All Get the Same Meanings From the Text

During our discussions I was delighted by Hillary's sociological analyses of the readings. I was similarly pleased by how Jackie routinely used the lens of race to make sense of the texts we were discussing. And I was always amazed by Anne's ability to get to the heart of the matter and thoughtfully articulate her positions. Yet, I was frustrated by students like Allison and Joseph who often didn't seem to "get it." And I worried about Tricia's rambling monologues about her school that didn't seem to relate to the discussion. When I reflected on our early discussions I fretted over what I saw as a rush to practice as some students preferred to relate texts to their classrooms rather than using textual evidence to support their claims, which was, after all, the point of Interpretive Discussion.

However, over the course of the semester I became more comfortable with these issues. I had to keep reminding myself, for instance, that the goal of Interpretive Discussions wasn't to *get* some predetermined meaning (i.e., *my* meaning), but to work together to make sense of challenging texts and to push students' thinking—in the case of the McDermott and Varenne (1995) article, to challenge the deficit thinking behind popular conceptions of disabilities. Consider, for example, the following excerpt from the "Culture as Disability" discussion. The discussion of "how do cultures disable?" has just begun. Colleen begins by citing text from the article to make her point, followed by Allison who attempts to build on Colleen's claim:

> Colleen: "I think it kind of goes back to, like, why do we want people to acquire knowledge, and who sets that standard and all this because we're placing . . . judgment on what is more valuable, like what knowledge is more valuable."

> Allison: "I think it's right to put it in terms of fact versus opinion. I mean, to say that something is wrong can be a fact or it can be an opinion. To say that 2 + 2 is not 5, that's a fact. But wrong can easily be an opinion as well. But with disabled, if something is labeled, that's one thing, but that can also be an opinion. People could say I'm disabled because I'm barely five feet, so technically I'm disabled. But do I consider myself disabled? No, I don't. . . . If I lived in China I wouldn't be considered short at all. . . . I think it has a lot to do with facts versus opinion, and then the judgment base there and then the label that's put on. And I think that those labels change with what she's talking about within the culture you are in. . . . But sometimes we're in classrooms or groups where it is an

isolated culture, and how does that change what we consider a disability or an ability? Or what type of disabilities count as disabilities? Like in a reading class, is a kid in a wheelchair disabled? No."

At the time I was perplexed by Allison's comment (and I've left out some of the more confusing parts). First, Colleen's previous claim didn't seem to have anything to do with "fact versus opinion." But with the luxury of being able to read the transcript of this discussion, it is obvious that Allison makes a couple of useful points: what counts as disabled depends on the context (she wouldn't be considered short in China), and disabilities aren't salient in all contexts (being a wheelchair user has no relevance in a reading class). So disabilities aren't just about *deficits*. Allison isn't as articulate or as intellectually sophisticated as some of the other students, nor does she cite any sort of textual evidence to support her claim. Certainly she doesn't draw on neo-Marxist theory to articulate her claims as Hillary often did. But she does make a couple of worthy claims that indicate that the text pushed her to reconsider deficit thinking, something that was not always evident in previous discussions.

Students didn't all get the same meaning from the text because they started in different places and brought different perspectives to make sense of the text. And practice was a lens several teachers in my class routinely drew on to make sense of our readings. Tricia, for example, suggested that the parents she works with who insisted their children be labeled to gain some sort of accommodations were a factor in the cultural construction of disabilities in her school. This wasn't a point explicitly taken up in the "Culture as Disability" article, but it certainly builds on McDermott and Varenne's (1995) claim that disabilities must be understood in terms of the cultural context, not student deficiencies. Similarly, Nancy cited children she'd worked with who came to see themselves as "disabled" only after they'd been given a label to support her claim that disabilities didn't necessarily reside in students. As with Tricia, Nancy makes an argument drawing on evidence beyond the McDermott and Varenne (1995) text but is absolutely consistent with the idea that disability is a cultural construct.

The tendency of those students in my class who were practicing teachers to make sense of texts primarily in terms of their practice, rather than in terms of textual evidence, frustrated me early in the semester since one of my goals was for students to use textual evidence—not personal experience—to support their claims. But this seems to have been a useful way for these students to make sense of the texts we discussed, and, as the semester progressed, I expanded my sense of Interpretive Discussion to make room for students to connect the readings to practice, even allocating the last 5–10 minutes of every discussion to consider the instructional implications of the readings. This reinforces an essential point about successful discussions: authentic discussions make room for a range of possible answers, although all responses should be supported by some kind of evidence.

I Used Particular Strategies That Kept Discussions Moving and Focused

Because I approached this as an action research project, I regularly reflected on our Interpretive Discussions and debriefing sessions with an eye toward making these discussions more effective. After listening to our first discussion, for example, I wrote in my research journal that I often spoke too quickly and worried about students who didn't participate. Over the course of the semester, I continued to review our discussions and worked to improve them. To get students to address their comments to each other, for instance, we began to use name cards so everyone could refer to each other by name. I worked to slow down discussions at various points so students could gather their thoughts ("Okay, let's take some time write a response to the basic question.") or locate places in the text that were being cited ("Wait until everyone has found the place in the text."). I also used wait time and other moves ("Anyone we haven't heard from yet?") to encourage more students to participate. I routinely restated the basic question and used follow-up questions to keep discussions moving and focused. I occasionally summarized the discussion for the same purpose. I used *revoicing* ("So you're saying . . .") to ensure clarity and understanding. I regularly requested textual evidence to keep the discussion focused on the text ("What do you think McDermott and Varenne [1995] would say? Is there a place you can point to in the text that supports your claim?"). But I also learned to value other kinds of evidence, including students' experience in their classrooms.

My review of the transcripts also indicates things that I did not do that contributed to student engagement. For example, I never evaluated students' responses, nor did I ever offer my own interpretation of the texts we discussed, which would have amounted to an indirect evaluation of my students' interpretations. What's particularly notable about the discussion of "Culture as Disability" is how few turns I took in this discussion. There is one stretch where students took 20 turns without an interjection from me, and there are many other segments of five to seven turns without any comment from me. Moreover, my turns tended to be short and focused mainly on revoicing (six turns); restating the question(s) (five turns); invitations to participate (four turns); summarizing (three turns); and asking people to slow down and give everyone a chance to locate the place in the text they were referring to (seven turns). This pattern of turn-taking is somewhat different from our earliest discussions where I took more turns focused on learning the practice of Interpretive Discussion. For example, in earlier discussions, I took more turns intended to keep the discussion focused and asking for textual evidence. But by the time we discussed "Culture as Disability," my students were more comfortable participating in an Interpretive Discussion. And, as I've already noted, I relaxed my standards for what counted as evidence.

Still, I've found many places in the transcripts where I might have done better, places where I ought to have asked for clarification, occasions when I should have asked for textual or other kinds of evidence to support students' claims, or where I think I waited too long to refocus the discussion. I have been mindful of these lessons as my students and I used Interpretive Discussion to interpret other texts this academic year in other courses I teach.

I'd like to make one final observation. Overall, I think my action research project demonstrates the potential of Interpretive Discussion to overcome bottlenecks like deficit thinking by engaging students in rich, meaningful discussions of challenging texts. In the case of "Culture as Disability," for example, students drew on their careful reading of the text as a means of seriously engaging the question: How can disabilities—and deficit thinking more generally—be viewed as cultural constructs? It's worth pointing out that preparing for our Interpretive Discussions also led students to much more careful readings of course materials than in previous courses I have taught.

However, preparation for and execution of Interpretive Discussions is hard work. Getting ready to lead an Interpretive Discussion, including creating basic and follow-up questions and managing the discussion itself, requires multiple readings of the text. Facilitating the discussion requires careful attention to what students are saying, who is and isn't speaking, how the discussion is flowing, and so on. Learning to create the conditions for an effective discussion also requires careful reflection, including, perhaps, listening to audio recordings of discussions. Arguably, managing an Interpretive Discussion is much more difficult—and more tiring—than lecturing. But with careful preparation, Interpretive Discussion is an approach that greatly increases the probability that *powerful readings*, like "Culture as Disability," actually engage, challenge, and, in some cases, transform students' thinking.

Notes

1. Haroutunian-Gordon (personal communication, November 30, 2009) argues that all students should participate in every Interpretive Discussion. I made a conscious decision not to require participation, reasoning that my students are adults who should make their own decisions about whether to participate in discussions. I was also mindful that I increasingly receive documentation from my students of anxiety disorders that limit their ability to speak in public settings. I did talk with my students during debriefing sessions, however, about how to increase their participation, and it was from such discussions that strategies like giving students time to reflect on the basic question by writing and talking with someone else emerged.

2. I have changed the names of students throughout this chapter.

3. Students wrote anonymously.

References

Dillon, J. T. (1994). *Using discussion in classrooms*. Philadelphia, PA: Open University Press.

Hardman, F., & Mroz, M, (1999). Post-16 English Teaching: From Recitation to Discussion. *Educational Review, 51*(3), 283–293.

Haroutunian-Gordon, S. (2009). *Learning to teach through discussion: The art of turning the soul.* New Haven, CT: Yale University Press.

MacIntosh, P. (1989). White privilege: Unpacking the invisible knapsack. *Peace and Freedom*, July/August.

McDermott, R., & Varenne, H. (1995). Culture as disability. *Anthropology & Education Quarterly, 26*, 324–328.

Michaels, S., O'Connor, C., Hall, M., with Resnick, L. (2002). *Accountable talk: Classroom conversation that works* (CD-ROM set). Pittsburgh, PA: University of Pittsburgh.

Paugh, P., & Dudley-Marling, C. (2011). "Speaking" deficit into or out of existence: How language constrains classroom teachers' knowledge about instructing diverse learners. *International Journal of Inclusive Education, 15*(2), 1–15.

6

TEACHING AGAINST ESSENTIALISM AND THE "CULTURE OF POVERTY"

Paul C. Gorski

Grandma tends to stretch vowel sounds, drawing extended air time out of them in her sweet Appalachian twang. Where D.C.-born folk like me give a door a push, she gives it a *poosh*. Where I crave candy, she offers sweeter-sounding *cane-dee*. Her vocabulary, as well, is of a western Maryland mountain variety, unassuming and undisturbed by slangy language or new age idiom. To her, a refrigerator is still a Frigidaire; or, more precisely, a *freegeedaire*; neighbors live *across the way*. Her children, including my mother, say she's never cursed and only occasionally lets fly her fiercest expression: *Great day in the mornin'!*

Despite growing up in poverty, Grandma isn't uneducated or lacking in contemporary wits, as one might presume based upon the "culture of poverty" paradigm that dominates today's understandings of poverty and schooling in the United States. She graduated first in her high school class. Later, the year she turned 50, she completed college and became a nurse. I've never been tempted to "correct" Grandma's language, nor do I feel embarrassed when she talks about how my Uncle Terry's *gone a'feesheen'*. She doesn't need *my* diction or vocabulary to give meaning to her world. She certainly doesn't need to be freed from the grasp of a mythical "culture of poverty" or its fictional "language registers." What needs *a'fixin'* is not Grandma's dispositions or behaviors, but those of a society that sees only her poverty and, as a result, labels her—the beloved matriarch of an extended family—as a culturally deficient representative of an essentialized (assumed to be monolithic) group.

I have found, in my 15 or so years teaching social justice teacher education courses, that this notion of cultural deficiency—and, in fact, the tendency to locate explanations for all sorts of phenomena in amorphous and stereotypical notions of "culture" (Ladson-Billings, 2006)—is prevalent among my students, regardless of what sorts of inequities we are exploring. For example, conversations about racial equity invariably are redirected by concerns about baggy clothing or "self-segregation" among students of color. The term *girl culture* has entered the education lexicon, stereotyping and problematizing the ways young women interact and behave. I have struggled to find pedagogical tools to help my students, predominantly teachers-to-be, shake themselves out of a tendency to lean on this "culture" default, whether we're discussing race, religion, language, or even sexual orientation or gender.

However, despite growing up with a mother and grandmother of poor Appalachian stock and a father of working-class urban stock, I have struggled mightily to find ways to help my students rethink an increasingly epidemic obsession with the notion of *class* cultures and, in particular, the "culture of poverty." This is due in part, I am sure, to the more general uneasiness people in the United States experience when talking about class (Kincheloe & Steinberg, 2007). When it comes to pre- and in-service teachers, though, the mental grip the culture of poverty paradigm maintains on the collective consciousness has been hastened, as well, by the proliferation of a framework for understanding poverty introduced by Ruby Payne (2005), today's most prominent culture-of-poverty torchbearer. A bevy of activists and scholars have identified Payne's books and workshops as among the most influential *and the most dangerously inaccurate* staples of teacher professional development in circulation (Bohn, 2007; Bomer, Dworin, May, & Semingson, 2008; Gorski, 2008a; Ng & Rury, 2006; Osei-Kofi, 2005).

Whatever the reasons for the stubborn persistence of the culture of poverty paradigm, despite decades of research in all sorts of contexts demonstrating that *there is no such thing as a culture of poverty* (more on this later), one thing is certain: my students and I weathered a lot of stumbles, scrapes, and pedagogical slips—years of them, in fact—trying, failing, and trying again to identify experiences to help them rethink the validity of the "culture of poverty." The most formidable challenge in this process has been overcoming a sort of learning bottleneck wherein my students, on average, cling so tightly to culture-obsessed explanations for outcome inequalities (i.e., test scores or graduation rates) that they struggle to understand these phenomena in their larger sociopolitical contexts, particularly when it comes to matters of economic justice.

I have found over the years that one of the most important concepts—one of the *threshold* concepts—students must grasp to push their way through the bottleneck is "essentialism." The practice of essentialism attributes stereotypical characteristics to large swaths of people based solely on a single identity dimension such as gender, race, or class. As I discuss later, essentialism lends itself to deficit thinking because it encourages us to look for the source of problems, such as the disproportionate dropout rate of low-income students, in stereotyped understandings of the "cultures" of those students rather than in the educational and social systems that repress them. When we fail to "catch" ourselves in this essentialism process, we risk missing the sociopolitical altogether; we risk never accounting for the fact that what looks like a dropout often is a *push-out*. My students tend to "get" this conceptually once we've spent a little time on it. *Of course, it's ludicrous to attribute an individual behavior to an entire community of people.* What they struggle with—and what I struggled for years to help them do—is to find the essentialism in their own thinking.

I offer in this chapter a synthesis of these trials and tribulations and how they eventually led me to construct an effective process for helping students spot and reconsider their tendencies to essentialize low-income families.

The Trouble With the "Culture of Poverty"

By now many people know that the "culture of poverty" hypothesis was introduced in the 1950s by Oscar Lewis (1959). Lewis (1961) expanded on the notion in the early 1960s, arguing, based upon an ethnographic study in one Mexican village, that poor people, by virtue of being poor, can be assumed to share a common set of beliefs, behaviors, and dispositions, many of which appeared several decades later in Lewis's (2005) list of attributes of the "mindset of poverty." These include a lack of orientation toward the future (or a need for instant gratification), substance abuse, a propensity for violence, and disinterest in education.

Sometimes, however, it's what we *don't know* that renders us susceptible to fallaciousness. For instance, did you know that by the late 1960s, the culture of poverty paradigm largely had been dismissed by social scientists, some of whom were troubled by Payne's extrapolation from a single village to the global population, and others who tried unsuccessfully to replicate his findings in other regional contexts (e.g., Ryan, 1971; Valentine, 1968)? Did you know that the idiom "blaming the victim" was coined in 1971 by William Ryan *as a criticism of the culture of poverty hypothesis*? Ryan (1971) explained that such paradigms "concentrate on the defects of the victim . . . and ignore the continuing effect of victimizing social forces" (p. 8).

The trouble with the "culture of poverty," beyond the fact—*and shouldn't this be enough?*—that four decades of research have shown that *it does not exist* (Adeola, 2005; Baetan, 2004; Gorski, 2008b), is twofold. First, it *essentializes* poor people, suggesting that all we need to know is that my Grandma is poor and, equipped with that information, we somehow can "know" virtually everything else about her (Bomer et al., 2008). Second, it misdirects class equity efforts by mistakenly identifying the problem to be remedied, as in the case of the socioeconomic "achievement gap," as existing within a shared "culture" of poor people (which, again, does not exist).

Such diversions serve privileged communities well, ensuring inattention to the conditions that underlie economic injustice, such as inequitable access to high-quality schooling. And they are an easy sell based, as they are, on stereotypes that, thanks to the myth of meritocracy in the United States (Borrego, 2003), already are embedded in the popular consciousness. Certainly, most of my teacher education students enter my classes convinced that the culture of poverty, or at least the general assertion behind it, is real.

Trial and Error and Trial Again

The difficulty, of course, is that scholarly attempts to debunk common understandings generally prove to be of little mitigating consequence against mass perception. This is particularly the case, in my experience, when it comes to matters of class. It's even *more particularly* the case among people who overwhelmingly do not know the strain of economic hardship, when they are socialized, as most of my students are, to associate their inexperience with poverty as the evidence of their merit (Adeola, 2005; Weigt, 2006; Williams, 2009).

Unfortunately, when I think I lack the pedagogical tools to engage students constructively around a concept or problem, my impulse is to perform a fact-dump. For years I used this approach with class and poverty. I required reading after reading: anything I could find that challenged the false assumptions with which I predicted a majority of students would enter the conversation. Some students—the few who respond with intrigue to this sort of passive-aggressiveness—might be energized by being buried in quantitative studies assigned primarily to reveal to them their ignorance. *Most* of my students, however, do not respond well to a fact-dump. What that approach fails to do, even when followed by in-class processing, is to encourage students to participate openly and fully in the construction of deeper understandings about poverty and their positionalities relative to economic justice. In fact, many students responded by entering class defensively, hackles up, or tentatively, afraid to offend.

Many of the common stereotypes that comprise the culture of poverty paradigm—*poor people are lazy; poor people don't value education*—are embedded too deeply into popular perception to be overturned in this manner. These stereotypes, and the fairly ridiculous notion that we can know how a student learns or what supports he or she needs or how his or her family communicates based upon a single dimension of the student's identity, have become part of the "common sense" of teaching. Like most people, including me, my students want to believe whatever confirms their existing mental models, and, like most people, they prefer to do so without acknowledging that they have mental models. What I needed were strategies to help reveal to my students their mental models rather than strategies meant to "correct" their thinking.

This has been most evident during in-class conversations about family involvement. Many students enter my classes indoctrinated with a belief in the dire significance of "parent involvement." For the most part, though, because they have been led to believe—incorrectly, it turns out (Jennings, 2004; Li, 2010; West-Olatunji, Sanders, Mehta, & Behar-Horenstein, 2010)—that single dimensions of identity (low socioeconomic status, for instance) predict rates of family involvement, many assume poor families simply are not invested in their children's education. So I can present them with facts: "Well, so and so (e.g., Li, 2010) found that poor families are just as involved in their kids' learning as wealthier families." Or I can go straight to the systemic: "Well, so and so (e.g., Holcomb-McCoy, 2010) found that the problem isn't a lack of desire to be involved, but that events like Back to School Night are constructed around assumptions that all families have transportation and access to affordable childcare." Whichever way I cut it— and believe me when I say I have cut it in innumerable ways—these approaches, based on the faulty assumption that a lifetime of social conditioning can be erased with the right combination of convincing data, have not worked.

What I came to understand is that many of my students retain and defend two conflicting views at once: (1) that there are socioeconomic-based inequities in access and opportunity, and (2) that meritocracy is real. It wasn't until, prodded by students' repeated references to the "culture of poverty," that I understood how many of them manage to hold these views simultaneously. *Of course inequities existed*, they concede. Overwhelmingly, though, these inequities are attributed not to economic injustice, but instead to the behaviors of individuals. The implication is that the inequities are *deserved*, reflecting Herbert Gans's (1995) notion of the *undeserving poor*.

Through this long process of trial and error, I learned, among other things, that my students and I needed a new pedagogical approach, an opportunity to reflect on the ways we were socialized to see and experience class.

A Process for Encouraging an Essentialism-Free Class Consciousness

In this section, I discuss the pedagogical process I developed for helping students understand the notion of *essentialism*, particularly as it relates to low-income people. The process includes five steps: (1) exploring common perceptions of poor people; (2) reflecting on our perceptions and where we got them; (3) analyzing perceptions as symptoms of ideologies; (4) applying new lenses to the school environment; and (5) spotting insidious discourses of class privilege and economic injustice.

Step 1: Exploring Common Perceptions of Poor People

I begin by posing a question to the class: Why are poor people poor? Usually I ask students to respond in small groups, perhaps after a short free-write. Following 10 or 15 minutes of discussion, I open the floor, asking them to describe their perceptions as well as what they discussed in groups. Responses vary, of course, on a continuum between the deficit-laden (e.g., "they don't work hard") and the systemic (e.g., "capitalism requires poverty"). However, on average, they reflect the conflicted double understanding I described earlier: an ideology that acknowledges some level of inequity *qualified by* suggestions that inequities are deserved.

At this point in the process I resist the temptation to challenge students' essentialist thinking. I do so because the objective is to help students *reveal to themselves* where they are in their thinking, a crucial step on the path toward deeper consciousness. Instead, I ask them to consider what might account for divergences in their perceptions of why poor people are poor, implicitly raising a question about the objectivity of personal lenses.

Explaining that we are transitioning into an exploration of class bias, I then ask students to brainstorm a list of common stereotypes about poor people in the United States. To "permit" them to share prejudiced ideas without the threat of being labeled prejudiced, I clarify that they don't need to *believe* a stereotype to share it; rather, they only need to be familiar with it *as a stereotype*. I've done this activity dozens of times and never have found a group whose members couldn't fill a chalkboard with stereotypes. Students almost invariably identify "laziness" first; I am sure to point out this pattern because, in my view, this stereotype is the root of the culture of poverty mentality. Many responses are predictable: poor people don't value education; they use drugs; they have kids out of wedlock.

The most important aspect of this activity is that students are naming what they know; *they* are generating the fodder for reflection. Again, I do not use this activity to challenge essentialist thinking. I have written in the past about popular stereotypes regarding poor people (see Gorski, 2008b); I have studied and tested them. I know, for instance, that poor people have the exact same attitudes about education as their wealthier counterparts, despite the fact that they are cheated out of comparable educational opportunity. I believe, however, that the essentialism bottleneck is more vulnerable when students are facilitated through making that connection rather than when I impose it onto them.

Step 2: Reflecting on Our Perceptions and Where We Got Them

The second step in the process also begins with a question: Where do these stereotypes come from? This step helps students reveal to themselves their class lenses.

Generally I find that students answer this question in very broad terms: *the media, my parents, my church.* The key to scaffolding my students to more complex understandings of essentialism, I have learned, is encouraging them to answer this question with more specificity. If a student responds that the stereotypes come from the media, I ask that student to provide specific examples. "What are some of the explicit messages you see?" I might ask. Then, "What are some of the more implicit patterns?" This second prompt is crucial because explicit examples—what students see on shows like *Cops*, for instance—are easy to dismiss as sensationalized nonsense. The insidious stuff is much harder to dismiss, so I push for insidious examples: "What day-to-day messages did you receive from your family about poor and working-class people? What kinds of programs related to poverty, if any, does your synagogue (or church or mosque) sponsor? What do the objectives of these programs suggest, implicitly, about the 'problem' they are attempting to resolve?" I often conclude this step by asking students to do a short free-write about what they know about poor people in the United States and how they came to know it. I might ask them to choose one or two of the brainstormed stereotypes with which they grapple—perhaps those they actually believe. "How did you come to believe them?"

Step 3: Analyzing Perceptions as Symptoms of Ideologies

Another strategy I've used to help students reveal *to themselves* their socializations is to assign *them* the task of seeking evidence for their own stereotypes. In small groups, students identify the stereotype from the brainstormed list that they believe has been most present in their collective socializations. Most groups, educators-to-be that they are, choose "poor people don't value education," but others commonly choose laziness or substance abuse. Their homework for the next class is to use scholarly sources—journal articles, research reports, and the like—to determine the extent of the stereotype's accuracy. They are instructed to find at least three sources and not to include sources from for-profit or partisan organizations.

The truth is, there is a bit of manipulation at play here because I know what they are going to find: virtually none of the common stereotypes about poor people can withstand analysis. But the point, again, is that *they* discover this on their own.

I begin the next class by asking each group to report its findings. What sources did they find? How, if at all, did they adjust their perceptions based on the information they found? What I have found particularly interesting in this process is the humility many students demonstrate when sharing findings that conflict with what they thought they knew—humility and, in some cases, embarrassment or shame. A student in a recent class explained, "I was shocked. I always thought that poor people were mostly drug addicts. We learned, in reality, that wealthy people are more likely to be addicts than poor people, even though wealthy people can afford detox programs." I also find—and this has tested my humility—that students assign greater credibility to information when it comes from peers than when it comes from me.

Initially I found this unnerving; now I see it as a gift, an opportunity to share more power in the classroom.

As I mentioned, some students display shame or embarrassment during report-outs. Some even talk about being ashamed of how they've treated homeless people or of their assumptions about poor people in their own families. Certainly some educators would disagree, but experience tells me that some level of shame and embarrassment can be constructive. After all, disenfranchised communities, like those from the poor Appalachian region where my grandma grew up, receive near-constant messages from society that they ought to embody these feelings. I also know, however, that, absent any form of intervention, some people can be cognitively paralyzed by shame. To mitigate the potential for cognitive paralysis, I acknowledge the shame and try to reframe it as a cognitive triumph. I might say, "I sense some shame and embarrassment in the room. If that's where you are, I encourage you to feel what you're feeling profoundly, and then let it go. In the end, it's not about shame, but about knowing and responding. Now you know. And that's a triumph. The only question is, what will you do differently now that you know?" Some social justice educators might read this as coddling the privileged. I see it as setting the bar of expectations higher than it ever has been for students who are learning to grapple with their privilege. So if it is coddling, it's strategic coddling, and I will offer it to every student at some point, if not during this discussion, then during our exploration of ableism, linguicism, sexism, racism, heterosexism, or intersectional combinations of two or more of these oppressions.

Once all of the groups have reported their findings, we transition into a conversation about *perception*. "How," I ask, "have we become so misinformed? What does it mean when the most common understandings are based on false assumptions?" Students generally respond to these prompts by talking about the prevalence of bias and discrimination in fairly general terms. A common response: "It affects people's attitudes about poor families."

This, then, leads to a key moment of the process. I ask the students what I have come to see as a central question in any conversation about social justice: *To whose benefit?* I inquire, for instance, "Who or what do these 'culture of poverty' stereotypes protect? We know who they hurt, but who do they benefit?" Generally I divide students into small groups to grapple with these questions. The intention is to shift into a conversation, not about the "problem" of poor people's cultures, but about the "problem" of an inequitable educational system. In other words, by asking these questions, I am helping students through a cognitive shift, from focusing on "those poor people" to focusing on *that which represses* poor people. In many ways, this shift encourages students to practice raising ideological questions about an education system that, according to most of their socializations, is the "great equalizer." Again, students tend to respond in fairly general terms: *It protects rich people.* So the next step involves exploring how, particularly in regard to educational policy and practice, the culture of poverty paradigm and its essentialist nature protect the powerful at the expense of the disenfranchised.

Step Four: Applying New Lenses to the School Environment

As I described earlier, many of my students appear to hold two conflicting views simultaneously: that class inequity exists (at least on an interpersonal level), but that, given the meritocratic nature of U.S. society, class inequity is largely deserved by people who simply haven't worked hard enough. The work I do with my students in the first three steps of this process is meant to unsettle the essentialist stereotypes that underlie the myth of meritocracy and to reflect on how they've been socialized to uphold a stereotypic ideology regarding poverty. In the fourth step I engage students in applying their shifting lenses to a school environment.

I call the activity "Socioeconomic Class and School Opportunity." Students are divided into groups of four or five peers, and each group is assigned one of five characters, each a K–12 student from a unique socioeconomic situation. All five "characters" must complete the same school assignment, which is described on a handout. (Character and assignment descriptions are provided in the appendix to this chapter.) However, based upon each character's socioeconomic situation, connoted by the fact that she or he has also been given access to a specified amount of (fake) cash and has a variety of tasks to complete before starting work on the assignment, each character is afforded a certain level of privilege or hampered by certain drains on time. Privileges might include having a ride to the store to purchase materials or having a quiet place to work. Challenges, on the other hand, might include having to care for a younger sibling or having to walk to purchase materials. Each group is given only the information and financial resources for its character, so it doesn't know that other groups are receiving more or less "opportunity." They have 30 minutes to complete the project.

I set up a "store" in a building outside of the classroom so that students need to spend time acquiring their materials. The store includes a range of arts and crafts resources: construction paper, glue, crayons, and so on. It also includes snack items, which characters caring for younger siblings might need. Once they complete their other tasks—requiring some of the lower socioeconomic groups to spend time running make-believe errands—groups use their "money" to purchase items they need to complete the assignment. Of course, because the groups receive different amounts of money, they have access to different material resources; because they have different levels of privilege and challenges, they also have different lengths of time to complete their projects.

Once the groups return to class with their projects, I ask them, starting with the low-income group, to describe their characters, discuss the resources with which they began the activity, and share their projects. I use prompting questions to help them along: "What were you able to purchase with your allotted resources? How much time did you have to complete your project once you took care of other responsibilities? What challenges did you face?" Most students grasp the point of the activity after a couple of group presentations: opportunity matters. But more important, they begin to understand that access to financial resources facilitates access to other advantages, such as quiet places to work and time.

I largely focus the discussion following this activity on a single question: "How might this experience help us think differently about meritocracy?" The aha moments are plenty. A couple of semesters ago I recorded responses to this activity from student reflection papers. Several mentioned a broader understanding of "opportunity." One student noted, "I didn't realize that not having to care for siblings could be seen as a sort of privilege." Others zeroed in on the notion of "hard work." One student, a future early childhood teacher in the "wealthy" group, wrote,

> I grew up hearing "effort, effort, effort." But in reality, it didn't matter how much effort the group with the least resources put into their project because they couldn't even afford the materials that my group took for granted and they had all that extra stuff to do before beginning the project. I think I see what you mean now by the "myth of meritocracy."

I also believe it is important, when teaching against essentialist frameworks like the "culture of poverty," to provide a cognitive bridge that helps students understand the *implications* of the myth of meritocracy. After all, my understanding of its fallaciousness cannot undo the hold it has on mass consciousness. So I ask students to consider its implications in a school setting: "Assuming you believed that meritocracy was real, how might you, as a teacher, make sense of the varying quality of these projects? How, based on that assumption, might you treat lower-income students?" I also encourage students to think about other ways the assumption of meritocracy drives school policy and practice. "What role does it play in standardized testing? How does it affect teachers' expectations of students? How might it inform the sorts of pedagogies commonly used with specific groups of students?"

Obviously, some students continue to resist this reframing of meritocracy, insisting that people with fewer resources *just need to be creative*. I have found, though, that by this time in the process, the larger cognitive tide begins to turn—a shift evident by the fact that I no longer am the one raising questions about what most of my students thought they knew. Students, equipped with newly forming lenses, start to challenge each other to think more deeply.

Step 5: Spotting Insidious Discourses of Class Privilege and Economic Injustice

This is the point at which we work on spotting more implicit forms of economic injustice in the everyday discourses of education. This, I believe, is a particularly important competency. I know, after all, that students are subject to these discourses—the "culture of poverty," deficit ideology, and other essentialist messages—in and out of their teacher preparation programs, and that, given the popularity of Payne and other deficit ideologues, the barrage will continue when they become teachers. It's one thing to "see" that explicit inequities—charging fees for extracurricular activities, for instance—exist and are problematic. I argue, though, that most class inequity in schools is less explicit, buried in "the way things are."

Over the years I have used a variety of tools to help students practice "spotting" implicit, insidious class inequity and economic injustice; for helping them strengthen their abilities to see what they're socialized not to see. I have collected a dozen or so texts in a variety of media that demonstrate elements of dominant class discourses in more or less explicit ways, such as Bill O'Reilly's interview of Diane Sawyer about an ABC News feature on Appalachian children (available at http://therevivalist.info/bill-o'reilly-appa lachia-is-hopeless/). Without question, though, the most effective tools for this have been excerpts from Payne's work.

In the first of these, a one-page essay titled "Reflections on Katrina and the Gulf Coast Crisis," Payne (2006) manages to draw on virtually all of the common "culture of poverty" stereotypes, essentializing the people most affected by the hurricane. She states, for instance, "To survive in the situation in New Orleans required the ability to plan, but for the most part in generational poverty, one does not plan, one reacts" (¶2). Later, she explains,

> The violence was to be expected. Words are not seen as being very effective in generational poverty to resolve differences; fists are. . . . Furthermore, to resolve a conflict, one must have the ability to go from the personal to the issue, and the words largely are not there to do that [for people in poverty]. (¶3)

She continues, "In neighborhoods of generational poverty, two of the primary economic systems are prostitution and drugs. After Katrina struck, both of those economies were virtually wiped out overnight" (¶4).

I start by asking for volunteers to read the essay aloud, paragraph by paragraph: an opportunity for students literally to *hear* essentialist language. I ask students, in groups, to read the essay again, underlining examples of essentialism. After they have an opportunity to reflect on what they find in light of our earlier discussion of class stereotypes, I pose a question meant to continue the "implications" thread of our conversation: "On whom does Payne place responsibility for the devastation following Katrina?" (By posing this question, I introduce, even if implicitly, deficit ideology and its relationship with essentialist frameworks, a topic covered in greater depth by Dudley-Marling's chapter in this book.) I prod, "How does she do this?"

As we grapple with these questions, I try to focus students' attention on two primary forms of analysis. First, I want them to reflect on whether they previously would have noticed the essentialist nature of Payne's claims. "What makes these sorts of messages difficult to spot when we are not intent on spotting them?" The point here is that, because we are socialized to experience the world in particular ways, we must *work* to free ourselves from the constraints of "common sense." Second, I want to provide students an opportunity to reflect on the "null" content of Payne's texts: the messages she sends by suggesting that teachers need to "fix" a fictional "culture of poverty" while failing to address the systemic conditions of economic injustice. To this end, I point out that popular discourses are characterized by what they *include*, but also by what they *omit*. I might ask, "By focusing on what she identifies as deficits in poor people, what does Payne fail to address about Hurricane Katrina and its effects?"

I admit that I continue to struggle to some degree to help students make this transition smoothly. Some catch on quickly: "What about all the hiccups in the state and federal governments' communications leading up to and following Katrina?" Others seem cognitively stuck when it comes to examining the implications of "null" or omitted content. This, perhaps, is the next threshold concept with which I will grapple. In the more immediate term, I ask students what they perceive to be the relationship among the myth of meritocracy, their own class socializations, and deficit ideology's tendency to ignore systemic conditions: "Imagine a group of educators is tasked with developing a school-wide strategy for redressing class inequities. Given this web of influences, what are they likely to identify as the 'problem' to be fixed? How might this affect the policy and practice strategies they recommend?"

Unfortunately, although Payne's essay on Katrina was, until recently, available on her website, it appears as though she has removed it from circulation. However, among education folks, it shouldn't be hard to find an enthusiastic Payne fan from whom to request a copy.

Another useful excerpt from Payne's work, and one that *is* still available on her website (www.ahaprocess.com/files/Quiz-HiddenRules.pdf), is her series of checklists to "test your knowledge of the hidden rules of class." This one-page handout includes three checklists: "Could you survive in poverty?"; "Could you survive in middle class?"; and "Could you survive in wealth?" I like to have a bit of fun with that last one. "Before even looking at the checklists," I might say, "raise your hand if you believe you could survive in wealth." I always think about Grandma in that moment, and the ludicrousness of comparing her experience, in which survival could be a challenge, to whether a wealthy person can "survive."

I ask students to focus initially on the "surviving poverty" checklist, which includes fairly benign items ("I know how to find the best rummage sales") as well as fairly egregious items ("I know how to get a gun, even if I have a police record"). By this time, students generally "get" that the checklists exemplify essentialism, in their suggestion that all poor people have the same experiences. Nevertheless, to encourage students to connect their analysis of the checklists with previous conversations, I ask them to identify the items that reflect the stereotypes we discussed earlier. We talk about each item they identify. I might ask, for instance, "What percentage of poor people would you guess owns a gun?" My intention is to encourage them to consider the implications of their socializations. And so I prod, "For what percentage of a particular identity group must something be true for us to consider it part of their 'culture'?" I find these questions particularly instructive, not only for deepening our interrogation of the culture of poverty paradigm, but also for helping us reflect on popular essentialist discourses in schools, like those related to identity-specific "learning styles."

We turn, then, to the other checklists: "Can you find in the 'surviving in middle class' or 'surviving in wealth' checklists any similarly demonizing items, items that suggest moral deficiencies in middle-class or wealthy people?" Notwithstanding the occasional student who thrills me by pointing to items that suggest out-of-control consumption on the part of wealthy people ("I have at least two homes that are staffed and maintained"), students generally respond that no items on these lists demonize middle-class or wealthy people in the way that poor people are demonized in their checklist.

Again, I introduce the notion of null or omitted content: "What does the *omission* of these items suggest about the comparable morals of poor, middle-class, and wealthy people?" Here again, I challenge students to consider whether they would have noticed the demonizing nature of the "surviving in poverty" checklist before our engagement with these issues in class.

I generally end this activity by asking students to describe other ways they have witnessed essentialism in schools. Who are the targets? Those who have spent any amount of time in schools during their teacher preparation programs likely have witnessed the essentializing of low-income families and families of color, often in day-to-day chatter in teachers' lounges or during interactions with administrators. Others might describe gendered or racialized discourses about who is supposed to be talented in particular subjects. Alternatively, I sometimes ask students to describe ways they have been essentialized as students; in doing so I equip myself with a couple of dozen examples I can use as we discuss other equity concerns.

Final Reflections

I am not suggesting that these strategies are foolproof. I, as one fool, have managed to piece together a process that, with much tweaking, has helped my students and me analyze the culture of poverty paradigm and unpack "essentialism" as a threshold concept. I find by using this process that I have an easier time engaging students around several other threshold concepts: the insufficiency of the three-tiered (poor, middle-class, wealthy) class model (and the five-tiered one I use in the educational opportunity activity); corporatization of public schools; and the general imposition of neoliberalism on schools. This, I believe, is because they are better prepared to consider the possibility that inequitable conditions are purposeful—that they originate in discourses driven by those at the top of the power hierarchy rather than the supposed deficiencies of those at the bottom. Meanwhile, the process provides ample opportunities for self-reflection and for strengthening students' awareness about how their socializations inform their assumptions about, and expectations for, their future students.

Speaking more generally, I have culled some critical lessons from the years of trial and error that helped me hone this process. I am reminded of how important it is to be aware of my own triggers; of how, for example, my fondness for Grandma and my process of grappling with my own Appalachian identity makes it increasingly difficult to avoid imposing my ideologies on my students' learning experiences. Additionally, I have learned, once again, that if I remain dedicated to pedagogical mindfulness—to scaffolding and listening and coconstructing with students—I can trust not only the learning process itself, but also that my students will engage with an equal mindfulness and, semester after semester, wow me with their commitments to being equitable and just teachers.

References

Adeola, F. (2005). Racial and class divergence in public attitudes and perceptions about poverty in USA: An empirical study. *Race, Gender & Class, 12*(2), 53–78.

Baetan, G. (2004). Inner-city misery. *City, 8*(2), 235–241.

Bohn, A. (2007). A framework for understanding Ruby Payne. *Rethinking Schools, 21*(2), 13–15.

Bomer, R., Dworin, J. E., May, L., & Semingson, P. (2008). Miseducating teachers about the poor: A critical analysis of Ruby Payne's claims about poverty. *Teachers College Record, 110*(12), 2497–2531.

Borrego, S. (2003). *Class matters: Beyond access to inclusion.* Washington, DC: NASPA.

Gans, H. J. (1995). *The war against the poor.* New York: Basic Books.

Gorski, P. C. (2008a). Peddling poverty for profit: Elements of oppression in Ruby Payne's framework. *Equity & Excellence in Education, 41*(1), 130–148.

Gorski, P. C. (2008b). The myth of the "culture of poverty." *Educational Leadership, 65*(7), 32–35.

Holcombe-McCoy, C. (2010). Involving low-income parents and parents of color in college readiness activities: An exploratory study. *Professional School Counseling, 14*(1), 115–124.

Jennings, P. K. (2004). What mothers want: Welfare reform and maternal desire. *Journal of Sociology and Social Welfare, 31*(3), 113–130.

Kincheloe, J. L., & Steinberg, S. R. (2007). Cutting class in a dangerous era: A critical pedagogy of class awareness. In J. L. Kincheloe & S. R. Steinberg (Eds.), *Cutting class: Socioeconomic status and education* (pp. 3–69). New York: Rowman & Littlefield.

Ladson-Billings, G. (2006). It's not the culture of poverty, it's the poverty of culture: The problem with teacher education. *Anthropology and Education Quarterly, 37*(2), 104–109.

Lewis, O. (1959). *Five families: Mexican case studies in the culture of poverty.* New York: Basic Books.

Lewis, O. (1961). *The children of Sánchez: Autobiography of a Mexican family.* New York: Vintage.

Li, G. (2010). Race, class, and schooling: Multicultural families doing the hard work of home literacy in America's inner city. *Reading & Writing Quarterly, 26,* 140–165.

Ng, J. C., & Rury, J. L. (2006). Poverty and education: A critical analysis of the Ruby Payne phenomenon. *Teachers College Record.* Retrieved December 13, 2006, from http://www.tcrecord.org/Content.asp?ContentID = 12596

Osei-Kofi, N. (2005). Pathologizing the poor: A framework for understanding Ruby Payne's work. *Equity & Excellence in Education, 38*(4), 367–375.

Payne, R. (2005). *A framework for understanding poverty.* Highlands, TX: aha Processes, Inc.

Payne, R. (2006). Reflections on Katrina and the role of poverty in the Gulf Coast crisis. Retrieved June 22, 2006, from http://www.ahaprocess.com/files/HurricaneKatrinareflections. pdf

Ryan, W. (1971). *Blaming the victim.* New York: Vintage Books.

Valentine, C. (1968). *Culture and poverty: Critique and counter-proposal.* Chicago: University of Chicago Press.

Weigt, J. (2006). Compromises to carework: The social organization of mothers' experiences in the low wage labor market after welfare reform. *Social Problems, 53*(3), 332–351.

West-Olatunji, C., Sanders, T., Mehta, S., & Behar-Horenstein, L. (2010). Parenting practices among low-income parents/guardians of academically successful fifth grade African American children. *Multicultural Perspectives, 12*(3), 138–144.

Williams, W. R. (2009). Struggling with poverty: Implications for theory and policy of increasing research on social class-based stigma. *Analyses of Social Issues and Public Policy, 9*(1), 37–56.

SOCIOECONOMIC CLASS AND SCHOOL OPPORTUNITY ACTIVITY HANDOUTS

Midterm Group Art Project: Wealthy Student
This assignment is worth 86.4% of your final grade.

Who You Are

You are a *wealthy* eighth-grade student. Your parents are divorced. Your father, with whom you spend most weekends, works long hours as the CEO of a locally headquartered corporation. Your mother, with whom you stay during the week, works a part-time volunteer job and spends most of her remaining time at the golf and tennis club. She has hired a full-time, live-in nanny to take care of you and your older sister. During the week you live in a gated community five miles from the school, in a home where you have a large bedroom, a computer, and an intercom system so you can request snacks or other necessities from the nanny. The nanny drives you to and from school.

Your Assignment

You are to create a piece of art that tells a story about your socioeconomic condition—about what it's like to live as a person in your social class. The assignment will be graded based on the following criteria: (1) the number of colors you use—the more colors, the higher the grade; (2) the number of materials you use—the more materials, the higher grade; (3) the neatness of cutting, assembly, and so on; (4) the content (or how well you've depicted your own experiences). You may use *only the resources you purchase at the school supply store* (located in the Johnson Center lobby) with the money you have with you (in the envelope).

Your Task

You are to take the resources you have (what is found in the envelope you were given) and purchase the materials necessary for completing your art project. Your nanny will pick you up after school and drive you to the store (the Johnson Center) to purchase what you need. She then will drive you home (our classroom), where you can work on your project in quiet.

Rules of the Game

- You may use only the resources in the envelope to complete your assignment and handle your other duties!
- You may define "materials for completing your assignment" however you like: art supplies, sustenance (snacks or drinks), etc.

Midterm Group Art Project: Upper-Middle-Class Student
This assignment is worth 86.4% of your final grade.

Who You Are

You are an ***upper-middle-class*** eighth-grade student. Your mother works full time and travels a lot for work. Your father works half time from home so he can take care of you and your younger brother. You live in a single-family home where you have your own bedroom, your own desk, and your own computer. Your father drives you to and from school. You are struggling in math, but your family has hired a private tutor to help you two evenings a week. Due to the looming deadline for your midterm group art project, your parents paid the tutor a little bit extra to change your meeting time from tonight to tomorrow night.

Your Assignment

You are to create a piece of art that tells a story about your socioeconomic condition—about what it's like to live as a person in your social class. The assignment will be graded based on the following criteria: (1) the number of colors you use—the more colors, the higher the grade; (2) the number of materials you use—the more materials, the higher grade; (3) the neatness of cutting, assembly, and so on; (4) the content (or how well you've depicted your own experiences). You may use *only the resources you purchase at the school supply store* (located in the Johnson Center lobby) with the money you have with you (in the envelope).

Your Task

You are to take the resources you have (what is found in the envelope you were given) and purchase the materials necessary for completing your art project. Your father will pick you up after school and drive you to the store (in the Johnson Center) to purchase what you need. He will then drive you home (our classroom), where you can work on your project in relative quiet.

Rules of the Game
- You may use only the resources in the envelope to complete your assignment and handle your other duties!
- You may define "materials for completing your assignment" however you like: art supplies, sustenance (snacks or drinks), etc.

Midterm Group Art Project: Middle-Class Student
This assignment is worth 86.4% of your final grade.

Who You Are

You are a *middle-class* eighth-grade student. Your mother, who divorced your father three years ago, works full time during regular business hours. You live in a townhouse and walk to school. Your two younger siblings attend an after-school program. You love to do your homework at the local community center, which has a library that is a little quieter than your home (when your siblings are there) and because you can take occasional breaks from work and play basketball or ping pong.

Your Assignment

You are to create a piece of art that tells a story about your socioeconomic condition—about what it's like to live as a person in your social class. The assignment will be graded based on the following criteria: (1) the number of colors you use—the more colors, the higher the grade; (2) the number of materials you use—the more materials, the higher grade; (3) the neatness of cutting, assembly, and so on; (4) the content (or how well you've depicted your own experiences). You may use *only the resources you purchase at the school supply store* (located in the Johnson Center lobby) with the money you have with you (in the envelope).

Your Task

You are to take the resources you have (what is found in the envelope you were given) and purchase the materials necessary for completing your art project. So on your way to the community center, head to the shopping center (the Johnson Center) to purchase the materials you need for your project. Once you have the necessary materials, head home (Student Union Building 1) and begin working on the project. Make sure you turn your project in on time; late assignments will not be accepted.

Rules of the Game
- You may use only the resources in the envelope to complete your assignment and handle your other duties!
- You may define "materials for completing your assignment" however you like: art supplies, sustenance (snacks or drinks), etc.

Midterm Group Art Project: Working-Class Student
This assignment is worth 86.4% of your final grade.

Who You Are

You are a *working-class* eighth-grade student. Your mother works two jobs, and your father, who recently was laid off, has traveled north to try to find work. You are struggling in math, but your parents can't afford a tutor. You take the bus two miles to and from school. You, your older brother, and your mom live in a two-bedroom apartment. The walls are thin, so you hear a constant stream of noise while you're trying to concentrate on homework, but at least you have a little room to spread out.

Your Assignment

You are to create a piece of art that tells a story about your socioeconomic condition—about what it's like to live as a person in your social class. The assignment will be graded based on the following criteria: (1) the number of colors you use—the more colors, the higher the grade; (2) the number of materials you use—the more materials, the higher the grade; (3) the neatness of cutting, assembly, and so on; (4) the content (or how well you've depicted your own experiences). You may use *only the resources you purchase at the school supply store* (located in the Johnson Center lobby) with the money you have with you (in the envelope).

Your Task

You are to take the resources you have (what is found in the envelope you were given) and purchase the materials necessary for completing your art project. Unfortunately, before you begin working on the project, you need to stay after school to receive extra help from your math teacher, which means you'll miss your bus home. So head to your math classroom (Student Union Building II) for tutoring, then head to the shopping center (the Johnson Center) to purchase the materials you need for your project. Once you have the necessary materials, head home (Johnson Center basement) and begin working on the project. Make sure you turn your project in on time; late assignments will not be accepted.

Rules of the Game

- You may use only the resources in the envelope to complete your assignment and handle your other duties!
- You may define "materials for completing your assignment" however you like: art supplies, sustenance (snacks or drinks), etc.

Midterm Group Art Project: Low-Income Student
This assignment is worth 86.4% of your final grade.

Who You Are

You are a *low-income* eighth-grade student. Both of your parents work two jobs and are gone most of the day, and usually into evening. Your younger sister is a fourth grader at the elementary school down the street. You are responsible each day for picking her up, feeding her a snack, and taking care of her until your parents arrive home, often around 11 pm, after completing the evening shifts at their second jobs. Due to your family's financial condition, you share a small home with two other families, so often it is noisy and crowded, which makes doing homework difficult. But you persevere and do the best you can.

Your Assignment

You are to create a piece of art that tells a story about your socioeconomic condition—about what it's like to live as a person in your social class. The assignment will be graded based on the following criteria: (1) the number of colors you use—the more colors, the higher the grade; (2) the number of materials you use—the more materials, the higher grade; (3) the neatness of cutting, assembly, and so on; (4) the content (or how well you've depicted your own experiences). You may use *only the resources you purchase at the school supply store* (located in the Johnson Center lobby) with the money you have with you (in the envelope).

Your Task

You are to take the resources you have (what is found in the envelope you were given) and purchase the materials necessary for completing your art project. But remember, you also need to purchase a snack for your sister. And before you begin working on your project, you need to walk to the elementary school to pick her up. So go pick her up from school (Enterprise Hall, 4th Floor), then head over to the shopping center (the Johnson Center) to buy her snack and the supplies you need for your project. Then head home (Innovation Hall Main Floor) to work on your project. Make sure you turn your project in on time; late assignments will not be accepted.

Rules of the Game

- You may use only the resources in the envelope to complete your assignment and handle your other duties!
- You may define "materials for completing your assignment" however you like: art supplies, sustenance (snacks or drinks), etc.

7

DISRUPTING DENIAL AND WHITE PRIVILEGE IN TEACHER EDUCATION

Darren E. Lund and Paul R. Carr

O ur work for the past number of years has involved analyzing and unpacking White[1] privilege in the U.S. and Canadian education systems. Recent collaborations around these issues have included an edited book (Carr & Lund, 2007) and a retrospective analysis of some of the backlash we have encountered when raising issues of White privilege in societies that have difficulty facing the demons of their colonial pasts and remnants in their oppressive presents (Lund & Carr, 2010). We have presented our ideas at a number of conferences, primarily in North America, but also in Europe and South America. Further, the salience of our topic in light of ongoing public debates around diversity and discrimination has allowed us to speak in public venues, including newspapers and magazines, and on a number of call-in radio shows. Throughout our interventions we have been concerned by the extremely high resistance by many White people to considering their own racialized (White) identities as implicated in power and privilege. At the same time, we have continued to learn how others perceive *our* identities as White males of European origin, and how this can be both an advantage (in being able to connect with White people) and an area of concern (in presuming to be able, or attempting, to speak for people of color[2]). There are many accepted reasons *not* to address issues related to power, identity, and privilege—such as the learning "bottlenecks" around

---

Some of this is inspired by a previous piece (Carr & Lund, 2009) and has been significantly enhanced for this chapter.

which this book is constructed—but we believe that being silent only intensifies inequities and power differentials.

Both authors currently occupy faculty positions at universities in Canada and teach courses on social justice, diversity, identity, and democracy. Indeed, these themes tend to emerge in all of our teaching! The ongoing struggle to have White people place themselves personally within the web of oppression is fundamental to understanding oppression, discrimination, and racism, particularly in relation to sexism, classism, homophobia, and other social problems (Fine, Weis, Powell Pruitt, & Burns, 2004; Sullivan, 2006). Scholarly readings on racism and hegemony are one thing, but a personal implication in these issues fosters a great deal of resistance.

But really, why shouldn't it? Most of us (White people) have never been taught to think of ourselves as racialized beings, and certainly not to be part of the conversation on racism. Most of us never have been asked to examine our unearned privileges. Considering that most of our postsecondary students are White and middle class, this resistance is a significant obstacle and something worth paying sustained attention to if we are to seek its removal. Canada, not unlike the United States, represents a heterogeneous mix of people, and in both countries the majority of citizens will be people of color within the next several decades; Canada's three largest cities—Toronto, Montreal, and Vancouver—already comprise between one-quarter and one-half people of color, or "visible minorities," as referred to in Canadian government terminology. However, the vast majority of teachers, teacher educators, and educational administrators are White, despite the rapidly changing demography of students in the same schools.

To frame this chapter within the "bottleneck" theme, we share five guiding principles that may help the reader understand White privilege as a significant systemic issue and a barrier to achieving gains in the struggle for social justice. We place these principles within the context of teacher education, which is a clear intersection for stemming the inequities that invariably affect all sectors of society.

Principle 1: The backdrop of colonialism, imperialism, slavery, and racial discrimination is a shared experience, even for those who have never met anyone from another racialized origin, and we as White people must be concerned and implicated, despite the fact that White privilege has diminished the role of White people (in their own minds) when it comes to historic wrongs.

Principle 2: Neoliberalism enhances racial (and other) cleavages that are necessary for *economic growth* and *wealth accumulation* for the few at the expense of the many. It is increasingly difficult to critique racial problems because of the mythology that "we are all equal" and that "we are responsible for where we end up," thus further entrenching and protecting White privilege.

Principle 3: Critiques of race and racism often have been diluted and diminished because other inequities, such as sexism, classism, homophobia, religious persecution, and others exist, further allowing us to avoid White privilege as a central concern.

Principle 4: Many White people maintain that racism and White privilege cannot exist because "some of my best friends are Black/Jewish/Indian" and also because they can point to individuals (e.g., Barack Obama, Oprah Winfrey, or Tiger Woods in the United States, for example) to justify their belief that all members of a particular racial group have the same opportunities, which underscores that individual experience needs to be understood apart from collective experience.

Principle 5: One can be simultaneously good *and* racist, as evidenced by much of U.S. and Canadian history, in which many good programs, policies, initiatives, and events have taken place at the same time as dynamics that have perpetuated disenfranchisement, marginalization, and great harm.

We highlight these principles as a way of acknowledging that many in our society, especially White people, have been taught and encouraged to believe that White people are no different from anyone else (i.e., "we are all the same"); that we have no special privilege, advantage, or power; and that even discussing racialization should be avoided.

Thus, White students entering teacher education generally have been raised *not* to critique social difference and racism, which exacerbates the difficulty of doing meaningful, critical, and transformative social justice work. For students to be able and willing to reflect critically on the concept of White privilege, to break through this bottleneck, they need to come to terms with the possibility that their own experience may *not* be the universal one, especially for the racialized *Other*.

The Challenge

How can we teach about White power and privilege—what we label as Whiteness—without alienating White students, and without placing students of color in an uncomfortable, marginalized position? Is it possible to teach about Whiteness without being disruptive or causing paralyzing White guilt? Or, as Sleeter (2005) asks in much of her work, what type of preparation do White people need to engage in a critical examination of Whiteness?

Similarly, who should talk about Whiteness, how, in what context, and to what end? These questions frame the examples of the following activities that we believe are effective ways to begin critical reflection and movements toward antiracist action, in relation to Whiteness.

We know that no single list of activities or experiences will remedy the roadblocks emerging around social justice, multiculturalism, or diversity themes. Rather, we use an approach whereby students engage in critical reflection regarding their own identities and experiences, and then are drawn into a more dynamic, multifaceted, dialectical dialogue with other identities and experiences (James, 2010). Underpinning this philosophy and conceptual approach is a belief in Paulo Freire's (1970) understanding of education as intertwined with the political, economic, and sociocultural milieu. In sum, education is a political project (McLaren, 2007), and we encourage our students to be engaged—actively and critically—in that work. Avoiding addressing Whiteness can lead us to a more disenfranchised, antidemocratic society (Carr, 2010). Yes, teaching and learning about Whiteness can be uncomfortable, disconcerting, and difficult, but the aim is to move beyond guilt and shame to reclaim the possibility of engaging, understanding, and acting in an attempt to achieve social justice and transformation. We have sought to identify the proverbial "elephant in the room" by engaging in what some have called *disruptive pedagogies*. These are not to be read as a definitive list of activities that are somehow foolproof or "teacher-proof," as some curricula are packaged. Rather, they represent our attempts to document some promising approaches that help our students break through bottlenecks to a more critical understanding of our world.

Activities Toward/Seeking Awareness

We use a variety of activities to cultivate a sense of critical interrogation, engagement, and meaningful assessment of Whiteness. Beyond the activities, it is important for us to frame the context, prepare for diverse reactions, ensure that there is sustained activity, and recognize the range of discomfort that both White students and students of color might experience. Over time we have refined our practices, and we continue to consult with scholars, activists, and colleagues to better understand, appreciate, and reconcile what is happening around us. We share the following ideas for activities to illustrate an overall approach to this work rather than as exact ingredients for a perfect recipe.

Critical Self-Reflection Activity

One activity we recommend as a way of commencing dialogue about White privilege focuses on a critical self-reflection regarding identity. It is important for postsecondary students to tease out and unpack their own educational experiences to be able to appreciate what led them to become teachers, social workers, sociologists, nurses, or whatever profession is relevant to our particular courses. Carr has used this approach with his undergraduate education classes, asking students to write a short paper on five personalities, experiences, factors, issues, or events that have shaped their educational experiences. They are asked to reflect on, contextualize, and critique the five points they have identified in relation to discrimination, marginalization, social circumstance, and cultural capital.

When students present their papers in class, it is extremely powerful to discover that the *context* is as important as, if not more important than, the *content* in documenting their experiences. Students begin to make linkages with each other and to see how people's identities, and how they are treated based on those identities, are fundamental in determining educational success. Many students have had unfavorable elementary and secondary school experiences, and it is important to deconstruct, contextualize, and critique the meaning of social contexts in shaping these experiences. Others seem to have enjoyed a relatively barrier-free journey through school and into postsecondary education. These are not only rich areas for further analysis, but they also provide opportunities to consider students' own implications in larger social phenomena, such as bullying, dropping out (or being pushed out), teacher-student relations, and, significantly, racism, which many students articulate as a significant factor in light of our "color-blind," multicultural society.

Students are encouraged to identify trends that explain how some were marginalized, ignored, and diminished, whereas others seemed to have benefited from a relatively fluid, profitable, and enjoyable educational experience. All students are encouraged to understand the political nature of education; the non-neutral process of determining how it should be structured, organized, and managed; and how power is infused throughout our education system. The act of documenting what has shaped one's own educational experience is powerful, especially for future teachers, in that they can start to connect the relevance of their identities and cultural capital with their own experiences within the educational context.

During this process, we also critically interrogate what diversity looked and felt like. We quickly learn that, if diversity was dealt with at all, it often was approached in a superficial and primarily celebratory manner. We learn, too, that the absence of an explicit approach to social justice can be extremely traumatic for some students and neutralizing for others, highlighting the salience of identity. One of the focal points here is to determine how diversity shapes educational experiences and, moreover, how being White is not, as many of our White students assume, a neutral, raceless identity.

The aforementioned identity activity allows us to engage in a discussion about the lived experiences of people from a range of identities and, significantly, to problematize Whiteness, even if we start to do this through an analysis of social class and poverty. In predominantly White environments, a common refrain is that the *problem* of race does not exist, and, although we would argue that it is present and has shaped the White experience in relation to the *Other*, it is often more conducive to discuss other forms of disadvantage, especially classism and sexism, as a means to understand and make the linkage with inequitable power relations. Students have reacted strongly after hearing their colleagues present on their own educational experiences. They can see, despite the differences, the many common trends, themes, and issues in how their individual and collective experiences are framed, to varying degrees, by racialization. Some students may start by saying such things as, "I've never had contact with people of color," "It's never been an issue for me," "That problem doesn't exist for me," and "People are color-blind now." After this activity, they tend to realize that notions of race are all around them, even when they live in a mainly White community, and that negation of marginalized peoples requires great effort. This is where we try to excavate the normative, hegemonic qualities of Whiteness and, more important, what we can do about them. Being able to identify and talk about White power and privilege, therefore, is an important first step in addressing power differentials.

Ultimately, this exercise, when framed with critical questions about the pertinence of the context being as important as the content in the educational experience and the role of power, can help demystify the notion of meritocracy: that people succeed in education merely based on effort. The social construction of identity underpins the educational experience, and it plays a role in affecting attitudes and behavior, the organization of the school culture, decision-making processes, and the fundamental relationships that students develop in their formative years.

One cautionary note here is that we must avoid passing judgment on how students formulate the key events, personalities, issues, factors, and experiences they have highlighted. Some students might seem to become more entrenched in their assertion of a color-blind or postracial society while others might feel empowered, having been given a chance to reframe their own lives through another lens. Emotions could run high and students have complained that "this isn't what we signed up for," but creating equitable learning environments is a core tenet of our vision for social justice teacher education. Responding empathetically to each student is crucial, but what is more important is to extract an analysis and seek a more critical and engaged vantage point, which will be indispensable as these students become teachers or other professionals.

"Unpacking the Invisible Knapsack"

Lund uses a similar activity, usually in combination with distributing the influential Peggy McIntosh essay, "Unpacking the Invisible Knapsack" (1988). Before students have had a chance to consider McIntosh's take on White privilege, they are invited to write as many descriptors of themselves as they can. *How would you describe yourself?* At this point we assure students that their responses will not be handed in, graded, or shared with others. A brief discussion of the descriptors students have listed at this point allows them to see the wide range of categories their peers have identified, and perhaps to add to their lists. Some students note "hidden" aspects of their identities such as sexual orientation, ethnicity, a learning (dis)ability, or physical condition. They are invited to reflect on which dimensions of identity each of us is most likely to notice, highlight, ignore, or avoid. Some people produce long, detailed, and multifaceted lists while others struggle to include even a few broad descriptors.

Students then are asked to list common identity "errors" that people make about them, based perhaps on appearance, dress, or behavior. Some students talk about being mistaken as being gay, being an immigrant, being an ethnicity different from their own, and the like. They also are invited to note which identities are more hidden and which they are more likely to share willingly with people, and under what circumstances.

Lund then has students mark each item on their list with " + " or " − " or "?" depending on whether each descriptor is usually positive, negative, or more neutral or variable. He typically shares a few examples from his own list, including that he comes from an immigrant family (not apparent, as he is not from an ethnicity that typically faces discrimination because he is White) and grew up in a working-class neighborhood. Modeling specific examples allows students to expand their categories and gives White students ideas about how to describe themselves beyond the "normal" or "average" markers they may have assumed.

Students then are asked to think of specific examples of *reversed* situations—that is, times when the positive identity markers could work *against* them, and the negative ones could become *privilege* markers. For example, a turbaned Sikh male once shared that he might face discrimination in seeking employment, but enjoys an "insider" status at Indian weddings. A gay student felt vulnerable when waiting for public transportation but was comfortable among trusted friends at gay-friendly events. The activity is followed with informal discussions in pairs and small groups to talk about anything interesting they noted, surprises, and emerging understandings about the hierarchies of identity markers. This leads to a larger class discussion about the possible implications of identity and its saliency in their professional lives and in the lives of their students. Our colleague, Mara Sapon-Shevin (2004), has developed a DVD with provocative dramatic vignettes on diverse identities in educational settings, and these short clips may also be used to open this conversation with students.

After engaging in complex and candid dialogue among classmates on hidden identity issues, one pre-service teacher shared with Lund how a particular student in her science class who had been struggling with gender identity issues. The activity in class had opened her mind, she reported, to attend more carefully and sensitively to the student, a self-identified male who got his period suddenly in her class. Her handling of the incident without judgment prompted the student to tell the teacher that she may have saved his life with her calm understanding. He had been contemplating suicide and told her that she helped him believe in his own self-worth. She shared this experience with Lund to show the personal impact that an "enlightened" teacher may have on the lives of students whose marginalized identities leave them with few allies in typical school environments. It was a poignant reminder that any opportunities we can find to encourage students to engage in this challenging work of overcoming personal bottlenecks on identity issues can be invaluable to their professional and personal lives.

Multicultural Surveys Activity

Another strategy with university students involves multicultural "quizzes," such as one of this book's editors, Paul C. Gorski, has developed, to stimulate discussion on what we do and do not know, and why; these are meant to challenge some students' notions that oppression no longer exists. It is important for students to work in small groups, debating the items and trying to work through what answers to questions *should be*, and then come together as a larger group to discuss the correct answers. One technique Carr has used is to ask one group to read a question, emphasizing group members' collective experience, and then to have another group share its answer with a justification for that answer. Other groups are then invited to offer their analyses before the instructor reads the answers. Using Gorski's (2011) basic *Equity and Diversity* quiz with 20 questions, the entire activity takes about an hour to complete.

The instructor should leave time after each answer is revealed to seek critical interpretation of how those who chose the incorrect answer came to believe another conceptualization. This exercise allows students to critique what they learn in schools and elsewhere, including through the media, often resulting in stereotypes and fictitious images related to social justice and injustice. It is important to consider how White people are portrayed in general and how examining Whiteness is integral to addressing racial discrimination.

While this activity can be a friendly and fairly benign icebreaker, it also can reinforce the salience of knowledge construction and the epistemology of identity. When does identity matter, and when does it not? How and why do we maintain that we are "color-blind" when there is overwhelming evidence of racial discrimination and injustice? For some students, these activities can cause an existential crisis in which they are forced to rethink long-held beliefs. Anger and defensiveness are common and need to be handled with tact. This activity also encourages reflection on the socially constructed identities that are prevalent in the mainstream media, as well as how something as ubiquitous as the news can have an impact on teaching and learning.

Carr has seen students struggle with answers to questions that arguably should form part of their fundamental school learning, including U.S. military power around the world, poverty rates, racialized peoples, and the law. The point is not to have the "right" answer but, rather, to explore critically why questions about these topics seem to be so universally discouraged in mainstream education and media systems. Students sometimes feel a sense of embarrassment about what they do not know. We encourage them to reflect more deeply on what they know, and why they know it, through critical epistemological interrogation. Our discussions flow into identity: if we do not know about militaristic, political, and economic realities, then we must be able to accept that people who embody diverse (socially constructed) identities different from our own might also have different experiences despite living in the same society.

Media Literacy Activity

Another disruptive activity relates to the media and seeks to heighten awareness of the importance of media and political literacy. Do we teach media literacy in our schools? What are the implications of doing so or not doing so? How do the media pervade what we know and how we think? The media can create a normative, universal presence for White people and, as a corollary, may enhance stereotypes and discrimination. Since the media do *not* name or address White privilege, one might conclude that it does not exist.

The activity is structured as follows: the class is divided into five groups, each with a different task. One watches the news as it normally would; one times and documents news items and breaks; one focuses on political messages; one monitors the news anchors, journalists, and others on the screen; and one focuses on racial issues.

We watch a 30-minute nightly news program as a class. It does not make much of a difference what channel or jurisdiction is selected; the patterns tend to be consistent. After watching the news, each group, in the order outlined previously, reports on what it saw. It is important to layer the observations and analysis that each group shares and not to engage in discussion until each group has presented.

What Carr has found when using this activity with graduate students at the master's level is that they generally are surprised, and also disheartened, to see how little analysis the news provides and, moreover, how much it resembles entertainment more than a critical inquiry into social conditions. Students start to question how the stories are selected and presented and why they are not critiqued or contextualized in a meaningful way. Often, students observe a clear racialized organization to the news regarding who delivers the news, and the angle, the lack of critical discussions of race, and prevalent images generally reinforce Whiteness as the norm.

Following this activity, we find that students are more likely to think critically about how they address issues such as war, conflict, poverty, and injustice, among others, in their own classrooms. They begin to comprehend the effect of the mainstream media in their lives, even if they do not watch television, as school culture, values, curriculum, and pedagogy are all influenced by how neoliberalism shapes what we know.

A key feature of this activity is allowing students to analyze and discuss what they've seen—first individually, and afterward, collectively. Some students claim that media or popular culture does not affect them at all, and this is a point worth addressing directly with examples from contemporary media sources, preferably by focusing on local issues. By layering diverse voices and ideas, we can start to appreciate how we are all biased and how our identities influence what we experience. This is an important learning experience for White people and people of color alike, and can lead into the critical deconstruction of a common event. At the same time, it allows us to delve into the theoretical underpinning of Whiteness in an attempt to explain why we, as a society, generally resist undertaking critical analyses of White power and privilege.

Newspaper Activity

Lund uses a similar disruptive media activity with the local daily newspaper, leading students through an analysis of the photos of people appearing throughout an entire edition. At first the assignment seems awkward and inappropriate; after all, we have been taught that it is not polite to mention color or race, and here we are asking students to do a very simplistic kind of sorting. Students usually seem surprised and squirm in their seats. However flawed, the data generated through this assignment can be powerful. Whose faces do we see and what roles do they play in our community? How fairly do newspaper representations reflect the community's demographics? Invariably, the predominant images depict (apparently) White people, shown in a wide range of roles in the city and around the globe, while images of people of color appear mainly in the sports and entertainment section, as the exotic *other* in global stories, or positioned as criminals. Which articles or advertisements do students classify as more positive and desirable?

Lund has seen students become angry or suggest that attending to people's identities in this manner must be racist. However, the unsettling dimension of the assignment invariably leads to deeper self-evaluation and growth among many students. For White students the disruption can be particularly unsettling. Many never have looked critically at the racialized nature of media, and a "factual," numerical counting and critique of faces seems to fracture what they thought they knew. A typical comment after this activity is that some students "can never enjoy reading a newspaper or magazine again" without guilt or critical racial analysis. Lund counts this as a breakthrough—pushing through a bottleneck. The discussion is invariably rich and layered and, as with most activities, students should have ample time to sort out their emerging understandings, perhaps using private written reflections.

This print media activity, and the television news media activity, also raise questions about why the media expend so much time on trivial matters, most typically about which Hollywood star has been seen with whom. By leading our students through these critical and discomfiting exercises, we can start to assemble a picture of how racialized power works and, significantly, how White power and privilege are maintained in very explicit and complex ways. Students also are encouraged to start to reflect on what is omitted from the media—and school textbooks—and to question the effect of these omissions. For example, many Canadians are unaware that Canada also had slavery—although it was different and not as widespread as slavery in the United States—or the extent to which White Europeans committed heinous acts toward aboriginal peoples on both sides of the border (Lund, 2006). A "successful" pedagogical result is students' beginning to seek out additional resources to use in their subsequent teaching assignments, to supplement or counter the material in mainstream textbooks.

Moving Forward Activity

A more embodied activity involves students finding themselves physically engaged in an exercise about privilege that Lund adapted from an activity developed by a colleague, David Este, at the University of Calgary. We share the activity with his permission. The exercise is most powerful when followed by a comprehensive debriefing by a skilled instructor. Participants should be led to the exercise site silently, hand in hand, in a line. At the site, participants can release their hands but should be instructed to stand shoulder to shoulder in a straight line, without speaking. They should close their eyes as well.

Participants are instructed to listen carefully to each sentence the facilitator reads and take the step required if the sentence applies to them. They may be told there is a prize at the front of the site for which everyone is competing. Participants are asked to remain in their positions, and to look at their positions at the site as well as the positions of the other participants. Participants are then asked to consider who among them would probably win the prize.

The facilitator reads the students a number of prompts that ask them to take a certain number of steps forward or backward according to their life experiences. Many of the prompts address race, class, gender, and sexual orientation issues and can be adapted for specific instructional purposes. For example, a prompt might ask students to "take one or more steps *forward* if:

- you graduated from high school;
- you were encouraged to attend college or university by a parent;
- there were more than 50 books in your home when you grew up;
- a parent told you that you could be anything you wanted to be;
- you have ever inherited money or property;
- people of color worked in your household as servants, cleaners, nannies, or gardeners;
- one or both of your parents were professionals; or
- you studied the culture of your ancestors in elementary school, and so on.

Prompts requiring at least one step *back* might include if:

- you believe you have ever been followed by store personnel because of your race;
- you believe you were ever denied employment because of your race, class, ethnicity, gender, or sexual orientation;
- your parents did not grow up in this country;
- your home language was other than English;
- you had to rely primarily on public transportation;
- you often saw members of your race, ethnic groups, gender, or sexual orientation portrayed on television in degrading roles;
- you believe you ever have been paid less or treated unfairly in a workplace because of your race, class, ethnicity, gender, or sexual orientation;
- you were ever stopped or questioned by the police because of your race, class, ethnicity, gender, or sexual orientation;
- you were ever called names because of your race, class, ethnicity, gender, or sexual orientation;
- you were ever discouraged from pursuing academic programs or certain jobs because of your race, class, ethnicity, gender, or sexual orientation; or
- you have ever felt uncomfortable about a joke related to your race, class, ethnicity, gender, or sexual orientation but did not feel safe confronting the situation, and so on.

When they open their eyes, students see who has stepped toward the front of the room and who remains toward the back, perhaps even behind the starting line. As we might imagine, the front-runners typically include White, heterosexual, able-bodied males. Their responses are interesting and may include excuses or anger that they can't help that they had advantages. The activity also uncovers interesting anomalies that refute assumptions about people's identities; we can't always tell by looking at somebody what that person has experienced. Lund has followed this exercise with a variety of processing questions, from the general and broad to the specific and prodding: How did this exercise make you feel? What have you learned from this experience? As a graduate student, educator, or community worker, what can you do with this information in the future?

In response to this exercise, one student reported that he never had realized that other students didn't share advantaged backgrounds similar to his own; he noted that he always had thought of his life as "just a normal family" situation. In this sense, this exercise has offered students a revealing window into privilege.

However, using this sort of activity entails a great deal of potential emotional risk. Occasionally, and for a variety of reasons, students experience this exercise in a very emotional way; some at both ends of the privilege spectrum may feel "exposed." These responses should be handled with extreme sensitivity. Difficult or complex lessons are often emotionally powerful experiences. As instructors trying to help students question past assumptions and beliefs, we know that the work is risky *and* highly rewarding. As Kumashiro (2009) argues, these moments of discomfort are the ideal times for education to occur. We find these personally transformative experiences can assist students in viewing *their* students with greater sensitivity and in questioning their assumptions about families and students. We underscore, though, the importance of preparing adequately before facilitating these exercises with people who might experience denial, shame, guilt, regret, anger, or other negative emotions.

A Note on Disruptive Pedagogies

We emphasize that, with each of these disruptive approaches, content is important, but taking *context* into account is equally critical. Understanding that White people might reject an analysis of privilege because of their exposure to the hegemonic, normative ideologies that have pervaded our societies, and that people of color might experience discomfort when asked to expose their experience with injustice, is fundamental in doing this work effectively. We must be open to learning about how people have come to adopt "color-blindness." We must challenge and refute people's perceptions with a great deal of caution. In our experience, it is more effective to have people come to their own heightened understanding of identity over time. In other words, a one-hour teacher workshop on Whiteness with no follow-up could entrench existing viewpoints. We have found that, over the course of a 12- to 16-week semester, students can be exposed to a range of readings, videos, assignments, and activities, such as those outlined previously, to construct knowledge on their own identities and experiences as well as those of others. Although it is arduous, complex, and challenging work, it is a necessary undertaking, especially for those of us in teacher education.

Furthermore, we emphasize that the previous activities require planning and latitude. Groups vary, and sometimes certain concepts, anecdotes, metaphors, and descriptions work better with one group than another. We have experienced this firsthand in Canada, where many people are quick to insinuate that the United States has much more serious racial justice problems, as if to justify their own lack of engagement. The historical relationship between colonizing White people and aboriginal/First Nations People/American Indians underlies the so-called "discovery" of Canada and the United States and continues to be underexamined in these societies. Facing this past is crucial to inform our work in undoing racism and understanding White privilege. Moreover, the legacy of slavery and histories of systemic discrimination against many racialized groups grounds the lived experiences we all have.

In addressing these fundamental issues, we have learned that it is important to avoid being "preachy" or claim to have the "right answer" and, instead, to be sensitive to complex issues and experiences. We have learned a great deal through this work and have sought to be honest about how much we do *not* know and how our bodies may convey meanings in ways of which we are unaware. We often stumble, make mistakes, apologize, reflect, find patience, and try again. Students are remarkably understanding and open to a spirit of shared inquiry on difficult and uncomfortable topics. This approach toward teacher education is not simply about "bringing White people around" to a new understanding; it is also about interrogating how we *all* are immersed in a way of life in which inequities and injustices are embedded. In this spirit, we are committed as well to examining Whiteness in relation to its intersectionalities with gender, sexual orientation, class, religion, language, and other identities.

Conclusion

In this chapter, we have discussed disruptive methods, strategies, and activities to engage students in a critical exploration of privilege, identity, and Whiteness. We have cautioned that the context is as important as the content, and we alluded to our own starting point as two White males working in this arena. We wish to conclude by highlighting how important it is to seek out marginalized, alternative, and multiple racialized voices in this discussion. While we believe that we have been able, to a certain degree, to explore intimate and personal subject matter with White students because we are White, we also are cognizant that working collaboratively and respectfully with all colleagues and students who are not White is extremely important.

Before starting our *Great White North Project* in 2006, we sought the views of important scholars of color to determine how they would react. We were concerned how we might be extending our privilege in implicit ways. We were reassured when our colleagues encouraged us to push on and work in collaboration with them. With so much excellent scholarship on race, racism, and racialization—most of it typically focused on people of color and *their* challenges—we sought to identify how White people and White privilege fit into the race equation. While we recognize that race does not define everything, we are convinced that race is a central component for understanding historical and contemporary contexts in Canada, the United States, and elsewhere.

Particularly in teacher education, understanding this history and our personal implication in racism is essential, even if it may cause discomfort among White students (Howard, 2006; Sleeter, 2005; Solomon, Portelli, Daniel, & Campbell, 2005). All students and instructors will experience some unease and awkwardness and stumbling, and these are to be worked through as we strive collectively to squeeze our way through this bottleneck. In this spirit, we continue this project in a quest for more social justice, more engagement, more transformation, and more critical work, in general. Whiteness and privilege are, after all, central to the discussion of these questions: *What type of education, for whom, and how?*

Finally, we emphasize that our disruptive approach to teaching and learning aimed at better understanding, contextualizing, and addressing

White privilege is *not* about developing lists of words to avoid, images to reject, or music to boycott. Rather, it relates to finding a better understanding of how power works; how it is infused in our societies; and how it is used to acknowledge or negate difference, racialized lived experiences, and social inequalities (Dei, 2008). The fact that the United States now has an African American president does not diminish the lived reality of racism for many people of color, nor does it mean that power is necessarily exercised in a more democratic, equitable way for all citizens. The presence and symbolism of Obama is important and a visible advancement in the struggle for civil rights. However, it does not mean that the fundamental conditions underpinning a highly racialized society—including residential segregation, dropout rates, unemployment, incarceration rates for some racialized groups, and visible power differentials at political levels—have changed. These issues must continue to be critiqued through critical engagement within education.

Ultimately there are myriad differences among and within all racialized groups, and the study of White privilege is a way of becoming more sensitized to these and other complex differences that characterize the sociocultural and political landscape for all people. We wish readers the very best in their ongoing educational journeys and encourage them to undertake disruptive teaching toward promoting social justice in spite of the many forms of resistance to this important work.

Notes

1. The word for the racialized identity category of "White" is capitalized in this piece mainly to differentiate it from the name of the color.

2. The authors acknowledge the inadequacy of the phrase "of color" but also concede its widespread use to denote a wide range of racialized identities that are not White. Rather than use "non-White" as a descriptor that suggests a lack of something, we use the former, albeit with reservations.

References

Carr, P. R. (2010). *Does your vote count? Critical pedagogy and democracy*. New York: Peter Lang.

Carr, P. R., & Lund, D. E. (Eds.). (2007). *The great White north? Exploring Whiteness, privilege and identity in education*. Rotterdam, The Netherlands: Sense.

Carr, P. R., & Lund, D. E. (2009). The unspoken color of diversity: Whiteness, privilege, and critical engagement in education. In S. Steinberg (Ed.), *Diversity and multiculturalism: A reader* (pp. 45–55). New York: Peter Lang.

Dei, G. J. S. (2008). *Racists beware: Uncovering racial politics in the post modern society*. Rotterdam, The Netherlands: Sense.

Fine, M., Weis, L., Powell Pruitt, L., & Burns, A. (2004). *Off white: Readings on race, power, and society* (2nd ed.). New York: Routledge.

Freire, P. (1970). Pedagogy of the oppressed. New York: Continuum.

Gorski, P. (2011). Diversity awareness quizzes. *EdChange: Professional development, scholarship and activism for diversity, social justice, and community growth* [Online resource]. St. Paul, MN: Author. Retrieved from http://www.edchange.org/multicultural/quizzes.html

Howard, G. R. (2006). *We can't teach what we don't know: White teachers, multiracial schools* (2nd ed.). New York: Teachers College Press.

James, C. E. (2010). *Seeing ourselves: Exploring race, ethnicity and culture* (4th ed.). Toronto, Ontario: Thompson.

Kumashiro, K. K. (2009). *Against common sense: Teaching and learning toward social justice* (2nd ed.). New York: Routledge.

Lund, D. E. (2006). Waking up the neighbors: Surveying multicultural and antiracist education in Canada, the United Kingdom, and the United States. *Multicultural Perspectives, 8*(1), 35–43.

Lund, D. E., & Carr, P. R. (2010). Exposing privilege and racism in the great White north: Tackling Whiteness and identity issues in Canadian education. *Multicultural Perspectives, 12*(4), 229–234.

McIntosh, P. (1988). White privilege and male privilege: A personal account of coming to see correspondences through work in women's studies. Wellesley, MA: Wellesley College Center for Research on Women (Working Paper No. 189).

McLaren, P. (2007). *Life in schools: An introduction to critical pedagogy in the foundations of education* (5th ed.). Boston: Pearson Education.

Sapon-Shevin, M. (Producer). (2004). *And nobody said anything: Uncomfortable conversations on diversity* [DVD]. Syracuse, NY: Newhouse School of Public Communications, Syracuse University.

Sleeter, C. E. (2005). How white teachers construct race. In C. McCarthy, W. Crichlow, G. Dimitriadis, & N. Dolby (Eds.), *Race, identity and representation in education* (2nd ed.). New York: Routledge.

Solomon, R. P., Portelli, J. P., Daniel, B-J., & Campbell, A. (2005). The discourse of denial: How white teacher candidates construct race, racism and "white privilege." *Race, Ethnicity and Education, 8*(2), 147–169.

Sullivan, S. (2006). *Revealing whiteness: The unconscious habits of racial privilege*. Indianapolis: Indiana University Press.

8

TEACHING ABOUT CHRISTIAN PRIVILEGE IN THE TEACHER EDUCATION CLASSROOM

Warren J. Blumenfeld

When I was young, I sat upon my maternal grandfather Simon Mahler's knee. Looking down urgently but with deep affection, he said to me: "Varn" (he pronounced my name "Varn" through his distinctive Polish accent), "you are named after my father, Wolf Mahler." I asked where Wolf was, and Simon told me that Wolf, along with my great-grandmother Bascha and most of my grandfather Simon's 13 brothers and sisters, was killed by people called "Nazis." In shock, I asked why the Nazis killed them, and he responded, "Because they were Jews." Those words have reverberated in my mind, haunting me ever since.

I later learned that the Nazis shot many of my Polish relatives and dumped them in a mass grave in Krosno; they eventually shipped others to Auschwitz and Belzec, where they murdered them. Hitler rationalized his methods in resolving the "Jewish question" by fabricating "racial" arguments in his claims that Jews came from inferior "racial" stock and, therefore, they must be exterminated to prevent genetic and social contamination to so-called "Aryans."

A crucial point that cannot be forgotten, however, is that Nazi philosophy and justification for murdering Jews rested on a foundation of Christian religious claims against the Jewish people. For example, Hitler wrote in *Mein Kampf* (1925), "Today I believe that I am acting in accordance with the will of the Almighty Creator: by defending myself against the Jew, I am fighting for the work of the Lord" (Vol. I, p. 60). Nazi *racialization* of Jews and

Judaism rested upon misinterpretations of Christian *religious* texts. In addition to the Christian Bible, Hitler acknowledged the profound impact Martin Luther had upon his own attitudes about the Jewish people. In his 1543 treatise, *Von den Jüden und jren Lügen* (*On the Jews and Their Lies*), Luther characterized Jews as a "base, whoring people, that is, no people of God, and their boast of lineage, circumcision, and law must be accounted as filth."

While social realities in Nazi Germany and the contemporary United States clearly differ, some parallels exist in the symbiotic relationship between Christian privilege and religious oppression: oppression toward non-Christians gives rise to Christian privilege in majority-Christian communities and nations, and Christian privilege maintains oppression toward non-Christian individuals and faith communities. Based on Peggy McIntosh's (1988) pioneering investigations of White and male privilege, we can understand Christian privilege as constituting a seemingly invisible, unearned, and largely unacknowledged array of benefits accorded to Christians, with which they often unconsciously walk through life as if effortlessly carrying a knapsack tossed over their shoulders. This system of benefits confers dominance on Christians while subordinating members of other faith communities as well as nonbelievers. These systemic inequities are pervasive. They are encoded into the individual's consciousness and woven into the fabric of our social institutions, resulting in a stratified social order privileging dominant ("agent") groups while restricting and disempowering subordinate ("target") groups (Bell, 1997; Miller, 1976).

Following McIntosh's inventory outlining the manifestations of White privilege, scholars have developed parallel lists summarizing examples of Christian privilege (see, e.g., Clark, Vargas, Schlosser, & Alimo, 2002; Schlosser, 2003). As Clark et al. (2002) assert: "[T]he fact remains that all Christians benefit from Christian privilege regardless of the way they express themselves as Christians in the same way that all White people benefit from White privilege" (p. 12). I have defined *Christian privilege* (Blumenfeld, 2006) as:

> the overarching system of advantages bestowed on Christians. It is the institutionalization of a Christian norm or standard, which establishes and perpetuates the notion that all people are or should be Christian thereby privileging Christians and Christianity, and excluding the needs, concerns, ethnoreligious cultural practices, and life experiences of people who are not Christian. Often overt, though at times subtle, Christian privilege results in oppression by intent and design, but also it comes in the form of neglect, omission, erasure, and distortion. (p. 196)

Just as there is a spectrum of Christian denominations and traditions, so too is there a hierarchy or continuum of Christian privilege based on historical factors, numbers of practitioners, and degrees of social power (Blumenfeld, 2006). In this regard, in a U.S. context, though the gap in privilege between Christian denominations is apparently shrinking, White, mainline Protestant denominations may still have greater degrees of Christian privilege relative to some minority Christian denominations: African American, Latino/a, and Asian American churches; Amish; Mennonites; Quakers; Seventh-Day Adventists; Jehovah's Witnesses; Eastern and Greek Orthodox; adherents to Christian Science and to the Church of Jesus Christ of Latter Day Saints; and still in some quarters, to Catholics.

Christian Privilege as a Threshold Concept

Across the European colonized world, Christian hegemony historically has been used to justify oppression and genocide against minoritized peoples. It provided rationalizations for the slave trade, the colonization and confiscation of land and resources (e.g., the notion of "Manifest Destiny"), forced Christian conversions, and restrictive immigration laws. Given this history, I have come to believe that, even to develop a critical understanding of White and male privilege with a strong historical grounding, my students must grasp the Christian antecedents (and their contemporary manifestations) on which these forms of dominant group privilege rest.

This has raised considerable challenges for me as a teacher educator: "How can I distinguish Christian privilege and the *misuses* of Christian doctrine from Christianity itself? How do I assure students that we are investigating Christian privilege stemming from the *actions of people*, not challenging or criticizing Christian religions and doctrine overall?"

Until fairly recently, I have lived in relatively heterogeneous areas of the United States in terms of race, ethnicity, religion, socioeconomic class, sexual and gender identity, and other demographic markers. I accepted a faculty position in 2004 to teach courses focused on social justice in the School of Education at Iowa State University, a large research, tax-supported, state land-grant institution located in Ames, Iowa. I primarily teach a course titled "Multicultural Foundations in Schools and Society" on a campus and in a state in which the overwhelming majority of people are White and self-identify as some denomination of Christian. Virtually all students registered for my courses, which are mandatory for students in the teacher education program, are pre-service teachers raised in homogeneous rural communities.

I understood not very long into my work in Iowa that this position would pose a number of challenges not prevalent in my previous teaching experiences. On a final course paper, one student wrote that, although she enjoyed the course and felt that my graduate assistant and I were knowledgeable and had great senses of humor, she felt obliged to inform us that we will spend eternity in Hell for being "practicing homosexuals." Another student wrote on her course paper that homosexuality and transgenderism are sins in the same category as stealing and murder. She said I will travel to Hell if I continue to act on my same-sex desires, insisting that I will not receive an invitation to enter Heaven, *regardless* of my sexual identity and behavior, if I do not accept Jesus as my personal savior. She concluded that the real Christian privilege is "To suffer and die for the name of Christ."

Non-Christian Students

In a private meeting in my university office, a student said that, although she would like to speak during our discussions about religion in education, and specifically on the issue of Christian privilege, she feels "unsafe" doing so because she identifies as Wiccan. If word got out about her religious beliefs, she explained, schools in Iowa might disqualify her for employment. I could see the anger and sadness in her face as tears streamed down her cheeks.

A Jewish student told me that, since coming to our campus, he has gone into a "religious closet." To avoid marginalization, he tells his peers that he was raised Methodist since he often has heard other students express cruel anti-Jewish sentiments regarding Hitler and the German Holocaust as well as everyday expressions such as "Don't Jew me down" and "That's so Jewish."

A Muslim student felt marginalized and silenced when he engaged in online campus discussions about religion:

> Our campus atmosphere often stifles the discussion of such issues because of these personal attacks. Now that my time at Iowa State is complete, I cannot help but sympathize with the students who feel isolated for their ideas because I, too, have felt this way. (Mahayni, in Hansen, 2007)

This student discussed how he resents the many times Christian evangelists enter his dorm room attempting to convert him to Protestant Christianity.

A small number of students in my courses over the years have identified as atheist or agnostic. The vast majority of these students decided at some point to abandon the Christian faith communities of their families, sometimes experiencing rejection from family and friends as a result.

My discussions with these students made it extremely clear that I needed to find ways to discuss issues related to religion in education that empower students to find their voice.

Conceptual Foundations

As I mentioned earlier, a large proportion of students at Iowa State come from small, rural, largely White and Christian communities in which they had limited contact with people racially or religiously different from themselves. Very few have considered racial or religious power differentials. Many are resistant to reading and talking about social inequities and how these inequities affect educational and societal outcomes.

Students primarily enter the course conceptualizing "multicultural education" as the study of people from around the world. They initially take the so-called "festivals, foods, and folk songs" perspective often referred to as "cultural tourism" (Stebbins, 1996). In addition, many students come to the course expounding a "human relations" (or "liberal multiculturalism") approach, which emphasizes that "we are all people, and we should be able to get along," and "social identities are not important," as opposed to the "critical multiculturalism" (Kincheloe & Steinberg, 1998) perspective on which I build the course.

I use Robert Kegan's (1982) three-stage teaching model sequence. In the initial stage of Kegan's model, called "Confirmation," the educator meets learners "where they are"; solicits ideas, beliefs, and knowledge; listens and legitimizes; invites elaboration; and asks questions. The first paper I assign is the "Multiple Identities Project." I ask students to use themselves as "texts." They describe and analyze themselves from at least four vantage points: (1) Body Identity (physical description); (2) Social Identities (socially constructed identities both ascribed and achieved); (3) Moral/Ethical/Affective Identities (values and beliefs); and (4) Educational Experiences (their experiences as students in P–12 schools and how their *social identities* may have affected their understandings of diversity in schools). Overall, this assignment allows for individual voices to be heard and identities to be articulated, acknowledged, and affirmed.

Dominant Group Privilege

After I have confirmed where students are in terms of their backgrounds, experiences, and social identities (Kegan's first stage), a few weeks into the course, I provide students with concepts that for many have the effect of "contradicting" (Kegan's second stage) or expanding prior understandings around questions related to inequities in schools and society.

I first introduce the theme of dominant group privilege (which itself is a potential bottleneck concept) using Allan G. Johnson's (2006) book *Privilege, Power, and Difference*. Johnson provides an accessible and powerful interconnection among many forms of dominant group privilege (White, male, heterosexual, ability, socioeconomic class) in a style that does not elicit the guilt and blame that can shut down the learning process. Along with Johnson's book, and especially when I assign its second chapter, "Privilege, Oppression, Difference," I distribute Lewis Schlosser's list enumerating the forms of Christian privileges (http://convention.myacpa.org/archive/pro grams/Boston10/Handouts/446/ChristianPrivilegeHandout.pdf) since Johnson's discussion of this form of privilege is not developed in detail.

By presenting multiple forms of dominant group privilege simultaneously rather than initially highlighting one particular form, and by touching upon the multiple forms of social identities and privilege, Johnson's approach tends to unclog some learning bottlenecks that might hamper students' understandings of Christian privilege. For example, some of the White women in my class often are uncomfortable studying White privilege, but immediately understand male privilege. Through this process they begin to connect how they are simultaneously advantaged and restricted. In this way, they tend to explore more fully the multiple issues related to the *socially constructed* categories of identity that grant them power as well as constrain them.

I also assign a book, Joel Spring's (2010) *Deculturalization and the Struggle for Equality*, that begins to contradict (Kegan's second stage) many students' conceptual understandings of the historical roots of the United States. By exploding some of the misinformation students learned from their previous educational experiences, this history demonstrates how White privilege *connects alongside and often derives from Christian privilege and religious oppression in the United States*. Therefore, issues and discussions of Christian privilege emerge seamlessly and often spontaneously from Spring's analysis.

Meanwhile, I give students a two-part assignment to be completed by the following class session: the first part poses a question for critical contemplation; the second part includes a research exercise. The question: "Did

Christopher Columbus discover what has come to be called the United States? Why or why not?" I tell students that, after they reflect on this question, they should identify and read articles exploring Native American perspectives of Christopher Columbus and Columbus Day.

Usually students fill the room with frenetic energy the next time we meet. I ask them to divide into smaller groups to respond to the following prompts:

1. Discuss how you initially had answered the question: "Did Christopher Columbus discover what has come to be called United States? Why or why not?"
2. Discuss what you learned from Native American perspectives of Christopher Columbus and Columbus Day. What did you already know? What surprised you? What insights did you gain? What, if any, emotions arose for you? What questions do you still have?

Following 20 minutes of lively small-group discussion, we reconvene for a large classroom conversation. Many students express anger over the ways their teachers and textbooks portrayed Christopher Columbus during their early schooling. These students feel that they somehow "had been lied to" through the history commonly taught in schools. One semester a geology major responded with her own questions:

How could Columbus have *discovered* what would later be called "America" when Indians have lived on this land for 23,000 to 25,000 years . . . ? How can one "discover" people who have been here so long? Actually, Indians discovered Columbus on *their* land!

A number of students nod their heads in silent agreement. Other students articulate their love for their Christian faiths, but express shock and disbelief over the murder and forced conversions perpetrated by European explorers, missionaries, and settlers.

I also ask students to interrogate the concept of "European settlers." "If this was Indian land, how accurate is the term *European settlers*?" This question confuses some students; others understand the contradiction immediately. A few semesters ago, for instance, one student offered an analogy: "Say I own a house, and someone knocks on the door, walks in, pushes me outside, and claims: 'I like your house, and I am settling here. Be on your way.' Then he slams the door in my face."

That same semester, after the class during which we had these discussions, one enraged student remained behind to talk with me. "You and the geology student have disrespected my culture," she declared. "My culture teaches me that God created the universe six to seven thousand years ago. So, I ask you, how could Indians have lived here for thousands and thousands of years before God created the universe? Also, since Christians are called to bring God's message to all the nations of the world and spread the word of Jesus Christ, I take offense with the claim that Europeans *forcibly converted* anyone!" I thanked her for raising concerns that she certainly was not alone in having. I asked her if I could raise her concerns, while not referring to her by name, at our next class session. She agreed.

Throughout the course, I continually reconnect the elements and processes of multicultural education and reiterate that the course connects theory with practice by asking students to engage critically with the material, each other, and their professor as we all come to a deeper understanding of the importance of multicultural education. I often refer to Sonia Nieto (2002), who likens multiculturalism to a great tapestry:

> A tapestry is a hand-woven textile. When examined from the back, it may simply appear to be a motley group of threads. But when reversed, the threads work together to depict a picture of structure and beauty. A tapestry also symbolizes, through its knots, broken threads and seeming jumble of colors and patterns on the back, the tensions, conflicts, and dilemmas that a society needs to work out. (p. 270)

I began the next class discussion by referring to these ideas before introducing the student's concerns over our previous class discussion. Some students provided scientific evidence for the approximate age of the universe, others discussed their religious teachings. Some discussed the theological imperative to spread the word of Jesus, others talked about their frustrations and resentments when others attempt to convert them to Christianity.

I introduced the notion of "culture clash," in this instance the opposing beliefs, that, for some people, sharing the word of Jesus is an act of bestowing a great gift on the "unbeliever" while, for others, it is an imposition, annoyance, provocation, or worse, a form of oppression.

Coincidentally, I had prepared to introduce this day the concept of "cultural pluralism." The notion of "culture clash" provided a good segue into a discussion of Horace Kallen (1915), a Jewish immigrant and sociologist of Polish and Latvian heritage who coined the term *cultural pluralism* to challenge the notion of the "melting pot," which he considered inherently undemocratic. Kallen envisioned the United States as a great symphony orchestra, one in which all cultural and identity groups play in harmony while retaining their distinctive tones and timbres. Kallen believed that all groups have a "democratic right" to retain their own cultures and to resist the "ruthless Americanization" being forced upon them by segments of the native White Anglo-Protestant population.

I asked students to reflect on Kallen's vision: "Reflecting on the history and expressions or non-expressions of religion in the United States, can you imagine us attaining genuine religious pluralism? If so, what would this look like? If not, why not?"

Many students said that the United States was founded on and had attained Kallen's conceptualization of true religious pluralism. Others, while acknowledging that we are not yet at that point, hoped that someday we would attain Kallen's goal. A number of other students, however, asserted that we are now and always were meant to be "a Christian nation," and that the notion of religious pluralism runs contrary to their religious teachings. One student articulated this view best:

> [A]s a Christian I am called to not be tolerant. I am not called to be violent, but am called to make disciples of all nations. When I look through all of the information I have been given . . . I come to the conclusion that America was founded as a Christian nation. . . . Separation of church and state was created to keep the state out of changing the church, not to keep the church out of the state.

This student referred to his interpretation of Christian scripture, which commands him to spread the word of Jesus.

> *Matthew* 28:16–20: (16) Then the eleven disciples went to Galilee, to the mountain where Jesus had told them to go. (17) When they saw him, they worshiped him; but some doubted. (18) Then Jesus came to them and said, "All authority in heaven and on earth has been given to me. (19) Therefore go and make disciples of all nations, baptizing them in the name of the Father and of the Son and of the Holy Spirit, (20) and teaching them to obey everything I have commanded you. And surely I am with you always, to the very end of the age." (from the King James Bible)

Students also discussed warnings from their pastors and Christian leaders regarding the threat to their faith associated with attending secular educational institutions. One student referred to Brannon Howse, president and founder of the Worldview Weekend Foundation, which I investigated further:

> Where do most Christian students get their perspective on history and sociology or learn about the question of origins? The frightening reality is that most take in the steady diet of Secular Humanism served up in our public schools. And in college, it only gets worse. Worldview Weekend speaker Kerby Anderson puts it this way: "When a student enrolls in Philosophy 101, it could just as easily be called Atheism 101. A class in Sociology 101, should really be called Postmodernism 101. A class on Religion 101, is really a class that should be called Religious Pluralism 101. And a class in Biology 101, would more accurately be called Evolution 101." It's little wonder that more than three out of four young people from Christian homes deny their faith before graduating from college. Parents must prepare their children to counter the lies of Secular Humanism, the New Age Movement, and bizarre forms of mysticism finding their way into our churches. (Howse, 2007)

Strategies for Teaching About Christian Privilege

I value the importance of learning not only the numerous successful pedagogic strategies, classroom activities, resources, and assignments, but I find it also instructive to discuss the strategies that may have shown promise but, in reality, failed to produce the desired results. One such strategy in the latter category initially surprised me, but following critical reflection, became obvious.

Several years ago I wrote a historical and theoretical essay on the concept of Christian privilege in the United States (Blumenfeld, 2006). Due to the positive feedback I have received on the essay from students and educators, I decided to incorporate it into my courses.

When I assigned the essay, some students refused to read it. A number of students who did read it came to the next class session defensive and angry. I asked students to discuss the essay in small groups. Although some of what they shared during their report-outs was positive and reflective ("I never really understood the historical roots of Christian privilege and religious oppression in the United States"), much of the feedback either denied the extent of the problem or justified Christian proselytizing ("The article shows the author's bias against Christians"). A few students noted this reading on their course evaluations. One student wrote, for instance, that he "was sick and tired of the Christian bashing by the professor."

What I learned from this experience was that, because the issues related to Christian privilege and religious oppression are so volatile, I needed to reflect on my use of the essay. For example, although it presents what I believe to be an important historical overview, my authorship tainted the pedagogical efficacy of the essay. I also was reminded that, during any discussion on dominant group privilege, I need to be clear that what we are interrogating is power, control, and domination, not *identities*.

As a White man, I find that I can help students distinguish between issues of power and issues of identity regarding race and gender without engendering a lot of defensiveness. I am never accused of "hating White men." However, when I challenge heterosexual or Christian privilege, some students suggest that I hate heterosexuals or Christians, transfiguring themselves into the *victims* of oppression rather than the recipients of its unearned privileges. This is a common strategy in the psychology of dominant group denial. By labeling the targets of oppression as the perpetrators, as with the terminology of "reverse discrimination," those with privilege can feel secure in the belief that they are not oppressors, that the United States epitomizes the truest meritocracy.

I find that one way I can minimize this response is to allow students to "hear" about these issues from somebody other than myself. So rather than assigning my own essay, I have students read Charles H. Lippy's chapter, "Christian Nation or Pluralistic Culture: Religion in American Life" (2007), which has mitigated students' resistance to reading their professor's work and to exploring religious oppression and Christian privilege.

What I also learned from this experience was that many students understand issues of power, control, and oppression, but only on the individual level. They often fail to understand the institutional and larger societal (systemic) basis of oppression. Therefore, over the past few years, I have begun the "contradiction" of students' prior learning (Kegan, 1982) by dividing students into two sides for a debate in which I ask each group—the "pro" side and the "con" side—to argue the following question: "Is the United States a meritocracy?" Along with students researching this question for the debate, I assign a five-page paper due at the end of the class session on the day of the debate. In the paper they are to enumerate the points each of them hopes to make during the debate, followed by a critical analysis of where they actually stand on the question.

Christian Role Modeling: Social Norming

A strategy that has been particularly useful for helping students understand Christian privilege and other forms of dominance has been profiling dominant group members and organizations that have worked for social justice by exercising their power in positive ways. I advance this aspect of social norming (Perkins & Berkowitz, 1986) in a variety of ways. For example, inviting such speakers into class to share their experiences has proven extremely successful, particularly in helping to move students out of their comfort zones on the topic of Christian privilege.

For example, I often invite my colleague, Dr. Ellen E. Fairchild, into my class. Ellen, like many of my students, grew up on a small Iowa farm in a religiously and politically conservative Protestant family and community. She speaks about the critical incidents during her early years that helped her understand how surrounding herself with people who looked, believed, and thought like she did limited her vision of the world. As a child, she explored the local public library for books that transported her to other lands and introduced people she had never imagined. She investigated books describing religions other than her own and, in the process, experienced a sense of enrichment and empowerment. She talks about how she came to consciousness regarding her Christian and White privileges. She articulates for students the meaning and value of acknowledging, accepting, and acting to share dominant group privileges—in this instance, Christian privilege—to level the playing field by distributing power, rights, and responsibilities equitably. She also points out that not doing so can have negative implications for members of dominant groups as well as minoritized groups.

Bringing It Back Home (to the Classroom)

Because the majority of my students are pre-service teachers, I anticipate the spoken and unspoken questions students will raise: "What does this all have to do with teaching? Why do I need to have a critical consciousness about my social identities and 'positionality'?" To address these questions, I always try to bring our discussions back to the teaching profession and the classroom.

I often require students to read *We Can't Teach What We Don't Know: White Teachers, Multiracial Schools*, by Gary R. Howard (2006), who as a White educator provides a personal, insightful, and compelling argument for why all teachers, and in particular White teachers—the primary focus of his book—need to practice social justice and multicultural education. He calls on teachers to undertake the "inner work of personal growth" and transformation necessary to accomplish this important task. In doing so, Howard encourages "an examination of the role White educators can and must play in understanding, decoding, and dismantling the dynamics of White dominance" (p. 7) as well as other forms of oppression and privilege.

One year, during our unit on "Religion and Education," I invited a graduate student from my department to speak with the class about an incident at her daughter's elementary school. She and her daughter are Muslim. Recently, her daughter asked permission to go to the school library or remain in her classroom for lunch period during the Muslim holy month of Ramadan in which it was her practice to fast from sunrise to sunset. The school, however, had a *written* policy mandating that students must be present in the cafeteria during lunch breaks. After repeated discussions with the school principal, the mother of this student at last convinced the principal to allow her daughter to go to an alternate space during Ramadan while her classmates ate lunch.

Our visitor then discussed an encounter between her and her daughter's physical education teacher. The teacher forbade her daughter to wear a traditional Muslim full-body swimming garment during instruction in the school pool, but ordered her, instead, to wear a Western-style bathing suit, which would force the student to act in defiance to her faith. After much discussion, the principal finally agreed to permit the student to wear a swimming garment of her choice, though he warned the mother that the child would most likely incur angry and mocking epithets from classmates.

These examples highlighted for students the reality that responsibility often falls to parents to request accommodations at school for their children's religious practices. The process the family had to go through to secure accommodation is an example of Christian privilege: students and their families who are not Christian must justify to those in authority that they are entitled to accommodations, whether they involve the wearing of religious symbols or garments, being absent from school to observe religious or spiritual events or services, or other issues. Even calling attempts to create an equitable learning environment for this Muslim family an "accommodation" suggests a sort of Christian hegemony, normalizing Christianity and further defining Islam as "the Other."

In addition to inviting guest speakers to provide narratives about their experiences related to religion in education, I invite former students of mine who serve currently as teachers in local public schools to discuss what is occurring in their schools related to multicultural and social justice concerns. This gives students some insights into the on-the-ground realities related to equity and social justice they will face as teachers.

Toward the end of our section on religion and education, I ask students to apply all they have learned through these experiences in an essay assignment. I also provide them with a list of questions around which they might build their essays:

- Should public schools teach intelligent design and/or creationism alongside evolution?
- Should students recite the phrase "under God" in the Pledge of Allegiance? Should students recite the Pledge of Allegiance at all in schools?
- Should schools celebrate religious holidays like Christmas, Easter, Hanukkah, or Diwali, even when doing so is of little or no *educational* value?
- Should public schools have the right to incorporate prayers into their sporting events, student assemblies, and graduation ceremonies?
- Should sexuality education be taught in public schools? If so, beginning at what grade? What should or should not be taught, and in which subject area(s)? In your analysis, be sure to provide perspectives from various religious denominations, national and local organizations, advocacy groups, and others.
- Should public schools have the right to discuss family planning and distribute birth control information and birth and disease control devices like birth control pills, uterine devices, and condoms?

Conclusion: Social Justice as a Lens of Perception

I have never forgotten one essential point my educational psychology professor made in my class at San José State University when I was working toward my secondary teacher certification. His point crystallized for me the intent of meaningful learning. He explained that the word *education* is derived from two Latin roots: *e*, meaning "out of," and *ducere*, meaning "to lead" or "to draw."

"Education," he said, "is the process of drawing knowledge *out* of the student or leading the student *toward* knowledge, rather than putting or depositing information into what some educators perceive as the student's waiting and docile mind"—what the Brazilian philosopher and educator Paulo Reglus Neves Freire (1970) called the "banking system" of education.

I believe that, for genuine learning to occur, for it to be transformational, it must be student-centered—grounded in the shared experiences of learners—and composed of at least two essential elements or domains: the affective (feelings) and the cognitive (informational). I design and teach my classes with a dialogic approach within a social justice framework in which students and educators cooperate in the process, whereby all are simultaneously the teacher and the learner. Educational psychologist Lev Vygotsky (1990) referred to this process as *Obuchenie.*

Education, as I have learned from Freire, is a path toward permanent liberation in which people become aware (*conscientized*) of their position, and through *praxis* (reflection and action) transform the world. Educators, to be truly effective, must spend many years in self-reflection and must have a clear understanding of their motivations, strengths, limitations, "triggers," and fears. They must come to terms with their social identities (sometimes called "positionality"): both the ways in which they are privileged and the ways they have been the targets of systemic inequities. They are not afraid of showing vulnerability and admitting when they are wrong or when they "don't know." They have a firm grasp of the content area, and they work well with and are accessible to students and their peers.

A foundational element in critical multiculturalism or social justice education is social reconstruction, in which the educator's role is to help prepare future citizens to reconstruct society to better serve the interests of all groups of people, and to transform society toward greater equity for all. This has been my intention as I have crafted and recrafted my curriculum and pedagogy toward helping my students see and understand Christian privilege.

References

Bell, L. A. (1997). Theoretical foundations for social justice education. In M. Adams, L. A. Bell, & P. Griffin (Eds.), *Teaching for diversity and social justice* (pp. 3–15). New York: Routledge.

Blumenfeld, W. J. (2006). Christian privilege and the promotion of "secular" and not-so"secular" mainline Christianity in public schooling and the larger society. *Equity and Excellence in Education, 39*(3), 195–210.

Clark, C., Vargas, M. B., Schlosser, L. Z., & Alimo, C. (2002). Diversity initiatives in higher education: It's not just "Secret Santa" in December: Addressing educational and workplace climate issues linked to Christian privilege. [Electronic version]. *Multicultural Education, 10*(2), 52–57.

Freire, P. (1970). *Pedagogy of the oppressed* (M. Ramos, Trans.). New York: Seabury.

Hitler, A. (1925). *Mein kampf.* (My struggle). Vol. I. Reissued edition (1998, September 15). New York: Mariner Books.

Howard, G. R. (2006). *We can't teach what we don't know: White teachers, multiracial schools.* (2nd ed.). New York: Teachers College Press.

Howse, B. S. (2007, February 7). Make Worldview training a sweet deal for your kids. *Worldview Times.* Retrieved December 20, 2010, from http://www.world

viewweekend.com/worldview-times/article.php?articleid = 1518. Retrieved March 15, 2012.

Johnson, A. G. (2006). *Privilege, power, and difference* (2nd ed.). Boston: McGraw-Hill.

Kallen, H. (1915). Democracy versus the melting pot. *The Nation, 100*(2590), 190–194, 217–230.

Kegan, R. (1982). *Theory of human development: The evolving self.* Cambridge, MA: Harvard University Press.

Kincheloe, J. L., & Steinberg, S. R. (1998). Introduction: What is multiculturalism? In J. L. Kincheloe & S. R. Steinberg, *Changing multiculturalism*, Philadelphia, PA: Open University Press.

Lippy, C. H. (2007). Christian nation or pluralistic culture: Religion in American life. In J. A. Banks & C. A. McGee Banks (Eds.), *Multicultural education.* (6th ed.). Hoboken, NJ: John Wiley and Sons, Inc.

Luther, M. (1543). *Von den Jüden und jren Lügen* (*On the Jews and their lies*). In H. T. Lehmann, ed., *Luther's works.* (1971). Philadelphia, PA: Fortress Press.

Mahayni, B., in Hansen, M. (2007, September 6). Cross debate at ISU prods young minds. *Des Moines Register.*

McIntosh, P. (1988). *White privilege and male privilege: A personal account of coming to see correspondences through work in women's studies.* Wellesley, MA: Wellesley College Center for Research on Women.

Miller, J. B. (1976). *Toward a new psychology of women.* Boston: Beacon Press.

Nieto, S. (2002). *Critical perspectives for a new century.* Mahwah, NJ: Lawrence Erlbaum Associates, Inc.

Perkins, H., & Berkowitz, A. (1986). Perceiving the community norms of alcohol use among students: Some research implication for campus alcohol education programming. *International Journal of the Addictions, 21*(9/10), 961–976.

Schlosser, L. Z. (2003). Christian privilege: Breaking a sacred taboo. *Journal of Multicultural Counseling and Development, 31*(1), 44–51.

Spring, J. (2010). *Deculturalization and the struggle for equality: A brief history of the education of dominated cultures in the United States* (6th ed.). Boston: McGraw-Hill.

Stebbins, R. (1996) Cultural tourism as serious leisure. *Annals of Tourism Research, 23,* 948–950.

Vygotsky, L. (L. C. Moll, ed.). (1990). *Vygotsky and education: Instructional implication and applications of sociohistorical psychology.* Cambridge, UK: The Press Syndicate of the University of Cambridge.

9

FROM LITERACY TO "LITERACIES"

Using Photography to Help Teachers See What Youth Can Do

Kristien Zenkov, Athene Bell, Marriam Ewaida,
Megan R. Lynch, and James Harmon

"How the Police Work"

This picture of a police car reminds me of feeling safe. I feel safe in the United States more so than I did in Mexico. In Mexico there are a lot of gangs and not enough police, but in America, there are police everywhere. In America, I feel safe going to school because there are police officers in my school and it is not dangerous. Reading and writing for me is safe inside school because the teachers help me and tell me to read. When I go home, I read and write, but not all the time. I feel unsafe reading and writing because I don't have a lot of help at home.

—Emmanuel

Emmanuel was an eighth-grade student in the language arts class for English-language learners Marriam taught last year. Kristien spent every Tuesday with this class, facilitating a photography and literacy project through which we were asking students to *show* and *describe* what they thought about school. Like so many of the urban and English language learning youth with whom all of the authors of this chapter have worked throughout our careers as teacher educators, teachers, and researchers, Emmanuel often struggled to engage with school and the literacy activities Marriam and Kristien

were sharing. With his photograph and reflection above, Emmanuel depicted and detailed what we now know are some of the greatest literacy challenges our students face: a general sense of insecurity, in and out of school. This difficulty actually represented something different and greater, though—a social justice bottleneck around the concept of "literacy" itself.

Even after multiple decades as teachers, we continue to wonder why our students are so challenged, and we are still hopeful that we might learn more about the specifics behind their difficulties so we can help them to find success in our classes and in school in general. Emmanuel was born in Mexico and had been in the United States for less than two years and already enrolled in two different schools in his new country in a little over 13 months. The result, it seemed to Marriam and Kristien, was that he understandably approached the development of both his English proficiency and our language arts instruction with a fear of failure. We had witnessed this phenomenon many times before, with both youth whose first language was English and those young adults for whom English was a new tongue, all of whom had experienced many struggles in English language arts classes. Many seemed to feel much safer feigning indifference in our classes, even staying silent and maintaining some semblance of pride. The only other option appeared to be facing colossal embarrassment because much younger children all around them, in our classes and schools, seemed to be so much smarter than they were.

As a consequence, Emmanuel, like so many of our middle- and high-school students, exhibited what might typically be interpreted as *resistance* to engage with our classes and activities when he was actually just profoundly *reluctant* to do so. In addition, the literacy proficiencies Emmanuel did possess—in Spanish, popular media and technology, the visual and musical elements that were so much more prominent in his native culture than in his new American one—simply did not have much of a home in most of the classrooms he had encountered . . . or often were even forbidden in our tradition-bound schools, in our English-only state, and in most contemporary classrooms and schools across the United States. Finally, and perhaps most important, while he and his family members had great interest in gaining these new literacy and language skills, many of the members of his community had had even fewer opportunities to learn this new language, to develop literacy skills in it or their native tongues, and similarly faced a very steep cultural learning curve.

But Emmanuel found some of the greatest success in our language arts class when we began with explicit inquiries into his perspectives on school and reading and writing. Although we were the *named* experts in these topics in our classrooms, we realized that this expert stance was neither entirely accurate nor useful to our students' learning or our teaching success. With these inquiries we appealed to his proficiency with visual and multimodal tools as starting points for our writing activities. These projects relied on broader notions of literacy and called on him to share his experiences with school and English class as a starting point for his engagement with these educational settings. Most important, this approach allowed us to mitigate some of the fear he and our other diverse and English language learning students often feel when we call on them to complete our literacy assignments.

This approach contrasts greatly with many standard English class activities that fail to honor diverse youths' cultures, their often frustrating experiences with school, and the still narrow contemporary concepts of literacy with which most teachers operate. As literacy and teacher educators, we have learned over the past decade how we might challenge teachers' restrictive concepts of literacy and their often negative perceptions of youths' reading, writing, speaking, and listening abilities. For us and our students, these out-dated concepts of literacy represent an oppressive stance toward youth and their cultures and a cognitive "bottleneck" in our students'—future teach-ers—understandings of literacy and how they conceive of their own students' abilities. Appealing to these broader notions of literacy and related practices allows us to enact a social justice orientation in our K–12 settings and teacher education courses.

Contexts

Like many teachers in the United States, we do not look like, do not have cultures similar to, and in many cases do not speak the same first languages as the majority of our students. We are middle- and high-school language arts teachers and teacher educators working in urban and exurban communi-ties in the Midwestern and mid-Atlantic United States. Our communities have experienced significant demographic shifts over the past two decades, with our city settings becoming racially majority-minority, now consisting primarily of African American students. At the same time, our exurban com-munities have shifted from 5% to almost 50% ESOL (English for Speakers of Other Languages) students, with these families arriving from as close as our major city's inner-ring suburbs—where housing costs make such com-munities unaffordable—and as far away as Guatemala, El Salvador, Sri Lanka, and many other nations. Our exurban community also borders one that has been deporting citizens perceived to be "illegal" immigrants, making ESOL youth difficult to track. Suffice it to say that our historically White communities and schools have not embraced this increasing diversity.

We and the future teachers with whom we work—as their literacy meth-ods course instructors, university supervisors, and school-based mentor teachers—face troubling school attendance trends that challenge students' abilities even to show up for school, not to mention demonstrate interest or achieve in their English classes. The dropout—or "push-out"—rate in diverse and urban U.S. settings has remained higher than 50% for more than four decades, a statistic that is frighteningly consistent across African American, Latino/a, and English-language learner demographics (Children's Defense Fund, 2008; Greene & Winters, 2006; National Center for Educa-tional Statistics, 2009). Too often the future teachers with whom we work see these statistics and blame these youth and their families for the often limited relationships to school that such numbers represent. Rather than working to understand the structural causes behind these percentages and trends, they count these as confirming some of the damaging stereotypes about these young people and their communities common in popular media.

Yet considerable research and analyses of school attendance and achievement patterns have illustrated how schools' organizations and curricula and even the latent effects of segregationist policies have marginalized generations of our nation's most economically impoverished students of color and non-English-language learners from school. This research demonstrates how "dropping" out and being "pushed" out of school are actually reasonable reactions to unresponsive, culturally irrelevant, and "blaming the victim" stances toward students and families of color as well as economically disadvantaged students and families. These trends, which are painfully illustrated for us by the apprehension that Emmanuel described in this chapter's opening quote, are felt by many immigrant families—both undocumented and "legal" immigrants—who frequently do not send their children to school for fear of drawing the attention of truancy officers and other law enforcement authorities.

For us as literacy teacher educators, the primary challenge these demographic shifts and the lack of cultural awareness of both pre- and in-service teachers pose is how to confront teachers' traditional, incomplete, and even oppressive concepts of literacy. While many literacy theorists and educational psychologists have attempted to offer broader, more responsive, and more social justice–oriented notions of literacy by which *all* teachers should be guided, too often these ideas are dismissed as novelties, outside the domain of most content area teachers or simply irrelevant to the ultimate evaluations of youths' academic achievement and teachers' professional performance: high-stakes assessments. These concepts of literacy become tangled in the social justice bottleneck we now explicitly and frequently attempt to address with middle- and high-school students and the pre-service teachers who one day will serve these youth.

New Notions of Literacy

For generations, educators around the United States and in every diverse educational setting, from preschools through graduate schools, have struggled with the concept of "literacy" and their roles in addressing students' literacy development. Teachers working with our youngest children often encounter pupils who have not had the benefit of families who have regularly read to them, so these teachers frequently lament that youngsters have no "concept of print." High-school subject area teachers in our nation's most economically impoverished and academically underperforming communities habitually dismiss their responsibility for helping students to appreciate and comprehend their math, science, and social studies textbooks. Traditional school literacy position suggests to teachers—and, sadly, to students—a learning pathology, that low-income students of color and English-language learning youth arrive in our classrooms with some *deficit* and that individually and collectively they are responsible if they fail to achieve in school. Of course, teachers and schools *never* explicitly frame children in this way, but most pedagogical approaches still assume that youth must be "fixed" by the traditional school and literacy content that teachers possess and curricular materials contain. For example, most teachers' and many wealthier and White students' proficiencies with academic language and school procedures are considered "normal" rather than the result of generations of privilege and experiences with these traditions.

Almost as a rejoinder, "progressive" university- and school-based teacher educators share broader notions of literacy with future teachers who encounter school curricula and testing systems that disregard these expansive theories and the "texts" these concepts recognize that our students value, produce, and manipulate. Understood as a foundational element of every academic exchange, this narrow, school-oriented notion of "literacy" is normalized. And the multimodal concept of "literacies" is the threshold social justice concept with which many future teachers struggle, because the most basic assumptions about what *counts* as literacy often rely on these pathological ideas about children's and young adults' abilities to read, write, speak, listen, present, and create. Educators, school systems, and our academic evaluation methods unwittingly operationalize this deficit orientation daily.

Fortunately, for the past three decades, literacy researchers the world over have provided not just alternative theoretical lenses on literacy but also numerous examples of the teaching and assessment practices through which P–12 students' literacy capacities might be viewed, supported, and engaged by our assignments and assessments. "Literacy" now is understood as a "new" and "multimodal" activity (Alvermann & Strickland, 2004; Kress, 2003; Moje, 2008). Contemporary literacy theorists, researchers, and educators recognize that *every* person possesses a literacy capacity—or, in fact, a range of "literacies." These educators and thinkers argue, too, that the forms and content of these capacities should be honored and considered foundational to both the media through which we educate youth and the products we regard as evidence of their learning.

The texts and forms with which young people are now recognized as being literate include visual, electronic, musical, and cultural structures and media (Christenbury, Bomer, & Smagorinsky, 2009; Leu, Kinzer, Coiro, & Cammack, 2004). Curricula and pedagogies that rely on these concepts of literacy and appeal to these texts enhance youths' positive ethnic identities and provide them with understandings and tools that challenge the racism that permeates the culture of U.S. schools (Gay, 2010; Hanley & Noblit, 2009; Miller, 2006). For example, relying on an expanded set of texts—visual media and texts drawn from students' communities—allows young people who are not proficient with traditional school texts to recognize themselves and be recognized by their teachers as fluent, capable, proficient, and *literate*. Unfortunately, while numerous investigators have demonstrated how literacy educators might integrate these broader notions and examples of literacy into their pedagogies (Lankshear & Knobel, 2006; Morrell, 2007), these considerations remain the exception for most classroom teachers (Van Horn, 2008; Williams, 2008; Zenkov, 2009). They also are finding favor in fewer teachers' practices as high-stakes testing pressures narrow the curriculum (Herrington, Hodgson, & Moran, 2009). And, of course, these high-stakes assessments, which rely *only* on those traditional, narrow notions of literacy and texts, are increasingly thrust upon "failing" schools and students as the *only* evidence of their academic abilities.

Yet researchers have detailed how youths' proficiency with a range of untraditional texts—including visual media and photographic images—provides the groundwork for teaching methods and curricula that advance adolescents' appreciation for traditional literacy activities and new angles on their connections to school (Hibbing & Rankin-Erickson, 2003; Kroeger et al., 2004; Marquez-Zenkov, 2007; Moje, 2007). For example, by beginning lessons with these visual tools—which students typically do not perceive as "school" texts—young people have been able to forget and see past their self-perceptions and their characterizations as "struggling" readers, writers, and students (Streng et al., 2004). Even more important, students' literacy development plays a primary role in their decisions to remain in or drop out of school (Smyth, 2007), and studies have documented how schools' curricular responses to some populations' low traditional literacy rates contribute to overall school disengagement (Lan & Lanthier, 2003; Samuelson, 2004; Zenkov & Harmon, 2009).

The research on and documentation of these young people's capacities are substantial. And we, our middle- and high-school students, and our pre-service teacher interns are almost universally *relieved* when we begin to understand this broad notion of literacy: without necessarily being conscious of our students' "literacies," so many of us *know* they are capable of so much more than school often allows. As optimistic and as committed to social justice as most teachers and teacher educators are, we are hungry for a lens on literacy and our teaching that will allow us to appreciate and access these abilities. Finally, given the fact that so many of the middle- and high-school students with whom future teachers will work have developed a normalized disengagement from our English language arts pedagogies, it is essential that we provide these educators with alternative means for working with these youth.

Teachers and Multimodal Literacy

While in our work with veteran teachers we have encountered some considerable and often reasonable resistance to these broader notions of literacy—in the form of their absolute reliance on traditional, school-based forms of texts and assessments—we have discovered that pre-service teachers often appreciate these concepts. Younger teachers tend to be "digital natives," having grown up in an era when media forms have exploded and become increasingly accessible. Many veteran teachers are personally uncomfortable with all but the most rudimentary forms of technology, rejecting the latest and most popular text and multimedia tools as irrelevant to school and their subject matter. While they recognize that their young adolescent and young adult students generally have exceptional proficiency with visual and digital media and varied forms of texts, they rarely are able to appreciate or feel comfortable that these are capacities—*literacies*—that might have utility in their classes.

Unfortunately, almost all classroom teachers—pre-service and experienced educators alike—generally view these multimodal tools as paraphernalia to be used with outside-school or extracurricular projects rather than as mechanisms that a broader, multimodal, literacies-oriented, social justice approach calls on us to integrate. Our focus as educators has been on helping pre-service teachers to recognize, appreciate, and integrate broader notions of literacy and these tools into their teaching practices, resisting those restrictive and damaging concepts, curricula, and pedagogies that fail to honor or engage diverse middle- and high-school students. We have attempted several different pedagogical approaches to help connect pre-service teachers with this appreciation.

We began with what has become a fairly standard content literacy course assignment, the "literacy-mapping" activity. This activity allows future teachers to document their increasingly diverse students' abilities. But they also seemed to "ghettoize" these capacities further, to view them as novelties rather than legitimate abilities that might have a place in their classrooms, and to marginalize them as nontraditional and largely irrelevant interests and aptitudes.

In an effort to temper this perspective, we called on pre-service teachers in our content literacy classes, English methods courses, and student teaching internships to document not just their future *students'* literacies but also their *own*. We hoped that this dual focus would allow the next generation of educators to recognize that we *all* bring an assorted range of abilities to every educational setting, and to appreciate that our primary mission as teachers— especially educators driven by a multimodal, social justice–oriented literacies approach—is to honor these abilities, to bridge our own literacies with those of our students, and to use these links to promote students' English language arts and general school achievement.

With this second attempt at helping future teachers to understand a broader nature of literacy, we also integrated visual tools into these explorations. We called on pre-service teachers to work with young adults to document their literacies *visually*, and then in writing, and required them to document their own literacies through the same means. One of our most successful efforts with helping future teachers to appreciate this broader notion of literacy resulted from beginning with these visual tools, with which they were generally less comfortable and proficient than their students.

Our most effective attempt at promoting future teachers' appreciation for a broader concept of literacy has resulted—somewhat counterintuitively—from a project that does not explicitly address this notion or teachers' or their students' literacies. We now call on pre-service teachers to work with a few youth in the schools where they are completing field work hours to use photographs—specifically a "photovoice" method—to illustrate their own and youths' literacies and to document their own and the youths' ideas about why they come to school, what helps them to be successful in school, and what impedes their interest in and ability to attend and achieve in school. When we avoided the explicit exploration of future teachers' and middle- and high-school students' literacies, educators and the youth with whom we work both came to appreciate our literacy class and general school activities, and, at last, to recognize the social justice basis of a broad literacy concept and its utility in *all* classes.

Raising Pre-Service Teachers' Awareness of Students' "Literacies"

Our first effort at helping the future teachers with whom we work to understand this broad notion of literacy began with multiple classes of pre-service teachers in a "content literacy" course. Virtually every licensure program in the United States requires all future teachers—early childhood through high-school teachers, in every subject area—to take such a class. The general idea behind this course is that *every* teacher is a *literacy* teacher—that *every* teacher must help students to develop as readers, writers, speakers, listeners, and presenters. For our first few years working with pre-service teachers, across our university classes and in initial field work experiences in our middle- and high-school classrooms, we called on them to begin the course with a "literacy-mapping" activity, which we described in the following way:

Students' "Literacy Map" Assignment

Think about your students' upbringings, family and life experiences, educational experiences, etc., especially about the personal and cultural contexts of your students' lives. Think of each of these unique, formative events and environments as experiences with "texts" that have resulted in a "literacy" your students now possess. For example, Kristien is "literate" as a husband to his wife, and the "texts" with which he interacts—that help him learn that literacy and represent his proficiency with this literacy—include his marriage license, the many dates on which he and his wife Justine went prior to marriage, their wedding rings, photographs of their life together, and even his parents' interactions with each other, as these taught him a lot about what "marriage" means. So what are your students' "literacies," in and out of school? What are the environments, relationships, schedules, activities, materials, etc., with which students engage in schools and classrooms? What are the resources, buildings, homes, and institutions your students might encounter on the way to and from school? Help your students, yourself, and your peers understand the nature and origin of these texts and your students' literacies by describing, in a maximum three-page typed document, at least five of these literacies—the things your students best know how to do. Please note that a "literacy" is not necessarily a positive thing—it's just a *thing*, a capacity, a skill, or a knowledge base. Be sure to bring to class at least one "text" that relates to each of the student literacies you describe.

Of course, our pre-service teacher students most often would gaze at us with looks of profound confusion when we first assigned this project. But a quick discussion about the idea of this assignment always led to significant intrigue, and recognition, then apparent appreciation for, the *idea* that we *all* have a range of capacities, many of which our schools don't recognize or integrate. This assignment required pre-service teachers to interact with youth, something they were longing to do. And the results of these first attempts at raising young educators' awareness of the different capacities—literacies—their students possessed excited us greatly. The proverbial learning light bulbs almost blinded us.

The range of the literacies, "texts," and artifacts the pre-service teachers shared are too varied and numerous to describe in any detail here, but a few examples are instructive. Josh, a future social studies teacher, brought a photograph that Robert, one of the young adults with whom he worked, shared with him; it was a picture of Robert's own home, one of those now-sagging, wood-shingled, two-family units built as workers' cottages with a separate second-story rental unit, that were ubiquitous in our neighborhoods. With this image and Robert's brief reflection, Josh represented Robert's literacy in "family": "After I come from school, I go to a house that is across the street from where I live; I babysit. I babysit every day. I think of the kids as family."

Jamie, a pre-service science teacher, brought in a cardboard box she and one of her students, Deondre, had decorated, and then filled with items representing a range of Deondre's literacies—materials that the young man had made Jamie swear she would return to him the very next day. One item about which Jamie spoke, and that Deondre addressed, was a deck of cards, meant to illustrate Deondre's literacy in "relaxation": "My activities outside of school are playing cards, playing streetball, studying, and e-mailing. I don't like to sit in the house all the time so I go to hang out with my friends. I can talk to my friends over the Internet because I'm always on the computer just searching the Internet and getting new information about the world."

The artifact orientation of this project was one of its most significant elements: this focus seemed to help our future teachers recognize that they and their students learned through many media *other* than books. This awareness is a key component of a broad, social justice–centered concept of literacy. And, while our pre-service teacher students clearly learned a lot through this project about the young people who eventually would fill their classrooms—and about that expansive notion of "literacy" and "texts"—it did not take us long to see that this assignment was insufficient for helping future teachers to recognize, respect, and, most important, *integrate* these capacities into their teaching.

We had reached the level of intellectual infatuation with our students, but they were not yet taking a critical approach to this work. Again, they liked the *idea* that their students entered their classrooms with a range of capacities to which schools often did not appeal, but these still seemed like new *toys* to play with, and then discard, rather than new *tools* that might be foundational in their instruction. They did not yet appreciate that understanding their students' literacies was a *justice* issue: calling on these literacies in our classes—all of our classes—was our duty, if we wanted to respect and engage youth in the ways they deserved. Overall, this project seemed to move these diverse capacities—and, by extension, our diverse students—further to the fringe of our pedagogical practices.

Begin at the Beginning—With Your *Own* Literacies

In retrospect—even reviewing the original assignment description we provided to students—it seems obvious that the starting point for helping these pre-service teachers appreciate and integrate this broad notion of literacy should have been explorations and illustrations of their *own* literacies. These future teachers clearly had found success in school; most were actually in a graduate-level, master's licensure program. But they still likely had encountered challenges in school, which we knew were related to their own schools' and teachers' inabilities or choices not to integrate their "literacies" into instruction and curricula.

Thus we turned next to calling on these pre-service educators—again, mostly in our content literacy classes, but also in our university-based English methods courses and school-based student teaching internships—to document not just their future students' literacies, but also their own. We hoped that this dual focus would allow the next generation of teachers to recognize that we all bring an assorted range of abilities to every educational setting, and that our primary mission as educators—especially teachers driven by a social justice orientation—is to honor these abilities, to bridge our literacies with those of our students, and to use these links to promote students' literacy class and general school achievement. The result was the following opening assignment, a significant revision of the original "literacy-mapping" project explained earlier:

Your Own and a Student's "Literacy Map" Assignment

After our introductory activities on the first day of class—and for Part I of this assignment—think about your own upbringing, family and life experiences, educational experiences, etc. Think especially about the personal and cultural contexts of your life. Think of each of these unique, formative events and environments as experiences with "texts" that have resulted in a "literacy" you now possess. For example, Kristien is "literate" as a husband to his wife, and the "texts" with which he interacts—that help him learn that literacy and represent his proficiency with this literacy—include his marriage license, the many dates he and his wife had prior to marriage, their wedding rings, photographs of their life together, and even his parents' interactions with each other, as these taught him a lot about what "marriage" means. Please note that a "literacy" is not necessarily a positive thing—it's just a *thing*, a capacity, a skill, or a knowledge base. Help yourself and your peers understand the nature and origin of these texts and literacies by creating a visual "map" of them. Use photographs that you take or find to represent at least three of the literacies you recognize. Then, in a maximum three-page typed document, describe a "key" for this map. For Part II of this project, think about your students' upbringings, family and life experiences, educational experiences, etc.—and especially about the personal and cultural contexts of your students' lives. Again, think of each of these unique, formative events and environments as experiences with "texts" that have resulted in a "literacy" that your students now possess. So, what are your students "literacies," in and out of school? What are the environments, relationships, schedules, activities, materials, etc., with which students engage in schools and classrooms? What are the resources, buildings, homes, and institutions your students might encounter on the way to and from school? Help your students, your peers, and yourself understand the nature and origin of these texts and your students' literacies by using photographs to illustrate these literacies. Then describe, in a second, maximum three-page typed

document, at least five of these literacies—the things your students best
know how to do.

This second iteration of the literacy-mapping assignment seemed even
more engaging than the first. Our pre-service teachers not only seemed to
"get" that their students possessed a much more diverse range of capacities—
which school, teachers, and society rarely seemed to appreciate—but that
they did as well. While again, the number and range of the literacies and
photographs included in these projects are too voluminous to honor in any
comprehensive way here, a few examples are illustrative. Debra, a 40ish African American woman starting her second career, brought in a postcard of
her church, a historic structure with a century-old congregation, to illustrate
her literacy in "community," which she described in the following way: "I
spend a lot of my time in church. I am a member of the Usher Board. I
am involved with the youth group. I also have a part-time job working at
McDonald's. Between family obligations, church, and work, there is not
much time left." In the rest of her reflection she described how she already
recognized that her city students were literate in numerous capacities that
did not seem to have a place in school.

But Debra extended this project further, in a way that immediately
seemed like an obvious next step, but that we simply had missed in our
planning. We called on the pre-service teachers to *consider* their own and
their students' literacies, believing that this would scaffold them toward an
appreciation of these literacies, and, in turn, allowing them to welcome students into their classrooms and bridge them to academic engagement and
success, while enacting a more accepting, knowledgeable, and activist stance
toward the diversity the youth represented. But we had not called on these
future teachers actually to begin to make *explicit* connections between their
own and their students' literacies. With Debra's example we recognized that
such connections always had been one of the keys to our own success as
teachers, and that this literacy mapping assignment had to prod these teachers toward appreciating the similarities and differences between their own
and youths' literacies.

With this new lens in mind, we asked students in our next content
literacy course not only to complete the mapping of their own and a select
group of students' literacies, but also to *compare* these and detail how they
imagined they might integrate both sets of literacies into their teaching. We
explained to the pre-service teachers how we viewed the act of making such
comparisons as a demonstration of a deeper respect for their students, as an

effort to allow their own and their students' most complete selves to live and thrive in their classroom settings, and as a very practical attempt at making their teaching—regardless of subject matter—relevant to their students' lives. Janet, who had enjoyed a two-decades-long career as a chemistry researcher and now was pursuing a science teacher calling, depicted her literacy in "being a part of something bigger than yourself" through a high-school yearbook photograph of her in full band uniform at a football game, described in the following way:

> I spent four years in all sorts of bands including marching band. During the fall, I had marching band seven days a week. We competed against other bands and always had one big competition in another state. The camaraderie was the best part because we felt part of something great and were very proud of that. The discipline helped me in my future studies.

Then, working with Brittany, a high-school junior, Janet discovered Brittany's literacy in "self-sufficiency," illustrated with a picture of Brittany's purse and the following reflection: "I really like photography. My dad gave me an old Minolta and I take it almost everywhere with me. I work at the movie theater, too. It's boring, and I probably smell like popcorn, but at least I'm making my own money, right?" When Janet speculated on how she might bridge her own and Brittany's literacies through her teaching, she recognized that, on the surface, these "bigger than yourself" and "self-sufficiency" competencies were almost contrasting capacities, and that Janet might value collaborative small-group work in her teaching, while Brittany might be reluctant to partner with others. Janet described how she would scaffold her students toward productive group activities, perhaps even by asking them to research and describe the benefits of various types of group formations in educational settings.

The second significant revision we made to this assignment was the inclusion of photographs, rather than artifacts, to illustrate the "texts" that represented the literacies our pre-service teachers were documenting. Our use of visual tools was consistent with the principles behind a broad definition of *literacy*, which explicitly calls on us to appreciate that popular culture, media, and technology should be primary texts in our classrooms. But it also allowed these teachers to consider many literacies on which they otherwise might not have been able to focus, given the component of the earlier version of this assignment that required them to bring in actual artifacts related to these capacities. Through this simple shift, we provided our students with greater access to this justice-oriented notion of literacy—one that levels the educational playing field by avoiding a deficit perspective on students and appreciating that *all* youth arrive in our classrooms with capacities of some sort, and by helping these future teachers to develop a clearer awareness of how they might use both the more expansive set of literacies they were documenting and these visual tools in their own classrooms.

This concentration on visual tools also has been instructive in another, perhaps even more radical way. We have witnessed time and again how our middle- and high-school students are considerably more comfortable with visual and technology-oriented tools than are our pre-service teachers. Today's young people are simply more *literate* in these tools. Young adults, we find, generally are better able to illustrate concepts with images than most future teachers, including the 20-something pre-service educators who comprise the majority of our teacher education students. But incredibly few future teachers recognize that their students are *more* literate than they are in some capacity. Positioning these young people as experts challenges the very injustice of a deficit orientation that is the focus of this chapter. This change in the expert role and the discomfort these pre-service teachers feel turned out to be key elements for effectively challenging this social justice bottleneck.

Seeing Literacies by *Not* Looking for Them

Only after we had implemented the second version of this assignment did we discover a considerable research literature on the connections between this broad concept of literacy and the use of visual tools. Such arts-based tools are effective at enabling youth to articulate what they consider relevant to their school experiences and at promoting their writing and reading efficacy (Marquez-Zenkov & Harmon, 2007). Visual sociologists have used "photo elicitation" techniques to access adolescents' insights that language-centered methods cannot (Raggl & Schratz, 2004). These visually based methods provide our multimodally literate young people with tools with which they are already fluent, using them to bridge to language rather than beginning with traditional literacy forms. The visual arts draw on and develop students' abilities to observe, envision, and explore untraditional ideas and, simultaneously, to reflect on that process, and to engage in metacognition or the skills involved in stepping back from, and being able to describe and interpret, one's experiences, rather than simply *having* experiences (Hetland, Winner, Veenema, & Sheridan, 2007). Visual texts that are relevant to students' lives—particularly those *produced* by young people—motivate youth to engage in reading and writing tasks, and adolescents' proficiencies with these texts promote their sense of writing and reading efficacy.

But our use of photography took the most significant turn when we first viewed the photographs the future teachers brought in to illustrate their own and their students' literacies in the second iteration of our assignment. While sharing their photographs, these future teachers described literacies they and the youth with whom they were working recognized in themselves. But our audiences of other pre-service teachers and young people considered the same images and saw many *other* literacies represented. For example, Emmanuel's photograph with which we opened this chapter might have suggested that our students are literate in knowing the routes to walk their younger siblings to school, avoiding potential encounters with the local police. The most significant literacy, then, would not be in "safety," as Emmanuel described, but in knowing how to take care of the younger people in their communities. Thus, the photographs became a starting point for exploring literacies we, these future teachers, and the young adults in our classes might not have otherwise perceived. Simultaneously these pre-service educators and youth began to think more metaphorically, to consider how these alternative visual "texts" might lead to a wider range of interpretations, to richer conversations, and to improved engagement with writing than would traditional school texts such as books.

We began to understand that not only did we need to require pre-service teachers to use the very types of tools that were inherently part of a broader notion of literacy, but we also had to position them in an even more challenging *learning* stance, one so familiar to the students they would one day serve. We also recognized that, ironically, we were being too *literal* with our literacy-mapping assignments. Perhaps the way to understand the rich, practical, everyday notion and examples of this social justice–oriented, multimodal concept of literacy was to ask our students to inquire about something entirely different, or different enough that they would share their ideas about literacies while focusing on another topic with which they had much greater comfort. We now believe that this balance of relative comfort and profound uneasiness is at the core of any successful social justice education project.

With a group of youth in one of our high-school English classes, we developed and then implemented the "Perfect School" project. This assignment has evolved into the centerpiece of our literacy education efforts, a semester-long activity in our English methods and content literacy classes with pre-service teachers:

The Story of the Perfect Future School

As a "teacher leader"—a role we should expect all teachers to play, especially those committed to a social justice perspective—you will identify the characteristics of public schools that successfully educate all students and consider youths' points of view on school. For this assignment, you will *not* write a description of the qualities of this perfect school; rather, you will create a picture book that you can share with your future students. In your story, you will work with at least one student in your field work site to address the following questions—from both your own and this student's perspective:

- What is the purpose of school?
- What helps students to be successful in school?
- What gets in the way of students' success in school?
- How can all constituents of the school community—administrators, teachers, students, family members, etc.—get involved in supporting students' school engagement and achievement?

For this project you will be given a book kit to create a full-color, minimum 16-page volume. In addition to learning about youths' perspectives on school, the goal is for you to be a published author by the end of the semester and to use all of your creativity to develop an intriguing, relevant storybook that matters to you and at least one young adult with whom you've worked. Please let your brains hurt as you consider what you might create for this project.

The results of this assignment have been among the richest of our teaching careers. We have called not only on pre-service teachers to consider these questions, but we also have implemented this project (now called "Through Students' Eyes"; see www.throughstudentseyes.org) with hundreds of youth. In the stories of "perfect" schools and the images and reflections about school that these future teachers and youth share, we have encountered important, compelling ideas about what our schools, classes, curricula, and pedagogies should look like. And, of course, about what literacy means, what literacy curricula might address, and what literacy pedagogies might best serve our diverse young people. Here we offer one example from a preservice teacher and one from one our high-school students, both sharing their perspectives on these questions about school. While we do not offer examples of the final "Story of the Perfect School" projects, we believe these illustrations provide important insights into the stories our students—future teachers and current high-school students—have told.

"Trying to Be Cool"

> *Peer pressure with a capital P definitely got in my way [of school success]. A lot of my friends wanted to be cool. They adored the life of rappers and drug dealers—fast money, fancy clothes, and having many girlfriends. I didn't want those things but I wanted cool friends so I tried to identify with them. I did not want people to know that I was smart so I didn't answer questions or do my work. I'm convinced that some of my peers weren't doing schoolwork because they did not see how it would help them in life. Me, I knew the value but I just wanted to fit in. Just imagine how the kids would make fun of me if I showed them this side of me . . .*

> —James

James was a future English teacher in our urban-focused teacher licensure program. With the image and reflection shown here he offered us great

insight, not only into his perspective on school, but also into what many of our current high-school students—especially perhaps African American young men—are thinking about being *or appearing to be* "smart," in that traditional school sense. It is interesting that his perspective was complicated and contradicted by one of our current students—an African American adolescent—with the following photograph and narrative:

"Having Fun"

 Teens like to have fun with other teens and it is healthy to get out to enjoy yourself for just those couple of hours. It helps you relieve stress. First thing Monday morning, I wake up at 5 o'clock and get my sister up and ready for school, get her down to the rapid station by 6:00 and then I come back and make sure that my younger brother and another sister get up and dress by 6:45. My younger brother and I catch our bus and we get to school about 7:30. I call my sisters' schools and make sure that they made it there safely. During athletic seasons, I go to practice after school, then to work at 5:30. Then, I head home at 10:00. Before going to bed at midnight, I help my mom clean around the house.

—Markus

Markus was a happy-go-lucky junior and senior in high school when we worked with him. He was mature beyond his years, absolutely unflappable, and seemed resigned to the range of responsibilities in his life. He didn't have the mental or physical space or time to worry about being "cool," but he had his own reasons for not engaging in school in the way he and we hoped.

Of course, the future teachers' and young folks' responses to these questions provided us with great insight into the factors of their lives—to their "literacies," if you will. And calling on these pre-service teachers to inquire into and richly document adolescents' points of view on school allowed them to connect with young people—their future students—in novel, deeper ways. As we have noted at many earlier points in this chapter, the goal of a broad, social justice–oriented perspective on literacy is to allow future teachers and youth to appreciate that they have many more capacities—and strengths and challenges—than what school often recognizes. Again, while these photovoice and "perfect" school projects did not concentrate explicitly on young folks' literacies, these capacities are primarily what our future teachers discovered.

The visually based inquiries and the project of writing and illustrating a story of a "perfect" school also called on youth and future education professionals to *use* a range of literacy skills in richer, more engaging, and more authentic ways than in most of their school assignments. Our students and the future teachers willingly wrote about their ideas about school, used visual media to document their points of view, and talked with each other and their counterparts—teachers with youth, youth with each other, and pre-service teachers with each other. That is, they were both *developing* and *using* their traditional literacy skills while they were documenting examples of these more progressive forms of literacy.

Conclusions

The literacy bottleneck described in this chapter is foundational to our work as social justice educators, because a broad, progressive notion of literacy is central to future and veteran teachers' abilities to engage our increasingly diverse middle- and high-school students. Perhaps the primary lesson of the projects we have described in this chapter is that the development of a pre-service teacher's understanding and ability to implement this expansive notion of literacy must begin with practices that assume that young people have a range of constructive capacities, that they are the experts on their own learning and, ultimately, on our teaching. While the final "perfect school" project we have detailed does *not* focus explicitly on future teachers' understanding, appreciating, or enacting this broader concept of literacy, the outcome of this assignment is that pre-service teachers better appreciate our literacy education classes, an expansive notion of literacy and its implications for their instruction, and the social justice basis of this broad literacy concept and its utility in *all* classes. Perhaps most important, they seem to understand the larger contexts that make such a consideration of this broader notion so important, so necessary, so just.

The inquiry stance of this project in fact raises the question of literacies and opens conceptual and practical doors for future teachers. It allows them to empower the people who typically have the *least* authority in schools to consider authoritatively and with multiple media answer queries about the very existence and nature of the institution in which these literacies are appreciated, ignored, or denied. Perhaps such an inquiry stance is what is necessary when a threshold concept is so foreign at its core—that is, our world commonly counts people as literate or not, rather than as literate in potentially innumerable ways—and yet makes so much sense intuitively. That is, sometimes the best way through a bottleneck is to challenge teachers to engage with this concept through seemingly irrelevant means, some other topic entirely, through a question that has answers they assume they and the youth they serve already know. Perhaps we must engage them in the very threshold concept—with its own tools—to which we are attempting to introduce them.

This project and the pedagogical approach it represents also allow young adults to engage as proficient writers, to *own* the adult-like tasks of questioning the social contract of schooling, and to have their responses validated as contributions to authentic discussions of the purposes of school. These adolescents' engagement with literacy and life skills has been both a *product* and a *mechanism* of this project—outcomes and devices that these broad literacy-based activities readily promote. The most significant outcome of this project is that the abilities of our diverse, urban, and English language learning youths and their communities, which too often go unrecognized in current discussions about literacy and school achievement, have become more apparent to us, our adolescent and future teacher students, and the audiences for their visual and written efforts. And based on this project and its results, we have witnessed young people like Emmanuel approach school and its literacy tasks with less fear and with much greater confidence in their abilities to read, write, speak, and listen, in school and out.

References

Alvermann, D. E., & Strickland, D. S. (2004). *Bridging the literacy achievement gap: Grades 4–12*. New York: Teachers College Press.

Children's Defense Fund. (2008). *The state of America's children 2008*. Retrieved August 11, 2009, from www.childrensdefense.org/child-research-data-publica tions/data/state-of-americas-children-2008-report.html

Christenbury, L., Bomer, R., & Smagorinsky, P. (Eds.). (2009). *Handbook of adolescent literacy research*. New York: Guilford Press.

Gay, G. (2010). *Culturally responsive teaching: Theory, research, and practice* (2nd ed.). New York: Teachers College Press.

Greene, J., & Winters, M. A. (2006). *Leaving boys behind: Public high school graduation rates* (Civic Report #48). New York: Manhattan Institute for Policy Research.

Hanley, M. S., & Noblit, G.W. (2009). *Cultural responsiveness, race, identity, and academic success: A review of literature*. Retrieved July 10, 2010, from http://www .heinz.org/programs_cms.aspx?SectionID = 1&ParentID = 233

Herrington, A., Hodgson, K., & Moran, C. (Eds.). (2009). *Teaching the new writing: Technology, change, and assessment in the 21st century classroom*. New York: Teachers College Press.

Hetland, L., Winner, E., Veenema, S., & Sheridan, K. (2007). *Studio thinking: The real benefits of visual arts education*. New York: Teachers College Press.

Hibbing, A. N., & Rankin-Erickson, J. L. (2003). A picture is worth a thousand words: Using visual images to improve comprehension for middle school struggling readers. *The Reading Teacher, 56*(8), 758–770.

Kress, G. R. (2003). *Literacy in the new media age*. London: Routledge.

Kroeger, S., Burton, C., Comarata, A., Cobs, C., Hamm, C., Hopkins, R., & Kouche, B. (2004). Student voice and critical reflection: Helping students at risk. *Teaching Exceptional Children, 36*(3), 50–57.

Lan, W., & Lanthier, R. (2003). Changes in students' academic performance and perceptions of school before dropping out of schools. *Journal of Education for Students Place at Risk, 8*(3), 309–332.

Lankshear, C., & Knobel, M. (2006). *New literacies: Everyday practices and classroom learning* (2nd ed.). Maidenhead, UK: Open University Press.

Leu, D. J., Jr., Kinzer, C. K., Coiro, J., & Cammack, D. W. (2004). Toward a theory of new literacies emerging from the Internet and other information and communication technologies. In R. B. Ruddell & N. Unrau (Eds.), *Theoretical models and processes of reading* (5th ed.) (pp. 1570–1613). Newark, DE: International Reading Association.

Marquez-Zenkov, K. (2007). Through city students' eyes: Urban students' beliefs about school's purposes, supports, and impediments. *Visual Studies, 22*(2), 138–154.

Marquez-Zenkov, K., & Harmon, J. (2007). "Seeing" English in the city: Using photography to understand students' literacy relationships. *English Journal, 96*(6), 24–30.

Miller, C. J. (2006). Images from the streets: Art for social change from the Homelessness Photography Project. *Social Justice, 33*(2).

Moje, E. B. (2007). Youth literacy, culture and identity. In J. Flood, D. Lapp, S. B. Heath, & V. Chou (Eds.), Handbook of research on teaching literacy through the communicative and visual arts, volume II (pp. 207–219). Mahwah, NJ: Lawrence Erlbaum.

Moje, E. B. (2008). The complex world of adolescent literacy: Myths, motivations, and mysteries. *Harvard Educational Review, 78*(1), 107–154.

Morrell, E. (2007). *Critical literacy and urban youth: Pedagogies of access, dissent, and liberation*. New York: Routledge.

National Center for Education Statistics. (2009). *The condition of education: 2009.* Washington, DC: National Center for Education Statistics/Institute of Education Sciences.

Raggl, A., & Schratz, M. (2004). Using visuals to release pupil's voices: Emotional pathways to enhancing thinking and reflecting on learning. In C. Pole (Ed.), *Seeing is believing? Approaches to visual research* (vol. 7) (pp. 147–162). New York: Elsevier.

Samuelson, B. L. (2004). "I used to go to school. Now I learn.": Unschoolers critiquing the discourse of school. In J. Mahari (Ed.), *What they don't learn in school: Literacy in the lives of urban youth* (pp. 103–122). New York: Peter Lang.

Smyth, J. (2007). Toward the pedagogically engaged school: Listening to student voice as a positive response to disengagement and "dropping out"? In D. Thiessen & A. Cook-Sather (Eds.), *International handbook of student experience in elementary and secondary school* (pp. 635–658). Dordrecht, The Netherlands: Springer.

Streng, J. M., Rhodes, S. D., Ayala, G. X., Eng., E., Arceo, R., & Phipps, S. (2004). *Realidad Latina*: Latino adolescents, their school, and a university use photovoice to examine and address the influence of immigration. *Journal of Interprofessional Care, 18*(4), 403–415.

Van Horn, L. (2008). *Reading photographs to write with meaning and purpose, grades 4–12.* Newark, DE: International Reading Association.

Williams, B. T. (2008). Tomorrow will not be like today: Literacy and identity in a world of multiliteracies. *Journal of Adolescent & Adult Literacy, 51*(8), 682–686.

Zenkov, K. (2009). The teachers and schools they deserve: "Seeing" the pedagogies, practices, and programs urban students want. *Theory Into Practice, 48*(3), 168–175.

Zenkov, K., & Harmon, J. (2009). Picturing a writing process: Using photovoice to learn how to teach writing to urban youth. *Journal of Adolescent and Adult Literacy, 52*(7), 575–584.

10

TEACHING AND LEARNING ABOUT IMMIGRATION AS A HUMANITARIAN ISSUE

The Sociopolitical Context Bottleneck

Edward M. Olivos

Why don't you teach your students about Immigration law of these United States instead of Illegal immigration tricks? Methinks you should remove yourself back to California with the rest of the communistic politicians who believe in open border policies, sanctuary, over-population and the reconquista!

—Personal communication to author

These comments came to me in an e-mail in response to an August 2008 feature story in the *Oregon Daily Emerald*, the student-run newspaper at the University of Oregon (UO). The story profiled a special "field experience" course I had taught that summer in which I took a group of UO students to the U.S./Mexico border to witness "firsthand" what life was like on the "borderlands" for Latino/a (mostly Mexican) immigrants and their allies. While the comments of the irate e-mail sender might reflect the views and sentiments of a particularly ignorant and hypernativist member of our society (a sector of the population that appears to be growing rapidly), they are nonetheless an indication of the challenging work that needs to be done to educate people about the sociopolitical context that encourages immigration to the United States and the hate that accompanies that immigration (Bacon, 2008; Blandin, 2011; Vedadi, 2011).

The 2008 class was the first permanent offering of what would eventually become a whole series of required core equal opportunity (EO) courses for the undergraduate major in Educational Foundations in the Department of Education Studies (EDST) here at the UO. The goal of this particular EO course is to challenge many of the myths surrounding immigration by exploring, according to the syllabus, "the issue of immigration within the context of inequality in society and in social institutions and how one institution in particular, public education, has responded to [the] presence [of immigrants and immigrant students]." It is designed to engage students, all hopeful future teachers, in exploring the social, political, historical, and economic factors that contribute to the phenomenon of immigration and how the public school system has worked explicitly and implicitly to reinforce stereotypes and the subordinate status of immigrant students and communities.

Negative beliefs about immigration and immigrants often are embedded in and influenced by historical misinformation (Chomsky, 2007). These beliefs can be detected in arguments that view immigration as problematic, not for the immigrants themselves, but rather for the social and economic comfort of White Americans. These beliefs are reflected in discourses that: (a) frame immigration as solely an individual or group choice (as if someone woke up one morning and decided to risk his or her life to go to another country just for the adventure) rather than a complex social, historical, political, and economic phenomenon; (b) idealize a mythical glorified past ("my ancestors came to this country and learned English and assimilated because they wanted to be Americans") that ignores the historical, racialized exclusion of many past groups of immigrants (including African Americans and, ironically, even nonimmigrants like Native Americans); and (c) paint undocumented immigrants as lawbreakers and burdens on society while ignoring the financial benefits they provide to the U.S. economic system and how excessive consumerism directly encourages the exploitation of immigrant labor. The trouble with each of these views is that they lack *sociopolitical context*; that is, they are not based on an understanding of the social, political, and economic forces that inform not only immigration, but also people's responses to immigration and immigrants.

In this chapter I discuss how I teach about the sociopolitical context of immigration to help my students through a social justice learning bottleneck characterized by these misunderstandings. I argue that students need to grasp and contemplate several realities of the sociopolitical context of immigration to understand the complexity of immigration and the experiences of immigrants, including their children. I summarize these realities and misunderstandings in Table 10.1.

TABLE 10.1
Immigration Learning Bottlenecks Related to a Lack of Understanding of Their Sociopolitical Context and Implications

Sociopolitical Context	Misunderstanding (Bottleneck)	Implication
Immigration is the result of inequitable sociopolitical and economic policies and practices between "first world" and "developing" nations.	Students may view immigration solely as an individual act or choice without taking these policies and practices into account.	Students may fail to see how U.S. policies and practices (including the individual and collective politics and lifestyles of its citizens) contribute to the vast movement of people around the globe.
The United States has a long history of racial exclusion and exploitation, often reflected in historical immigration and citizenship laws and practices against non-Whites.	Students may view the United States as a great melting pot that has accepted and encouraged all immigrant groups equally.	Because current immigrant groups are portrayed as being on "equal footing" with past (mostly White) immigrants, students may interpret these groups' "failure" to assimilate and thrive in the United States as a result of their "separatist" ideologies or cultural deficiencies.
Unbridled consumerism and excessive corporate profit depend on the exploitation of laborers, particularly those who are the most marginalized, both globally and nationally.	Students may see individual consumerism as unrelated to broader global networks of human and environmental exploitation.	Students may see immigrants (particularly undocumented immigrants) as burdens, lawbreakers, and invaders who depend on U.S. taxpayers to support them rather than as exploited workers seeking to achieve U.S. level of materialism.

These are the types of critical reconsiderations I emphasize in my classes on immigration to help students reach a deeper understanding of this complex topic and how it will impact them, not only as future teachers, but also as socially responsible citizens. They are focused on two outcomes: (1) pushing students to understand the greater sociopolitical and economic context of immigration, and (2) challenging commonly accepted myths by providing a data-based counternarrative.

In the remainder of this chapter, I expand on these dimensions of the sociopolitical context of immigration and how I address them when teaching education students about immigration. I then detail the structure of the classes I teach and some of the techniques I use to try to work through the "bottlenecks" that exist around these concepts. I conclude by narrating some innovative approaches I have used to teach a predominantly middle-class, White student population the importance of sociopolitical context by examining immigration as fundamentally a human rights concern and not simply a legal one. In particular, I focus on trips I have taken to the U.S./Mexico border with UO students and the learning experiences we have had there.

Reframing Immigration Through Sociopolitical Context

What a great thing you and your students are doing Mr. Olivos.
Perhaps you will like it enough in Mexico to stay.

—Posting on *Oregon Daily Emerald* website comments section

Teaching about immigration is difficult in this era of changing demographics, increased xenophobia, and persistent anti-Latino/a rhetoric and sentiment (Passel & Cohn, 2011; Southern Poverty Law Center, 2008, 2011). Immigration, both documented and undocumented, is a controversial political and social issue. It is a lightning rod for debate. Emotions often are heightened during conversations about this topic; there is no neutral position on the subject (or on any social justice issue for that matter). The xenophobia and related misinformation is most notable in commonly voiced comments such as: "What is it about 'illegal' that they don't understand?"; "Why don't they just come here legally?"; "It's not that I oppose immigration; it's that I oppose 'illegal' immigration"; "If they want to come to our country, they need to assimilate to us and learn English"; "Immigrants are a drain on the economy"; and "They only come here for the services."

These comments reflect significant ignorance regarding how immigration is spawned and influenced by the impact of globalization and labor exploitation (Bacon, 2008). Additionally, these sentiments veil how our own individual choices and personal consumerism influence immigration. My course, "Equal Opportunity: Diaspora and Immigration," is a critical exploration of the "root causes" of immigration in that it seeks to frame immigration as the result (not the *cause*) of economic inequality and the exploitation of immigrants as a fundamental human rights violation (Patel, n.d.). Its goals echo Chomsky's (2007) assertion that the immigration "problem" needs a "humanitarian solution, [namely] the creation of a new model of global economic integration—one that redistributes the planet's resources more equitably among its inhabitants, and one that respects traditional" lifestyles and ways of being (p. 166). An additional course objective is to challenge the noble mission of the U.S. public schools that have traditionally been portrayed as the exclusive means by which immigrants are successfully integrated into U.S. society rather than as institutions that often strategically assimilate already marginalized communities into subordinate sectors of society. This course does so by helping students examine practices around language, family engagement, school reform, teacher expectations, and so on that disenfranchise immigrant students and their families (Suárez-Orozco & Suárez-Orozco, 2001).

In response to the lack of experiences with immigrants and immigrant communities with which the majority of my students enter the class, and to help them comprehend the immigration phenomenon authentically, I focus on the threshold concept of the sociopolitical context, attempting to guide my students through the conceptual bottlenecks and toward the new understandings detailed in Table 10.1. More broadly, my goal is to help students understand that immigration is more than a personal or legal act; it is a broad-scale humanitarian issue that impacts the most vulnerable of the world's population and is often influenced by the explicit and implicit actions and mind-sets of profit- and consumer-driven societies.

A Pedagogical Illustration: Problematizing "Illegals"

Granted, most students in my classes are well-intentioned and well-meaning folks. Very rarely have I encountered a student who purposefully and willfully vilifies and dehumanizes immigrants. Nevertheless, even "well-meaning" people are vulnerable to internalizing and perpetuating societal myths, biases, and intolerances. This can be seen, for example, in some of my students' cavalier use of the word "illegals" to describe undocumented immigrants or in their subtle "us versus them" mentality that underlies some of their comments or descriptions about immigrant communities without understanding the impact these comments can have on real people.

One example of the problematic use of this word actually occurred in another class I frequently teach at the UO called "Language, Power, and Education." During a discussion on recent trends in U.S. language legislation related to the elimination of bilingual education in some states, several students nonchalantly expressed how they could see how "some folks" (not them, of course, because *they* are caring future teachers) might consider "catering" to "illegals" or "illegals' children" as a drain on resources for already underfunded schools. This dialogue between students continued for a short while and ended rather uneventfully—or at least I thought so. While I personally was feeling uncomfortable with the students' use of the word *illegal*, I did nothing to stop it—at least during this particular class session. At the end of the class, however, a student came to me to express how horrible she felt during the discussion and how angry she was at the other students' arrogance and insensitivity. This student, a Brazilian immigrant, felt personally dehumanized by the students' comments, and particularly the openness with which they expressed their opinions about "illegals."

As a woman of African descent, the student (whom I knew prior to the class) often was identified mistakenly as a U.S. national (i.e., African American), so apparently the other students had expressed similar sentiments in their small groups not knowing that she was an immigrant as well as a second-language learner. What made this particular episode highly problematic was that she dropped the class after this incident. This unfortunate event provided me with several important teaching lessons. The first was that I must interrupt hate language in my classes regardless of whether the students are using it knowingly or "accidentally." The other lesson I learned was that I must work consciously to problematize language I believe to be harmful to others and provide students with "new" language options. As a result, one of the first activities I do in my immigration course is to discuss the problematic use of the word *illegals* to describe human beings (García, 2012).

Because the word *illegals* (short for "illegal aliens" or "illegal immigrants") is used so commonly in the media and among politicians, it is often difficult for students to understand why some communities find the word derogatory (García, 2012; Kellter, 2011; Lal, 2012). This, to me, is a key aspect of the sociopolitical context of immigration and a considerable bottleneck for my students: their subtle compliance with this decontextualized framing. To problematize this word, I begin by showing a powerful video by the Anti-Defamation League, titled *Code Words of Hate*. This short video shows actual clips from popular news networks and programs and concretely identifies how these types of framing (via language use) have been used to dehumanize and disenfranchise particular groups of people, often with the help of "well-intentioned" individuals.

Students' responses to this video are varied. Some find it incredible that there actually are people "out there" who believe "this stuff," from the media. Others find it appalling that "legitimate" news networks openly distort facts or manufacture public opinion based on hate and intolerance. In tandem with this video, my students read an article by the organization

Media Matters (2008), called "Fear and Loathing in Prime Time," which documents the troubling trend of political pundits using the airwaves to promote hate, and even violence, toward immigrant communities.

The video and readings are used for background information but they are also a lesson starter for exploring how word choice is not a neutral act. Thus, as a follow-up to the video, I ask the students to think of who comes to mind when we use certain problematic descriptors in our language— descriptors such as *terrorist, illegal,* or *welfare queen.* I write these words on the whiteboard and ask my students to say with whom they associate these words. It should come as no surprise that my students uniformly associate the word *terrorist* with Arab men or Muslims, while *welfare queen* (a term made popular by Ronald Reagan) is associated with African American women, and *illegal* with Latino/as, and more specifically, Mexicans. As an extension of this lesson, I encourage my students to think of this example in the context of being future teachers. For example, I ask my students to consider terms heard in school contexts such as *dropouts, at-risk students,* and *limited English proficient,* and the implications of using these terms to describe students' potentials.

Although the ultimate goal of this lesson is to help students problematize the word *illegal* (and other code language) for its fundamental anti-humanistic nature, I ultimately am unsure whether students actually "get it" or if they just quit using the word in class to humor me (I wish to explore this in future offerings of this class). Nevertheless, this effort to problematize hegemonic word use is an important first step toward my goal of humanizing the immigrant experience in that it helps students consider (at the very least) the subtlety of hate and oppression found in society and codified into language.

Finally, as part of this lesson, I have also learned that if I expect students to stop using or doing "something," then I have to provide them with options or alternatives. In the past students have asked me, "Well, if I can't use that word, what word can I use?" As a result, I present students with different terms that have been used in different contexts (such as *undocumented immigrant* or *unauthorized immigrant*). Although each of these terms can be seen as problematic in its own right, at least students can make a conscious decision, knowing the background of the different terms, which to use in class.

Exploring the Economic and Political Roots of Immigration

I believe that understanding the fundamental role financial interests play in the immigration phenomenon is critical to students' abilities to understand other issues related to the topic. Whereas a lack of this understanding might lead students to begin the conversation on immigration by scrutinizing the survival choices of poor or working-class immigrants, a more contoured understanding helps them imagine the immigration phenomenon as part of "the low-wage, high-profit [business] model" that exists to placate the consumerism of the "first world." It helps them imagine it as a result of how we rationalize the exploitation of "developing" nations, peoples, and resources (Chomsky, 2007). In other words, rather than focusing on the myth that immigrants come to the United States to take advantage of U.S. economic systems and cheat their way into a higher standard of living, I try to help my students learn what multinational corporations, banking institutions, and the governments that serve them do to maximize profits at the expense of poor and working-class communities, including undocumented immigrant communities. Thus, we consider how these entities exploit the natural and human resources of developing nations and negatively influence their political structures, environmental laws, and workers' rights for the sole purpose of maximizing profits and material desires. And on a personal level, we consider how we (as consciously rationalizing individuals) implicitly or even explicitly support these practices.

I have found several books and readings that do an admirable job of framing immigration around globalization (i.e., Bacon, 2008), yet over the last few years I have used primarily two texts to help students develop deeper understandings of this aspect of the sociopolitical context of immigration: *Confessions of an Economic Hit Man* by John Perkins (2004) and *"They Take Our Jobs!": And 20 Other Myths About Immigration* by Aviva Chomsky (2007). Although *Confessions* does not deal specifically with immigration, it does provide a fascinating first-person account of a former economic forecaster for a multinational consulting firm whose job was to inflate the projected economic returns of building projects in the developing nations (such as Indonesia or Ecuador) in which he did business. With the promise of high financial returns, these nations' governments took out large loans from international aid agencies and banks to contract U.S. corporations to carry out ostensibly money-making and economy-saving projects. When the promised returns did not materialize and the countries were in danger of defaulting on their loans, these corporations, and the U.S. government that serves them, helped themselves to the countries' natural resources, privatized their institutions, and influenced their political structures. Furthermore, as the condition of poor and working-class people declined as a result of their governments using more and more of their national budgets to pay back loans (thus cutting into national social programs), multinational corporations entered these markets, driving down wages, wiping out environmental laws, and exploiting workers for their (and U.S. consumers') benefit.

Since I want students to build a cognitive bridge between these conditions highlighted in the books and immigration, I base our discussions around a series of questions: What are the most vulnerable people in these countries to do under these circumstances? What are the consequences of these conditions on these countries' poor communities? Might immigration, under these circumstances, be a logical and even ethical response?

For many students in my classes, this is the first time they've been presented with a connection between displacement/immigration and economic exploitation and greed. For some of them, this "new" connection can be difficult to swallow; they might be inclined to believe that I am presenting a "conspiracy theory" or a convenient explanation for people's "illegal" actions. Some students, for example, question the legitimacy of the authors we read; others respond by saying that they have never heard of these events happening. In response to these doubts, I direct students to the news stories the authors reference in their books. The convenience here (from an instructor's point of view) is that most of these materials are easily retrievable, particularly on the Internet. I even try to refer to current events during these discussions so students see that many of the inequities we are discussing (economic exploitation, environmental degradation, and so on) are still occurring and to some extent even intensifying (Wallach, 2012).

Another common student response is to shift the blame. In these instances, some students focus blame on the sending countries' political and economic structures by arguing, for example, that "if Mexico wasn't so corrupt and they took better care of their people" there wouldn't be a need for Mexicans to emigrate from there. And although a case can be made that some immigrants are fleeing corruption, this oversimplification does not accurately reflect the complex relationship that exists between countries of unequal power and resources (as demonstrated in Perkins's book). Indeed, it is easy for students newly exposed to this economic and political roots argument to "otherize" and "externalize" the problems of exploitation; thus, it is important for students to see their actions as part of this sociopolitical context of consumerism and profit.

To facilitate this learning process, one activity I use is to ask students to investigate where their clothes were made. The instructions for this activity are fairly simple. I tell the students, "When you go home today, and as you undress for bed, look at the tags on your clothes and make a list of where the clothes were made. When you get dressed tomorrow, do the same thing with the clothes you put on." During the following class session I ask students to assemble in small groups and compare their lists. We then create a large-group tally of the places where students' clothes were made. Many students are surprised to see that most (if not all) of their clothes were made abroad in places like Mexico, El Salvador, India, China, Vietnam, Indonesia, or Bangladesh. I believe the biggest surprise arises from the fact that students simply don't think about where their clothes or other goods come from. In fact, I don't think many people in the United States take the time to think (or care) about where their clothing or food comes from and how these items make it into their hands.

During this clothing exploration lesson, we also specifically consider workers' salaries and working conditions. Questions I pose to my students (which they discuss in small groups) include: How much do you think the workers made for producing each article of clothing? What do you think the workers did before they worked in clothing factories? How much did you pay for these items? Who made the profit? These discussions prove to be important; the students begin to realize that most of the clothes on their bodies were made by poor underpaid laborers—maybe even children. Thus they begin to see that "local" and personal factors influence immigration.

Something I have learned from doing this activity, though, is that making the students feel guilty, angry, or helpless is not effective. Instead I focus on helping them understand that, in a globalized society, what we consider to be individual or local actions actually can have global implications. In other words, the process of considering our own tacit contributions to this system of exploitation—to the *sociopolitical context* of immigration—helps demonstrate to them that our actions have far-reaching consequences, many of which might be unintentional. As a result, immigration cannot and should not be viewed exclusively as a problem located in the sending country, nor should it be viewed as an "illegal" individual action.

This complexity is what makes immigration such a difficult topic for students to study. Therefore, in my classes on immigration, I must find ways to "backfill" important historical information (such as U.S. immigration exclusion laws); economic developments (such as the North American Free Trade Agreement and historical U.S. economic colonial relationships with developing nations—i.e., the banana republics of Central America); and military interventions (like the overthrow of Jacobo Arbenz in Guatemala, Mohammad Mossadegh in Iran, or Salvador Allende in Chile, and more recently Saddam Hussein in Iraq) for students even to begin to comprehend the factors that push immigrants to the United States.

Before proceeding, a caveat: In the past I have felt the "need" to provide students with a lot of historical, sociopolitical, and economic context—to the point of overwhelming them. This is when I have to remind myself (and my anxious students) that my class is not a history class, an economics class, or even a political science class. It is a class designed to give students alternative perspectives to the harmful and irresponsible portrayal of immigrants popularized by politicians, conservative talk show personalities, and the mainstream media. It's a forum in which students are introduced to the global and social context of immigration as a means to view immigration as a complex and interrelated phenomenon needing broad reforms, not just detention and deportation. As such, the "contextual" information is presented, not for memorization, but to help reframe immigration from a "legal problem" to a complex, interrelated, humanitarian problem (Chomsky, 2007). In short, it is a way to move the discussion beyond "blaming the victim" and toward a broader examination of our existing social structures.

Breaking Myths and Moving Toward Humanitarianism

By exploring concepts related to economic exploitation, political influence, and neocolonial "First World" and "Third World" relations, I try to break long-standing myths about immigration. In particular, I focus on making explicit to students that immigrating to a new country is often the last resort, something people must do to provide for themselves and their families. Additionally, we examine how many of the people we deem "illegal" have no option for "legally" coming to the United States (Flynn, Dalmia, & Colon, 2008), and that both documented and undocumented immigrants contribute greatly to the overall economic and social well-being of our country (Porter, 2005). Finally, we explore how immigrant families in the United States acculturate, on average, much more quickly (as by learning English) than have past generations, despite the fact that the U.S. racial hierarchy continues to pose serious challenges to immigrants of color (Portes & Rumbaut, 2001). This reality is particularly important for future teachers to understand because it might encourage them to stem elimination of programs, like bilingual education, that help immigrant students learn in public schools, but that often are the targets of racist and xenophobic political ideologies.

I rely heavily on Chomsky's (2007) fine book, *"They Take Our Jobs!": And 20 Other Myths About Immigration*, to help us examine and challenge these myths in class. Although the book addresses very complex issues, it does so with brief chapters and data. Our use of this book, however, is supplemented with data from research centers (such as the Pew Hispanic Center, the Migration Policy Institute, the Center for American Progress, and the American Immigration Council, to name a few) and government reports and data. These data are important because students are often skeptical of what they read when it contradicts long-standing myths that have been fed to them from the mainstream media and political campaigns and speeches. This also gives us an opportunity to discuss the deceptive nature of some of the "facts and figures" reported by anti-immigrant organizations such as the Federation for Immigration Reform (FAIR) and the Center for Immigration Studies (CIS), both of which the Southern Poverty Law Center (n.d.) has identified as hate groups or organizations tied to White supremacy and eugenics.

Debunking the common myths around immigration is difficult given the well-implanted beliefs that have long existed in many of our students' understanding of this topic. In these instances, it is important to present the students with a broad array of data and evidence that challenge these naive arguments. It is also important to have students view these myths through the sociopolitical context lens they are developing. Additionally, it is important to ask to students to assess who they believe is benefiting from these myths and stereotypes. It is hoped that by challenging these myths, students can begin to see immigrants from a more humanistic perspective, one that views immigration as a complex attempt to escape the ravages of unforgiving global capitalism.

Resources for Teaching About Immigration

Eugene, Oregon (home of the UO), is not the most diverse of communities. However, there are opportunities for students in my immigration courses to interact with people who have gone through an immigrant experience. Drawing from community resources has been an important part of the process of providing students with real stories of the successes and challenges immigrant families and students face. One activity I use, which is particularly helpful for my students, is to invite students from the local high-school chapter of MEChA (Movimiento Estudiantil Chicano de Aztlán) to class. These high-school students share some of the struggles their parents are experiencing in their attempts to make ends meet and provide for their children's well-being. They also discuss their own struggles in school, including their feelings of belongingness. The students do not focus only on the negative, however. They also share the wealth of values and cultural ties with which their parents endow them as well as the many positive interactions and relationships they've had throughout their educational experiences, often referring to particular teachers, activities, or clubs. They conclude by sharing what they would like future teachers to know about what it's like to be either an immigrant or from an immigrant family and what future teachers can do to be allies with students like them.

In addition to local resources and guest speakers, I have found several films that explore the complexity of immigration in the United States. Because it is virtually impossible to put students in others' shoes, I have found films and other multimedia sources to be useful resources for illustrating to students who are far removed geographically from the U.S./Mexico border the harsh realities associated with coming to the United States and the difficult conditions immigrants face once they have arrived. Table 10.2 provides a brief list of films and resources I have found particularly useful to teach about the sociopolitical context of immigration.

The films in this table are just a small sampling of good multimedia resources that can be used to "bring to life" the immigrant experience. They are good films in that they also address broader social complexities beyond blaming immigrants for their misfortune. Like all teaching resources, however, these films must be debriefed and the teaching concepts must be emphasized so that students do not just focus their attention on the victimization of the immigrants without understanding the broader social context.

In the next section, I provide a brief account of what I consider an "ideal" learning opportunity for students learning about immigration.

An Ideal Learning Opportunity and Experience

> *This class changed my life. And that's not a phrase that I throw around, because I want people to believe me when I say it. You don't plan to become an activist. You just come across information that you can't ignore and you have no other choice. And I feel like this is what this class has been for me.*
>
> —Student Travel Journal

In 2007, I explored the possibility of creating a class that would include a "study abroad" field work component, providing students with a more indepth analysis of immigration. I applied for and received a university grant

TABLE 10.2
Film Resources for Immigration Studies

Title	Synopsis	Teaching Concept
The 800 Mile Wall (Lorenz & Frey, 2009)	Documents the construction of the wall between the U.S. and Mexico and the consequences of U.S. policy to drive undocumented migrants through the U.S. Southwest desert between San Diego, CA, and El Paso, TX	Examines inhumane U.S. immigration enforcement policy that has resulted in the death of hundreds of undocumented immigrants along the U.S./Mexico border
Wetback: The Undocumented Documentary (Haynes & Torres, 2005)	Follows two undocumented Nicaraguan migrants as they attempt to traverse several Central American countries, Mexico, and the U.S. to reach Canada	Illustrates the difficult conditions undocumented immigrants travel through in the hope of reaching the U.S. for a better life and the factors that "pushed" them out of their countries
Which Way Home (Cammisa, 2010)	Narrates the story of Central American and Mexican children who attempt to cross undocumented into the U.S. to reunite with their parents or family members already living in the U.S.	Examines how immigration impacts the family, particularly children. It challenges the myth that all immigrants to the U.S. are men looking for work and highlights the desire for family reunification
Cartas del Otro Lado [Letters From the Other Side] (Courtney, 2006)	Filmmaker carries video letters between family members across the U.S./Mexico border in the post-NAFTA era. Personal stories of the families (women and children) left behind and the men working in the U.S.	Offers a humanistic portrayal of the aftereffects of NAFTA and how those "left behind" survive after their family life has been disrupted by free-trade capitalism and immigration
Sentenced Home (Newnham & Grabias, 2006)	Chronicles the experiences of three Cambodian Americans facing deportation due to their struggles with the law as youths in inner-city Seattle and the entanglement of the U.S. legal system	Offers a critique of inequitable and inconsistent immigration policies and the difficulties young people encounter as they try to "assimilate" to U.S. culture

(continues)

TABLE 10.2 (Continued)

Title	Synopsis	Teaching Concept
Made in L.A. (Carracedo & Bahar, 2007)	Documents a group of garment workers in Los Angeles who take on the department store Forever 21 in an attempt to create more equitable compensation and better work conditions for their labor	Illustrates how labor exploitation also exists in the U.S. and how immigrants suffer so the U.S. consumer can have affordable clothing and U.S. elites can maximize profits
Fear and Learning at Hoover Elementary (Trench & Simon, 1997)	Features the struggles of children and teachers in the aftermath of passage of Proposition 187 in California in the early 1990s	Explores the consequences of anti-immigration laws on children and their experiences in U.S. schools; also examines how schools are seamlessly connected to broader U.S. sentiments

to implement a "mini" travel abroad field work component to my immigration course. This component included a week-long visit to San Diego, California; Tijuana, Mexico; and northern Oregon. It was this class that drew the hate mail described at the beginning of this chapter. I received another campus award to repeat the trip during the summer 2010 semester with another cohort of students. A third trip took place in summer 2012.

These field work "study abroad" courses are structured as seminars. They begin on campus with a multiday course in which we explore the sociopolitical and economic factors that influence immigration and education. This is followed by approximately eight days of field work in San Diego, Tijuana, and northern Oregon. Experiences include field trips and discussions with organizations and individuals involved in working with immigrants on both sides of the Mexican border. Students, for example, tour the U.S./Mexico border with the border patrol, help place water in the scorching Imperial Valley desert with a group called *Water Station* whose mission is to prevent heat-related migrant death, and participate in a "search and rescue" with a group called *Los Angeles del Desierto*. In addition, students visit safety shelters in Tijuana and speak with recently deported Mexicans at the Mexico port of entry.

Each field experience is accompanied by an instructor-led seminar debrief. In 2008, the course concluded at the UO with individual and group presentations (open to the public) and discussions about what students had learned and how the experience affected them. We also discussed how their experiences will affect the children they eventually will teach. In 2010, the students did a series of campus presentations for classes, student organizations, and college faculty. It was their way to teach others about immigration and what they witnessed on these trips.

Student feedback for these travel experiences courses has been very positive, as demonstrated in the aforementioned comments. I argue that there is very little substitute for interacting with people who are living their lives as immigrants in the United States. Moreover, there is no substitute for experiencing at least a taste of the harsh conditions undocumented immigrants endure to enter the United States, as illustrated in the following student comments:

> Imagining what 3 days straight [crossing the desert] would be like with limited water supplies is impossible to imagine. Unlike the migrants crossing the desert, we had the luxury of having water at our disposal and being able to get into our cars with A/C. This definitely put things into perspective.

Obviously, most teacher educators are unable (due to financial constraints or logistics) to take their students to the U.S./Mexico border for a week. In this case, I encourage these instructors to seek out group-learning experiences, if not with immigrant communities in the immediate area, then with those from the closest available community of immigrants. You might take students to visit a local organization that assists immigrant communities with legal or personal matters. Or you might take them to a school to interact with *and learn from* students. You must prepare your students for these visits, however, by giving them information that helps them consider the social and institutional context of immigration. It is important, too, to discuss with your students how to engage with people they visit on equitable rather than patronizing terms.

Future Steps

To teach about immigration from a humanitarian perspective (both documented and undocumented) is to teach against the grain. The media abound with negative portrayals of and misinformation about immigrants (Media Matters, 2008). Television pundits and social conservatives use immigration as a wedge issue to divide voters, part of their attempt to enforce cultural hegemony.

One challenge I continue to encounter in my teaching and my work in general is avoiding the feeling of hopelessness that these humanitarian problems can produce. Indeed, it is one thing to treat immigrants well, to shop locally, and to have high expectations as a teacher; it is quite another to dismantle an entire interdependent global system of oppression and exploitation. Students can become overwhelmed by the enormity of social problems (corporate control, corruption, environmental destruction, and so on), so much so that many of them feel these problems are impossible to overcome. I approach these concerns delicately; I do not want my students to minimize the extent of the problem (as if buying only U.S.-made clothes will "solve" the immigration "problem"), but I also don't want them to become overwhelmed by it ("Nothing I do really makes a difference, so why even try?").

I constantly retool my class, understanding that students are not homogeneous and that many of their understandings about immigrants come from various, often undependable, sources. In the end, though, I find that personalizing the immigrant experience is the best way to help them understand the broader sociopolitical context that influences many of the injustices in the United States and globally, and how immigration fits into that context.

References

Bacon, D. (2008). *Illegal people: How globalization creates migration and criminalizes immigrants*. Boston: Beacon Press.

Blandin, V. (2011). Congressman Mo Brooks makes strong comments on illegal immigration law. *WHNT19 News*. Retrieved from http://www.whnt.com/news/whnt-congressman-mo-brooks-makes-strong-comments-on-illegal-immigration-law-20110628,0,1001498.story

Cammisa, R. (Producer/director). (2010). *Which way home* [Motion picture]. United States: Mr. Mudd.

Carracedo, A. (Coproducer/director), & Bahar, R. (Coproducer). (2007). *Made in L.A.* [Motion picture]. United States: Independent Television Service.

Chomsky, A. (2007). *"They take our jobs!" and 20 other myths about immigration*. Boston: Beacon Press.

Courtney, H. (Producer/director). (2006). *Cartas del otro lado [Letters from the other side]* [Motion picture]. United States: Front Porch Films and Independent Television Service.

Flynn, M., Dalmia, S., & Colon, T. (2008, September 24). What part of legal immigration don't you understand? *Reason Magazine*. Retrieved from http://reason.com/blog/2008/09/24/new-at-reason-mike-flynn-shikh.

García, C. (2012). Why "illegal immigrant" is a slur. *CNN Opinion*. Retrieved from http://www.cnn.com/2012/07/05/opinion/garcia-illegal-immigrants/index.html?hpt=hp_c1

Haynes, H. (Producer), & Torres, A. P. (Director). (2005). *Wetback: An undocumented documentary* [Motion picture]. Canada: Open City Works.

Kellter, B. (2011, December 13). Illegals. *New York Times*. Retrieved from http://keller.blogs.nytimes.com/2011/12/13/llegals/

Lal, P. (2012). It's more complicated than "legal vs illegal": An open letter to Ruben Navarrette. *New America Media*. Retrieved from http://newamericamedia.org/2012/07/its-more-complicated-than-legal-vs-illegal.php

Lorenz, J. (Producer), & Frey, J.C. (Director). (2009). *The 800 mile wall* [Motion picture]. United States: Gatekeeper Productions.

Media Matters. (2008). *Fear and loathing: Immigration myths and cable news*. Washington, DC: Author.

Newnham, N. (Coproducer/codirector), & Grabias, D. (Coproducer/codirector). (2006). United States: Independent Television Service.

Passel, J. S., & Cohn, D. (2011). *Unauthorized immigrant population: National and state trends, 2010*. Washington, DC: Pew Hispanic Center.

Patel, S. (n.d.). *Migrants' rights are human rights! Take the police out of immigration enforcement*. Retrieved from http://ccrjustice.org/migrants%E2%80%99-rights-are-human-rights!-take-police-out-of-immigration-enforcement

Perkins, J. (2004). *Confessions of an economic hit man*. New York: Plume.

Porter, E. (2005, April 5). Illegal immigrants are bolstering Social Security with billions. *New York Times*. Retrieved from http://www.nytimes.com

Portes, A., & Rumbaut, R. G. (2001). *Legacies: The story of the immigrant second generation*. Berkeley: University of California Press.

Southern Poverty Law Center. (n.d.). *Federation for American Immigration Reform* (Intelligence Files). Retrieved from http://www.splcenter.org/get-informed/intelligence-files/groups/federation-for-american-immigration-reform-fair

Southern Poverty Law Center. (2008, Spring). *Intelligence report*, issue 129.

Southern Poverty Law Center. (2011, Spring). *Intelligence report: The year in hate & extremism. Hate groups top 1000*, issue 141.

Suárez-Orozco, C., & Suárez-Orozco, M. (2001). *Children of immigration*. Cambridge, MA: Harvard University Press.

Trench, T. (Coproducer), & Simon, L. A. (Coproducer/director). (1997). *Fear and learning at Hoover Elementary* [Motion picture]. United States: Josepha Producciones.

Vedadi, N. (2011). Kennewick council candidate: Illegal immigrants should get death penalty. *KEPRTV.com*. Retrieved from http://www.keprtv.com/news/local/127495733.html

Wallach, L. (2012). NAFTA on steroids. *The Nation*. Retrieved from http://www.thenation.com/article/168627/nafta-steroids#

"YOU'RE GOING TO HELL!"

When Critical Multicultural Queer Affirmation Meets Christian Homophobia

Jeff Sapp

I just have to vent. Every semester I get evangelical Christian homo-phobes in my diversity courses and they are there because they want to be teachers. I mean, what am I supposed to do with them? They have a legal right to become teachers and I can't fail them for being homophobic. What drives me wild is that I know if we had some racist skinhead neo-Nazi in class, we'd be counseling him/her out in a blink because how could we expect a racist to effectively teach stu-dents of color? But when it comes to these I-disapprove-of-gay-people-because-of-my-religion folks, we are forced to tiptoe out of fear of a lawsuit. And believe me, I push them on it knowing full well I'll get creamed in my evaluations. Lately I've had to distance myself from them in order to keep my head on straight. I've stopped lashing out at them (which I used to do in a stern, teacherly kind of way), and all I can think to do is ask them, "How are you going to be an effective teacher of all of your students, even your LGBQT ones, espe-cially given what we learned about the connection between identity and good teaching?" Every semester some little piece of me dies know-ing that some gay-hating person passes my course and is going to get through the program and become a teacher and mess up some kids in the process. How do you handle it?

—Author's personal e-mail from a
prominent multicultural educator

I didn't appreciate his gay agenda.

—Student evaluation of the author from a course in which 28 of
29 students gave him a superior rating of "strongly agree" in all
categories; the student whose comment is shown here gave him a
rating of "strongly disagree" on every item

This chapter explores the bottleneck that occurs when some Christians who attend a required multicultural education course are met with an affirming queer curriculum, a curriculum their religious belief system wholeheartedly rejects. Often the students who experience this bottleneck have only one interpretation of Scripture and are rigid in their belief system that their beliefs come from an "inspired Word of God" and are in no way questionable. Not having studied Scripture in its original Hebrew and Greek, they may have relied on interpretations from others as the basis of their belief system; these interpretations are the focus of this chapter.

The bottleneck experience could, likewise, manifest itself in various ways for the instructors of the course who aren't familiar enough with religious texts to dialogue constructively with the Christian students. These instructor bottlenecks are demonstrated by the opening e-mail from my colleague who is struggling with how to get beyond his own negative reaction to students because they hold a drastically opposing belief system from what he is presenting in class. Opposing views may lead to unresolved conflict for both the instructor and the student. How do critical multicultural educators operationalize a humanizing pedagogy in regard to the conflicts around some Christian interpretations of Scripture and homosexuality?

Please note that the very first sentence of this chapter says "some" Christians and not "all" Christians. Like all terms in identity politics, the term *Christian* is politically charged. Not all Christians are homophobic. Some churches are queer-affirming. Some queer people are dedicated to their communities of faith. Certainly, though, many communities of faith are antigay and use the Bible as their foundation for antigay rhetoric. This chapter specifically addresses conservative Christians who use their faith and Scripture as weapons of homophobia.

Contextual Personal Narrative

I'm one of those queers whose early life was shaped by religious fundamentalism. I went to Jerry Falwell's Liberty Baptist College in the fall of 1977. I was 19. I was there when Anita Bryant sang her public song of antigay rhetoric. Bryant was a wildly popular singer in the 1950s and 1960s with multiple Top 40 hits; she also launched a campaign in Dade County, Florida, to repeal an ordinance that prohibited discrimination on the basis of sexual orientation. She once stated, "As a mother, I know that homosexuals cannot biologically reproduce children; therefore, they must recruit our children" and "if gays are granted rights, next we'll have to give rights to prostitutes and to people who sleep with St. Bernards and to nail biters" (Bryant & Green, 1978). I allowed Tim LaHaye's (1978) *The Unhappy Gays* to shape my view of what it meant to be gay. It didn't look good. According to LaHaye, a well-known evangelical author, gays were vile, militant, deceitful, and selfish; they carried disease and would die early deaths. I was there when Falwell began his political career and the Moral Majority was founded.

Launched in 1979, the Moral Majority was a political organization with an agenda of Christian-oriented political lobbying that campaigned for, among other things, opposition to state recognition and acceptance of "homosexual acts." I was on campus the day presidential hopeful Ronald Reagan came courting the Right. I was there surrounded by constant antigay rhetoric, judgment, self-loathing, and shame. I spent my early life in religious fundamentalism. It's not easy to get out of dogma's clutches. It's not easy to break with all you have ever known. But it's not easy living a lie either. Church is one of the greatest places for a gay man to hide because church demands you be a virgin until you marry. That way I never had to be faced with *any* kind of sexuality. I was the good, moral guy whom all the church mothers wanted their daughters to marry. I could not have planned a better closet.

The turning point that liberated me from this religious oppression was the methodology for my dissertation research. I chose a qualitative design that postulated that no one knows a topic better than one who has lived immersed in it. Suddenly I got it. Everything I'd ever known about being gay I had learned from heterosexual, conservative, Republican, evangelical Christians. Everything. I remember saying out loud, "How can someone who is not me name me?" I began reading everything I could get my hands on as long as it was written *by* gay people *for* gay people. It wasn't until 1993 that I saw the first glimpses of wholeness. That was when I began a daily journal practice that has stayed with me for nearly 20 years. Here is the very first thing I wrote on the very first page:

> This is my story about truth-telling. And what happens when you tell the truth. To yourself. To others. To the delicate relationships we all have.

I am queer.

I am not a sodomite. I am not a homosexual. I am queer. And I choose the term because I am tired of being named by the Other. How can the Other name me? How can the Other be the true chronicler of my world, of my experience. Only I can name myself and define and understand what that means. I am queer.

I discovered that a lot of people don't want the truth. People in the church left my life quickly. I was alone, but I finally felt like I had integrity, and the thing about integrity is that some people like it a lot more than lies. I soon had wonderful friends who loved me because I was a truth-teller, not because I pretended to be one. I discovered that you don't have to give up being spiritual because you're gay. Spirituality can coincide with beautiful queerness. That is my truth. I discovered that what you read matters. And whoever wrote what you read will impact you greatly. Mostly I discovered telling the truth is difficult but important. Truth-telling is the foundation of spirituality.

Coming out was a liberating and transformative experience steeped in the critical theory I was reading as a young doctoral student. Although finally out to myself, I remained in the closet to others until I finished my doctoral studies. Days after defending my dissertation I left rural Appalachia and headed for Los Angeles. When I moved to Los Angeles I became a queer activist and have spent the past 20 years as an activist and an educator. As an activist, I have focused on making public schools safe for all children. As an educator, each semester I come out anew to students, often disrupting their heteronormative worldview. As a scholar, I have written many articles on the queering of education and other gay issues.

Being Bilingual

I was a new assistant professor of education in 1994 and I had been out as gay for only a few months. I was still negotiating the wholeness of this new identity in those early years of teaching at the college level. Carlos was a student in one of my education courses and was well known as a Christian on our small Los Angeles college campus. One of the assignments in our Introduction to Education course was to begin building a professional library by choosing a professional book of interest regarding the teaching profession, reading it, writing a short synopsis of it, and presenting it to the class. I recall reading Carlos's paper, a paper meant for my eyes only, and being startled that he'd chosen the Bible as his professional book and that his paper focused on the sin of homosexuality and how homosexuals were damned to hell. I vividly recall sitting in a local coffee house staring at Carlos's paper for what seemed hours to me. "How do I respond to this?" I mused. I wrote something like this:

> It will come as no surprise that I disagree with everything you've written here. And since you want to bear witness of your faith to me, I am going to oblige you. Everything I know about God I am going to get from you. From your words, your tone, your nonverbal communication, your actions, your deeds. I give you the full responsibility of witnessing your faith to me and I invite you to show me the love of God.

I never had a conversation with Carlos about this, but his attitude toward me changed drastically and I now remember only a warm bond between us.

Just before our daughter (mine and my partner's) was born two years ago, I had another incident that left me unnerved. I had mentioned in a graduate course I teach on children's and adolescent literature that my partner and I had been attending adoption classes in preparation for our child. (We were viewing children's books that looked at different ways families were made, adoption being one of them.) A woman in class asked to see me after class one night; we walked out to a garden on our university campus and sat on a bench and she began to share. "I do not think you should adopt this child. And I do not think you should be with this man. I think you should marry a woman as God wants you to and have a child that looks just like you. This is what I am praying for you." It never ceases to shock me what people might say in the name of God's love. Here was a woman telling me not to love the most incredible man I have ever met. And telling me that he and I should not open up our hearts and lives to adopt a child being placed for adoption. It was so immensely disturbing. It is even more so now as our baby girl is two years old and is the joy and light of our lives. But, by this time in my career, I'd been through experiences like this many times. I didn't miss a beat. "And let me tell you what I pray for you," I said. "I pray that you will open up your heart to children in need, that you will show God's love without judgment, and that you will turn your concern to living your own faith instead of telling me how to live mine." I was careful to be calm, have hushed tones, and look her in the eyes.

It was the actual bottleneck experiences like these in my own classroom that caused a major epiphany for me. I realized that I was "bilingual." By "bilingual" I mean that I can speak both the language of religious fundamentalism and the language of critical multiculturalism and queer theory. This intersection of my past identity with my current identity aided me in negotiating what many of my multicultural colleagues, like the one I quoted at the beginning of this chapter, found quite difficult. Consequently, because of my "bilingual" ability, I have found myself regularly in the role of a cultural translator for colleagues who can't speak both languages. It is this role of "translator" that I draw upon in this chapter.

Bottleneck: The Clobber Passages

There are eight passages of Scripture that address homosexuality. They are *Genesis* 19:1–5; *Leviticus* 18:22 and 20:13; *Deuteronomy* 23:17; *I Corinthians* 6:9–10; *I Timothy* 1:9–10; *Romans* 1:26–27; and *Jude* 1:6–7. This chapter provides an example of how these eight passages—referred to by many in the queer community as "clobber passages" because queer people have been beaten up with them for so long—can be queered. By "queered" I mean moving past simple interpretations of Scripture that support people's homophobia and delving deeply into the text to find the modern hermeneutical meaning of the texts. Modern hermeneutics encompasses not only issues involving the written biblical text, but everything in the broader interpretative process as well, like verbal and nonverbal forms of communication, presuppositions, preunderstandings, the meaning and philosophy of language, and semiotics (Ferguson, Wright, & Packer, 1988). These examples of queer interpretations of Scripture are meant to give context to critical multiculturalists who receive student work that uses Scripture to underpin students' homophobia. They are also meant to invite Christian students to realize that there is more than one interpretation of Scripture.

This chapter puts forth a particular queer theology, but I make no claim that this is *the* queer theology. I only seek to add my voice to the many others who have questioned a single, narrow interpretation of Scripture. Here then is one thing that queer people growing up in antigay religious communities have that is of great advantage to themselves and to the broader community: Because of the cognitive and spiritual dissonance we feel regarding a loving deity and the violent rhetoric we hear from pulpits, we become scholars of the clobber passages at a very early age and study them our entire lives. The queering of Scripture offers a counternarrative to the patriarchal interpretation of the Bible we grew up with as impressionable children.

Queering Scripture "saves" us; it liberates us from spiritual violence (White, 1995). Oppression is often rooted in religious belief and ideologies of power (Soulforce, 2011), and spiritual abuse or spiritual violence can take on many forms, like a negative attitude toward anything feminine (sexism, misogyny), valuing the masculine over the feminine (patriarchy), or the violence of exclusion where many communities of faith prohibit queer people from fully participating membership in their worship.

I want to be clear that the audience for this chapter is professors in higher education who teach multicultural courses in teacher preparation programs. The purpose of this chapter is twofold. First, it is to give multicultural education faculty a critical understanding of something they may have never read about before in their professional lives, a queering of Scripture in the Bible that is often used to underpin some Christians' homophobia in the papers they write for that course. Second, I am sharing the strategies I've come up with over the course of my career that seek to liberate and open up discourse around this topic.

The primary tool we can use to interrogate and queer Scripture is, first and foremost, Scripture itself. To do this I refer to the numbering system used in *Strong's Concordance* (Strong, 1996). A concordance is an alphabetical index of all of the words in a text, showing every contextual occurrence of each word. *Strong's Concordance* is the standard, solid concordance and dictionary that biblical scholars have used for the past century (Kader, 1999). Every word in the Bible is assigned a number that corresponds to the Hebrew or Greek word actually used in the original language. You can look up the number for the word you wish to research, which will lead you to the actual word in the original language and give you its definition. This allows us to explore root words and cultural context. *Strong's Concordance* was written in conjunction with the King James Version (KJV) of the Bible, so I use the KJV to look at the clobber passages. The Bible is its own best interpreter. Although eight passages of Scripture are identified as clobber passages, I give only two examples (one from the Old Testament and one from the New Testament) because of the editorial limitations of a chapter in this book. Tables 11.1 and 11.2 are meant to aid you in the sometimes-dense translations from English to Hebrew and Greek.

> *Genesis* 19:1–5: (1) And there came two angels to Sodom at even; and Lot sat in the gate of Sodom: and Lot seeing them rose up to meet them; and he bowed himself with his face toward the ground; (2) And he said, Behold now, my lords, turn in, I pray you, into your servant's house, and tarry all

TABLE 11.1
Clobber Passage: *Genesis* **19:1–5**

Verse Being Addressed	Word(s) Being Interpreted	Strong's Concordance Number	Meaning of the Word(s) in the Original Hebrew
Genesis 19:1–5	"to know"	#3045	the Hebrew word *yada* means "to know, to be acquainted"
Genesis 19:1–5	"to know"	#7901	the Hebrew word *shakab* means "to lie down" and is used in a sexual connotation
Genesis 19:1–5	"men"	#582	"mortal" or "person" in general and it can be singular or plural
Genesis 19:1–5	"men"	#605	"male human being"

night, and wash your feet, and ye shall rise up early, and go on your ways. And they said, Nay; but we will abide in the street all night. (3) And he pressed upon them greatly; and they turned in unto him, and entered into his house; and he made them a feast, and did bake unleavened bread, and they did eat. (4) But before they lay down, the men of the city, even the men of Sodom, compassed the house round, both old and young, all the people from every quarter: (5) And they called unto Lot, and said unto him, Where are the men which came in to thee this night? bring them out unto us, that we may know them.

This *Genesis* verse is probably the most commonly known Scripture verse used to justify homophobia. What most of us have been told is that Sodom was destroyed because of homosexuality. A key to understanding these verses, though, lies in the interpretation of the two words, "to know." This is where the use of *Strong's Concordance* (1996) benefits us. The first definition of "to know" we'll look at is word #3045, the Hebrew word *yada*, which means "to know, to be acquainted." The second form of "to know" is word #7901, the Hebrew word *shakab*, which means "to lie down" and is used in a sexual connotation. Unfortunately for those who use the Sodom and Gomorrah story to condemn gays and lesbians, it is word #3045 *yada* that is used in *Genesis* 19 and not word #7901 *shakab*. This is one of the most deliberate misinterpretations of the story of Sodom and Gomorrah. Furthermore, if people would only read chapter 18 of *Genesis* they'd find that, according to Scripture itself, God had already determined that He was going to destroy Sodom long before the aforementioned altercation in *Genesis* 19:1–5. God says He is going to destroy Sodom because of its wickedness and He says nothing of homosexuality. In the story God and Abraham have bargained that if God can find 10 righteous people in the entire city then and only then would He spare the city. God sent angels to the city to see if it is indeed as wicked as He believes and it is these two angels that we read about in *Genesis* 19:1–5. Lot is offering the two angels lodging in his own home, as is the custom of the day. In other words, Lot is showing and offering hospitality to the two angels. What I find most amazing about this misinterpretation of Scripture—the replacing of *yada* with *shakab*—is that those who claim to use Scripture to condemn homosexuality are deliberately twisting the Bible to underpin their homophobia.

Another word in *Genesis* 19:1–5 that must be interrogated is the word "men" used in verse 4. There are multiple meanings for the Hebrew word *enowsh* that has been translated into English as "men." Word #582 *enowsh* means "mortal" or "person" in general and can be singular or plural. It is word #605 *enowsh* that means a "male human being." In *Genesis* 19:4, word #582 is used and, thus, it doesn't mean a mob of homosexual men, but instead it means all of the "mortals" in the city came to Lot's house; it means men, women, children, and the elderly all came to Lot's house. Furthermore, these "mortals" ask Lot where the other "mortals" are and again word #582 is used here. Therefore, all citizens of the city came and asked Lot to reveal who was in his house, not knowing whether it was men or women inside. And this crowd wanted to "be acquainted" with them (word #3045 *yada*). These verses of Scripture should be read as a mob coming to Lot's house to attack and/or murder his guests, not as a group of homosexuals seeking to rape the guests. The story of Sodom and Gomorrah has nothing to do with homosexuality. Ironically, it has to do with a people who were inhospitable to guests of their city—very like some of the inhospitable Christians we are writing about in this chapter! Is this why some Christians twist this verse to make it about the "sin of homosexuality," because in reality it is a verse that calls out their own "sin of inhospitality"? Ironically, it is inhospitable Christians who should be labeled "sodomites." The queering of *Genesis* 19:1–5 finds that there is nothing at all in this portion of Scripture about homosexuals.

Romans 1:26–27: (26) For this reason God gave them up to vile passions. For even their women exchanged the natural use for what is against nature. (27) Likewise also the men, leaving the natural use of the woman, burned

TABLE 11.2
Clobber Passage: *Romans 1:26–27*

Verse Being Addressed	Word(s) Being Interpreted	Strong's Concordance Number	Meaning of the Word(s) in the Original Greek
Romans 1:26–27	"exchanged"	#3337	the Greek word *metallassō*, meaning "to exchange one thing for another"
Romans 1:26–27	"natural"	#5446	the Greek word *physikos*, meaning "produced by nature, inborn," "governed by the instincts of nature"
Romans 1:26–27	"leaves"	#863	the Greek word *aphiēmi*, meaning "having forsaken," to "send away," to "lay aside" the instinctive use, to "leave" their natural use or to "yield up" their natural use of the woman
Romans 1:26–27	"burned"	#1572	the Greek word *ekkaiō*, meaning "to burn out," "to set on fire," "to be kindled, to burn"
Romans 1:26–27	"lust"	#3715	the Greek word *orexis*, meaning "eager desire, lust, appetite"

in their lust for one another, men with men committing what is shameful, and receiving in themselves the penalty of their error which was due.

Since *Romans* 1:26 begins with "For this reason" (which can be translated as "Because of this"), it is obviously connected to the verses before it and so it is important to know whom Paul is writing these verses for. In this Scripture, Paul is writing to the first-century Christian church at Rome. Paul is also writing to an audience that is both heterosexual and Christian. He isn't writing to a queer community of faith in the year 2012. Key to this passage of Scripture is the word "natural." In Greek, it means "produced by nature, inborn," or "governed by the instincts of nature." Today we'd refer to this as the sexual orientation you're born with. Thus, this passage of Scripture is writing about a heterosexual person exchanging his or her heterosexual orientation for homosexual behavior or activity, since you can't actually change your sexual orientation. They are doing what is unnatural to them. But, in the case of queer people, we are doing what is natural to us, falling in love and being intimate with someone of the same gender. What is unnatural to us is to have sex with the opposite gender. It's also interesting that Paul used the word "lust" in this text, and it translates as an "eager desire" in the Greek. The kind of lust Paul writes about here is an all-consuming, burning lust for sex. It reminds me of the ever so common political sex scandals where male politicians can't seem to keep their pants zipped up; that is, they burn in their lust for sex regardless of the consequences to their families or their careers. Once again, this verse is taken out of context and has nothing to do with committed, same-sex love in the twenty-first century.

Afterthoughts on the Clobber Passages

Those of us who regularly march in protests regarding equal rights for queer people often see an iconic protest sign. It says something along the lines of, *Here is what God says about homosexuality in the Bible* and then it has a set of empty quotation marks like this: "   "

There is nothing in the eight clobber passages that condemns homosexuality. That is the biblical truth.

So what's the problem, then? Good question. I think part of the answer lies in hearing only a single narrative about these verses over and over again. If it is all I have heard forever, then it must be true, right? Also, I would be surprised out of my wits if people really took the difficult effort to actually study the original Hebrew and Greek around any verse, let alone these eight clobber passages. Instead, they usually rely on a "man of God" (notice the patriarchy inherent in this term as there is never a "woman of God"), a preacher, to study and interpret Scripture for them. Preachers often study commentaries, a book that is a single author's series of comments, explanations, and annotations about a text. And if it is a single author's interpretation of Scripture, then it comes with that author's bias and if that author's bias is that "God hates fags," then so be it; that is what will be in the commentary.

Another afterthought to note that bears repeating is the difference between being a "literalist" and being a "selective literalist." As I wrote about earlier, people who use Scripture to underpin their homophobia proudly note that they believe in a literal interpretation of the Bible. They don't. What "I believe in a literal interpretation of the Bible" really means is that "I am pulling out this verse and that verse to underpin my prejudice." The latter is referred to as a "selective literalist."

Reading and studying Scripture is difficult work for anyone. Queering these clobber passages has been difficult, rigorous work and I hope I've done it well. Many others (Boswell, 1980; Comstock, 1993; Spong, 1990) have done a much better job than I have here, and texts on the topic of this chapter abound, just not in critical multicultural education circles. There are literally hundreds of books written on this subject by queer people of faith and queer scholars. I've attempted to synthesize what I've learned over the course of a lifetime in religious circles, but it is by no means comprehensive. This chapter seeks to *begin* to provide a counternarrative and to share personal strategies I've collected to alleviate the bottleneck that occurs when queer affirmation meets Christian homophobia in a multicultural education course.

Alleviating Pedagogical Strategies

How does a critical multiculturalist call out Christian homophobia without becoming an oppressor as well? What liberating practices can alleviate the conflict between queer affirmation and Christian homophobia? What practices don't work, that cause unresolved conflict? Steeped in the political and pedagogical concepts of Gandhi, Dr. Martin Luther King Jr., and Paulo Freire, the alleviating pedagogical strategies discussed will focus on humility, respect, problem-posing, and dialogue. These alleviating pedagogical strategies are based on my experience of negotiating this bottleneck in higher education for the past 20 years.

Be in solidarity. In my case, I can respond to people as their "brother in Christ," meaning that I made a profession of faith as a child and I am a Christian as well. This causes dissonance and is often difficult for some Christians to hear and understand if they've been taught their entire life that homosexuals are damned to hell. One way to be in solidarity is to introduce students to the websites of gays and lesbians committed to the same community of faith they attend. These sites abound on the Internet; two examples are Evangelicals Concerned (www.ecwr.org) and Dignity for gay and lesbian Catholics (www.dignityusa.org).

Affirm communities of faith. I find that people are just uncomfortable with religion and education being together and, consequently, refuse to speak of one in the company of the other. Many students are dedicated to their communities of faith, which comprise their entire social network where they have their friends, and find comfort, peace, and motivation to live their lives. Why would critical multicultural educators *not* want to affirm such rich diversity and bring it into classroom dialogue? Unless, of course, critical multicultural educators are uncomfortable with religion. If that is the case, then the weight of responsibility here is to broaden our own experiences. One of my favorite quotes from the poet Adrienne Rich says,

> When those who have the power to name and to socially construct reality choose not to see you or hear you, whether you are dark-skinned, old, disabled, female, or speak with a different accent or dialect than theirs, when someone with the authority of a teacher, say, describes the world and you are not in it, there is a moment of psychic disequilibrium, as if you looked into a mirror and saw nothing. (Maher & Tetreault, 1994)

How do you include communities of faith as a vibrant part of your multicultural curriculum?

Do dialogue, don't convert. Why would I want to convert you to my thinking regarding these passages of Scripture? If that were my goal, would I be any different from the Christian who seeks to convert me from my sexual orientation? Don't seek to "convert" Christians to the saving power of critical multiculturalism. The goal is dialogue, not conversion. I think this is critically important when this bottleneck is between a multicultural educator and, for lack of a better way to state it, a hard-core conservative Christian. The battle can become about winning the convert, not about bridging understanding. On the other hand, there will be people of faith in your classes who aren't hard core about this and who have always felt there was an incongruence regarding expressions of faith and how queer people are treated in their communities of faith. People on the fence, so to speak, may feel quite liberated by this biblical analysis. In providing some people of faith with this information, you aid in creating heterosexual allies in a movement for equity and justice.

Be humble. I once heard that confrontation should be the exercise of power with humility, but the reason most of us hate it is because we usually experience confrontation as the exercise of power with arrogance. I am always inspired by the work of Paulo Freire in *Pedagogy of the Oppressed* (1997), especially when he writes about dialogue and humility. "Dialogue cannot exist without humility. The naming of the world, through which men constantly re-create that world, cannot be an act of arrogance. Dialogue, as the encounter of men addressed to the common task of learning and acting, is broken if the parties (or one of them) lack humility. How can I dialogue if I always project ignorance onto others and never perceive my own?"

Watch your tone and nonverbal communication. Don't get into a fight with someone over his or her belief system. There is no reason to be in a power struggle with a student (where there is already a teacher-student power differential to begin with) and use a tone that is violent or nonverbally roll your eyes in disapproval. I learned as a young child in Sunday school that "more is caught than taught," meaning that I can say I am an educator committed to equity, but do students hear that in my voice and see it in my face? Am I congruent?

Use literature. Complement your dialogue with other pieces of literature that invite students to ponder the great questions of life. One of my favorites is from Rainer Maria Rilke (2009):

> I want to ask you, as clearly as I can, to bear with patience all that is unresolved in your heart, and try to love the questions themselves, as if they were rooms yet to enter or books written in a foreign language. Don't dig for answers that can't be given you yet: you live them now. For everything must be lived. Live the questions now, perhaps then, someday, you will gradually, without noticing, live into the answer. (p. 4)

Great pieces of literature can be another mirror to aid all of us in reflection.

Study holistic education, a philosophy of education that asserts that everything is connected; everything is in relationship. Holistic education seeks to educate the body, mind, and spirit. Fold knowledge of this philosophy of education into your course work as a logical way to include diverse spiritual communities.

Provide counternarratives. Invite speakers who are both queer and spiritual and let them speak on their own behalf. Try to find queer people who are ordained in their communities of faith. Organize a panel discussion of queer people of faith with a loving, rational person of faith who disagrees with homosexuality and let them model loving dialogue to students. Show students how dialogue is done, how disagreement can be done with grace and beauty. If you're especially nervous about discussing religion and homosexuality in a course, then this one is perfect for you because, face it, you're letting other people do the work and take the heat! Afterward, you facilitate and your task is accomplished! If you don't have anyone in your community to do this for you, check out my favorite documentary on the subject at www.fishoutofwaterfilm.com.

Out-Christian them. Sounds silly, I know, but if the Christians in your class are antagonistic—and some of them may be—then show them love, a basic tenet of their faith. Maybe I'm just too competitive, but I want to outlove them, showing them how faith is supposed to play out.

Speak about dispositions. Universities that prepare teachers are concerned about the dispositions of the candidates they prepare to be teachers. Dispositions, often referred to as the "squish things" that are harder to measure, include such things as caring; warmth; responsibility; being protective; embracing; and being helpful, positive, and well-informed. The National Council for Accreditation of Teacher Education (NCATE), founded in 1954 to ensure and raise the quality of preparation for the profession, defines professional dispositions as "professional attitudes, values, and beliefs demonstrated through both verbal and non-verbal behaviors as educators interact with students, families, colleagues, and communities. These positive behaviors support students' learning and development." When it comes to queer students and whether educators think they're fabulous or they're going to hell, conversations about dispositions are a way into discussions about sensitivity toward children of diverse backgrounds.

Grab the teachable moments. A principal in Tennessee recently made national headlines after she told her high-school student body that if they were gay they were going to hell and if they were pregnant their life was over. Unfortunately examples like this abound nationally and there are always plenty of horrible examples like this one to bring to students to discuss. What would they do if this hate happened on their campus? How can they respond to hate peacefully? Do students know their rights and a course of action if they hear hate speech from the adults in their school and community?

It's the law! Some states, like California, have laws that mandate educators to make schools safe for all children. Point that out. AB 537, the California Student Safety and Violence Prevention Act of 2000, changed California's Education Code by adding actual or perceived sexual orientation and gender identity to the existing nondiscrimination policy. This provides an opportunity to discuss bias at an interesting level with educators who resist affirming queer children in their classes because it expands the conversation to "actual or perceived sexual orientation." This is key. Ending homophobia and discrimination is crucial for all people, because, if you don't fit a narrow definition of gender expression—let's say a Barbie and Ken model of gender expression—then you, too, are in danger of being a target for gay violence even though you're heterosexual. Everyone knows someone who is heterosexual and is often thought to be gay or lesbian because of his or her gender expression. Also, educators have no problem pointing out special education law to candidates, making sure they know that federal and state laws protect children with special needs and knowing these laws aids educators and parents in advocating for this population. We should then feel equally compelled to point out laws in education codes in states where GLBTQ people are protected.

Out the curriculum! Erasure, the act or instance of erasing certain aspects of identities, is common in literature and curriculum. There is a wonderful classroom poster that says, "Unfortunately, history has set the record a little too straight"; it shows the photographs of 10 famous men and women throughout history who were gay and lesbian. It's so interesting to me that we'll contextualize someone like Sandra Cisneros and how she writes from the juxtaposition of her American English experience and her Latina Spanish experience, but educators rarely, if ever, contextualize people with their queer identities. So many people in the history and English canons were queer (James Baldwin, Willa Cather, Eleanor Roosevelt, Walt Whitman, Virginia Woolf) and, because professionals are timid about talking about sexual orientation, students don't know about these identities. I recently read, much to my surprise, that some scholars think President Abraham Lincoln could have been gay. I'm not saying he is or isn't, but I am saying that it makes for more interesting and engaging discussions that hook students' interest. Furthermore, in California, the governor recently signed a bill making it the first state in the nation to add lessons about gays and lesbians to social studies classes.

Watch your language! What I mean here is to become a serious student of the language you use, specifically words like "but," "should," "need," and "challenge." These semantically loaded words are conversation minefields. The word "but," for example, cancels or negates everything said previously. The person whose ideas are negated will focus on being invalidated, and the interchange of ideas can quickly turn into an argument or meaningless small talk. Instead, use the word "and" because it includes comments made by others who in turn will feel heard and acknowledged. This is more likely to open up discussion. The same is true of telling people what they "need" to do or what they "should" be doing. Folks, this language simply doesn't work. It pisses people off and either explodes the conversation or shuts it down. Instead of telling students what they "need" to do or "should" be doing, use language that suggests they "might" try this or "could" consider such-and-such. Words like "might" and "could" keep people positioned as the subjects of their own world. "Challenging" people doesn't work well either (it's not a sword fight, for heaven's sake). Instead, "invite" people to consider other possibilities. This is a difficult strategy as many of us have bad language habits. I suggest going as far as scaffolding this with the following stems until it becomes a part of your everyday language:

- "You're right and this is how I feel/think . . ."
- "That's okay and . . ."
- "That's true for you and what's true for me is something else . . ."
- "That's a really good point and I feel/think differently . . ."

Teach reflection. Hey, nothing gives me greater joy than to look out my window and get into someone else's business and go all judgmental on that person. It's fun. But, as teacher educators and specifically as critical multicultural educators, we are promoting and modeling the teacher as reflector of their practice and of themselves. Can I take that same critical eye I am using to look out the window and judge others and turn it to my own shadow in the mirror? After all, not having a balanced, honest, self-reflective view of self is such a bottleneck itself that many other chapters in this book are about students *not being able to* embrace facets of their privileged identities or biases in the mirror (i.e., White privilege, etc.). I love Parker J. Palmer's (1998) *The Courage to Teach*. He says,

> The question we most commonly ask is the "what" question—"What subjects shall we teach?" When the conversation goes a bit deeper, we ask the "how" question—"What methods and techniques are required to teach well?" Occasionally, when it goes deeper still, we ask the "why" question—"For what purpose and to what ends do we teach?" But seldom, if ever, do we ask the "who" question—"Who is the self that teaches? How does the quality of my selfhood form—or deform—the way I relate to my students, my subject, my colleagues, my world?"

Study the art of rhetoric. Being a student of *ethos*, *pathos*, and *logos* helps you to see exactly where students' arguments are coming from. We know that to be an effective writer we must understand these three terms, but I also believe it helps make us richer facilitators as well.

Push harder with research. A quick Internet search on how Christian antigay rhetoric leads to violence against gays and lesbians provides ample research showing that the two are linked. Point out this fact to students, provide research, show trends, and listen to the testimonies of survivors of violence.

Push harder with conversations about accountability. There will be some students you feel you can push harder than others. One of the most irritating things I hear from students who tell me I am doomed to hell because I am gay is that, "This isn't *me* saying this, it's God." This is an outright denial of responsibility for the horrific spiritual violence they are perpetrating. I absolutely tell them, "No way! You are the one speaking this violence to me, and I am holding you 100% responsible for delivering this violence to me personally. You are absolutely bearing witness of your faith to me right now, and I invite you to consider if this is really what you want to communicate to me."

Be prepared with materials for those who hunger for this information. I am teaching a multicultural education course this semester, and I have mentioned my work on this chapter several times in the class. Two students have e-mailed me privately asking if they could have access to this information immediately, one because his father uses the Bible for his antigay stance and the other wrote that he was curious about the possibilities of reconciling homosexuality with the Baptist Church. I have information ready and available for anyone who hungers to learn more and sometimes that is enough.

Note: Please don't use this chapter as a "clobber passage" for those Christians who believe that the Bible says gays are going to hell. A common occurrence I see in queer activism is queer people who hate, abuse, and are violent toward people of faith. How is that any different from spiritual violence against queer people? Let's not perpetuate a chain of violence.

Conclusion

In her stunning TED talk, novelist Chimamanda Adichie (2009) addresses the danger of a single story. She speaks of growing up in eastern Nigeria and of reading British and American children's books as a young reader. They were the only books she had available to her and she reflected on how they shaped her worldview. When she began to write her own stories at age seven, all of her characters were blond, blue-eyed, played in the snow, ate apples, and often spoke of how lovely it was that the sun had finally come out. She emphasizes how impressionable and vulnerable all of us are in the face of a single story, especially children. In her narrative, she grieves that her young self thought books were only about these blond and blue-eyed British children and not about "people like me, girls with skin the color of chocolate, whose kinky hair could not form ponytails." It wasn't until she read other Nigerian authors like Chinua Achebe and Camara Laye that she saw a counternarrative to the single story that had been illustrated to her in the early books of her childhood. Adichie's speech remains one of the most powerful I've ever heard as it illustrates and emphasizes how so many of the conflicts we see today are the result of the danger of a single narrative storyline: Muslims are terrorists; Mexicans are lazy; Asians are good in math; the 1950s were utopian; Democrats are bleeding-heart liberals; Republicans are Bible-banging NRA members; gays are pedophiles.

This chapter simply suggests that when it comes to the Bible and interpretation, that there is indeed a danger in a single story. Dogmatic, singular assuredness can lead to arrogance, and arrogance can lead to the shutdown of intellectual and spiritual inquiry. If I know "The Truth" (capital *T*) and you do not, I have placed myself in authority over you to control you. Consequently, we cannot enter into dialogue as equal subjects who are mediating the world with our words and deeds.

Last of all, in my "bilingual" role as translator between religious fundamentalism and critical multicultural educator, I find a common ground. Freire (1997) states,

> Dialogue cannot exist . . . in the absence of a profound love for the world and for men. The naming of the world, which is an act of creation and recreation, is not possible if it is not infused with love. Love is at the same time the foundation of dialogue and dialogue itself.

"And now these three things remain: faith, hope and love. But the greatest of these is love" (*I Corinthians* 13:13). Love demands equity and justice. Love is demonstrated through action, not just words.

I finish the final touches on this chapter on a Sunday afternoon. Our family has a Sunday ritual we observe. My partner, daughter, and I go over to my in-laws' every Sunday morning for a family breakfast. My in-laws, dedicated members of their Jehovah's Witnesses community of faith, take our precious girl to service with them every Sunday. We want our child exposed to as many communities of faith as possible so she may choose (or not choose) the one with which she feels most comfortable. Later in the day, my partner and I call my parents in another state after they get home from their church service, as they are dedicated Baptists. My partner and I have made concerted efforts in our 10 years together to interact with great respect toward our parents and surprise, surprise, surprise . . . our parents meet us with the same level of respect we so graciously offer to them. Neither of their communities of faith is queer-affirming, but they somehow transcend what they are taught and meet us in love. I'm sure at times they must see us as "radical queer activists" as we push the boundaries of equity and justice daily in our conversations and interactions. It is exhausting work. It is liberating work. And it is one model of what we long to see in the world around us—a model where people can believe differently, but interact with each other with dignity, grace, and love.

References

Adichie, C. (2009, July). *The danger of a single story*. Presentation at TEDGlobal 2009, Oxford, UK. Video retrieved September 20, 2011, from http://www.ted.com

Boswell, J. (1980). *Christianity, social tolerance, and homosexuality.* Chicago: University of Chicago Press.

Bryant, A., & Green, B. (1978). *At any cost.* Grand Rapids, MI: Fleming H. Revell.

Comstock, G. D. (1993). *Gay theology without apology.* Cleveland, OH: Pilgrim Press.

Ferguson, S. B., Wright, D. F., & Packer, J. I. (1988). *New dictionary of theology.* Downers Grove, IL: InterVarsity Press.

Freire, P. (1997). *Pedagogy of the oppressed.* New York: Continuum.

Kader, S. (1999). *Openly gay, openly Christian: How the Bible really is gay friendly.* San Francisco: Leyland.

LaHaye, T. (1978). *The unhappy gays: What everyone should know about homosexuality.* Carol Stream, IL: Tyndale House.

Maher, F., & Tetreault, M. (1994). *The feminist classroom.* New York: HarperCollins.

Palmer, P. (1998). *The courage to teach: Exploring the inner landscape of a teacher's life.* San Francisco: Jossey Bass.

Rilke, R. M. (2009). *Letters to a young poet.* Chicago: BN Publishing.

Soulforce. (2011). *Why religion?* Retrieved September 25, 2011, from http://www.soulforce.com

Spong, J. S. (1990). *Living in sin: A bishop rethinks human sexuality.* San Francisco: HarperSanFrancisco.

Strong, J. (1996). *The new Strong's concordance of the Bible.* Nashville, TN: T. Nelson Publishers.

White, M. (1995). *Stranger at the gate: To be gay and Christian in America.* New York: Plume.

BEYOND OPEN-MINDEDNESS

How "Overlaying" Can Help Foster Impactful Discussions of Meritocracy in Teacher Education Classrooms

Jody Cohen and Alice Lesnick

I n an undergraduate urban education class, we are discussing what children know—or don't know—in relation to what they are learning in school. One young man offers that in his family they used to play geography games at the dinner table. He muses that this probably isn't the case in the urban families we are studying, and that it's not the kids' fault. Other students share their own stories of expensive family vacations and other pricey experiences and exonerate the parents and children who are not privy to these advantages. At this moment, students in the class who come from poor or working-class families are quiet.

This all happens quickly. As facilitators, we might wonder if this situation should be treated as a "teachable moment." Might this uncomfortable exchange be mined to yield new insight? How might we move the group beyond recognizing a beneficial fit between some people's home experiences and schooling to consider different experiences as valuable in different terms? As social justice educators, we want to use the discomfort of such exchanges to help students examine their beliefs that some people's experiences are rightly used as a measure for all and justly occupy the top of the meritocracy.

How can we facilitate conversations that probe our core understandings of who we are and who our students and their families are?

This is an ordinary classroom story depicting what Oakes and Lipton (2003) call the "myth of meritocracy" in action. According to the myth of meritocracy, personal ability and effort lead to success. In other words, we have what we deserve. Our students, like us, are socialized in largely unconscious ways into this ideology by their families and communities as well as broader social messages that assign, for example, less value to careers involving manual effort than to other careers and more value to particular ways of speaking and living than others.

In this chapter we examine the challenge of teaching about the myth of meritocracy in our college education classrooms. We look at how the pressure to show an open-minded attitude can create a bottleneck that chokes off critical thinking about a complex and important topic. This pressure is social in the immediate context in that it drives students to avoid arousing discomfort or disapproval in their classmates and teachers, but it's also about broader issues of socialization, and in this sense pervades students' perceptions, thinking, and expression. Tracing our histories of trying to work with students on this concept, we arrive at an approach we call "overlaying" that we find useful in opening the bottleneck. This way of working helps our students look more directly and deeply at how meritocracy operates in schooling and more broadly.

Before we continue, we would like to situate ourselves, as we also do in our classes, which we teach at an undergraduate education and teacher preparation program in a small liberal arts college. Both of our family histories include various forms of labor and a move from working to middle class. Jody comes from a family that moved from being second-generation Eastern European immigrants from poor and working-class contexts into a middle- and later an upper-middle-class professional context. As an adult, although she has struggled with college tuitions for her children, she has been able to pay their way through school—a public university for one, a liberal arts college for the other—with the help of her college's tuition benefit. Alice's father's family followed the same trajectory as Jody's. He and his brothers were the first generation in their family to attend college; her mother's parents, though, were a social worker and a psychiatrist. By becoming a P–12 teacher and later a professor, Alice essentially went into what had become the family business, as her mother was a public school teacher and her father, a law professor.

In our experience as teachers, we often looked to the "teachable moment," with its emphasis on seizing an unexpected "slip" in which unconscious assumptions suddenly become explicit, as an opportunity to address meritocracy. However, we became increasingly uncomfortable with depending on such slips, which often are embarrassing for those who make them. We also came to see that the kinds of openings these slips create tend to disappear under the pressure to restore a sense of community and equilibrium, so they're not very useful to classroom inquiry over time.

We contrast the "teachable moment" approach with the approach that we call *overlaying*. By overlaying we mean working through a process to layer texts, stories, and perspectives—like the transparencies representing bodily systems in an anatomy text—in order to re-view their cross-connections and divergences and gain fresh, deeper, analytical understandings.[1]

We explore how this overlaying process holds promise for dealing with the bottleneck our students experience as they strive to act "open-mindedly"—how it helps us more effectively teach students to think critically about meritocracy.

While people's beliefs in meritocracy help to explain and justify inequities, part of the power of meritocracy is that it often is considered taboo to challenge it or name the way it works. We find that, at the very point at which critical dialogue might expose the shakiness of the concept, the conversation easily stalls, often due to students' commitment to "acting open-mindedly." In this sense, what we mean by acting open-mindedly is to display a nervously tolerant, sympathetic attitude toward people who lack privilege (whether oneself is privileged or not). While this attitude can come across as opposing a meritocratic ideology, we see it as a way this ideology speaks through our students.

Our students generally do not want to "blame the victim" for being poor or working class. They also do not want to *be blamed* for others' poverty or for being "classist." The threat of blaming or being blamed hinders students' abilities to engage in deeper analysis of class by triggering discomfort and pressuring them to appear open-minded. Helping students move through this bottleneck requires us to facilitate a stronger analysis of the relationships among social class hierarchy, schooling, knowledge, and power. This is a tall order because teaching for social justice entails helping people to see norms and understandings that typically remain unconscious. It entails moving, recursively, from a state of not knowing that we don't know to a capacity to know or be aware of what we don't know; awareness of what we don't know enables us to learn and make change (Howard, 1999).

Class discussion is a crucial public sphere for moving back and forth between unconscious and newly conscious understandings. It is also a key resource for helping our students use their academic work to gain new insights in our classes and as practitioners. The approach we call "overlaying" helps our students sit with uncertainty and spurs new understandings. Overlaying is a useful tool for helping students and ourselves see the gaps and cracks in the apparently coherent and complete—and thus enticing— pictures of reality the myth of meritocracy gives us. Although we focus here on discussion facilitation, this approach also threads through other dimensions of our work, including how we design curricula and respond to students' writing.

Most people assume that the point of school is to help people succeed within meritocracy, not to help them challenge or change it. For this reason school isn't a familiar place for the kind of analysis we're talking about here. This holds whether we're talking about K–12 schooling or college; in fact, many people see college access as *the* key to social and economic success. In this regard it's no surprise that the college curriculum provides little support for helping students analyze their individual experiences to understand them as part of a "meritocratic" system. Since a college degree represents upward mobility for many students, questioning the system might seem counterproductive.

Nevertheless, students often arrive in our classes with an uncomfortable awareness of different people's resources, power, and range of choices. We work to move this awareness from the edge of consciousness to the center, where we and our students can investigate what holds these differences in place. For example, our students know that children have different kinds of support at home for doing homework. Rather than assume a given value for either the homework or the support, we work with our students to look more closely at each and to see each as changeable.

Students also struggle to see the myth of meritocracy because it comes with its own bottleneck: pressure to feel and act open-mindedly before finding out more about other people's experiences in various contexts. This pressure to demonstrate a pluralistic attitude of universal respect actually inhibits learning. (For a discussion of "political correctness," a particular and oft-named manifestation of this bottleneck, see Howard, 1999.) We are distinguishing this performed but unearned stance of open-mindedness from actual open-mindedness gained through critical inquiry.

Inquiry asks us to hold various ideas open even when they are in tension. In contrast, the call to feel or act any particular way doesn't allow for this kind of complexity. Thus, in contexts where the pressure to feel and be open-minded is stronger than support for grappling with complexity, students are apt to avoid the complexity and in this way unwittingly protect the myth of meritocracy. Much has been written about the need for "safe space" when discussing charged topics of social justice. (See, e.g., Herman & Mandell, 2004; Pratt, 1998; Thompson-Grove, 2004.) For our purposes here, though, safe space can be as much a part of the problem as it is a solution. To strengthen analysis, we need to disable a mental and social safety catch that is in place to keep deeper critique from emerging. In the physical world, as with windows and guns, the safety catch protects against human error or ignorance. But in the cognitive realm, it polices "correctness" and in this way de-skills students at the very point when they need new skills to do social justice learning. Our interest is in how the effort to strengthen students' analysis of meritocracy is vexed by their fidelity to a particular notion of safety encoded in meritocracy itself.

In our classes, students of privilege try not to blame poor or working-class parents for their children's struggles and, to keep from offending anybody, they try to avoid asking frank questions about others' experiences. Those of us with class privilege might present ourselves as open-minded in order not to appear oppressive. Having made it to college, students from less-privileged backgrounds remain uneasy about social class. They tell stories of having "made it" to an elite college through the support of a wonderful mother or through college access programs. These students know many peers who did not "make it" out of their neighborhoods. These students may conform to the dominant mode of acting open-mindedly to fit in and succeed in the college environment.

In class discussions of social injustices that might expose their different positionalities, we've often had the sense that students feel pressured to appear comfortable with difference and to mask their discomfort. This makes the classroom seem like a safe community for exploring ideas, but without an analysis of meritocracy, it's actually neither safe nor intellectually challenging. Most immediately, students affirm that we're all here (at these selective institutions) now and in that sense it's a level playing field. Students often appeared to be in the grasp of the notion of meritocracy, but resist closely examining it.

The Trouble With the Teachable Moment

A *teachable moment* is an instance in a classroom when a student spontaneously and unexpectedly raises a hot or difficult issue. Such moments invite or even demand immediate attention. In our classrooms, teachable moments arise when students feel pressure to act open-mindedly in relation to conditions such as how individuals gain access to social and economic rewards. The problem is that, although the teachable moment can appear to provide a way of responding to the constraints of acting open-mindedly, it often depends on a speedy, compressed response in which students implicitly agree to honor the authority of select voices and "correct" answers. The moment may involve the revelation of unconscious assumptions, but it is often resolved by the reestablishment of the original dynamic rather than by the unsettling work of critical analysis.

Consider this example: during a discussion of affirmative action in college admission, a student tells the story of a high-school classmate who, it was widely rumored, claimed "mixed race" status, not during high school, but on college applications as a way of gaining a competitive advantage. Tension and suspense fill the room. It's as if we can read our students' thought bubbles: *Did this classmate game the system? Does race-based decision-making unfairly deny individual merit? Is the storyteller racist?*

As teachers, how do we work with these presumptions? Do we slow down and ask students to articulate what's in their minds? Do we step back and point out connections with broader historical patterns? Do we address meritocracy directly? While considering the options, we, as facilitators, are also aware of a sense of threat and fear in the group. Although in a way it's unproductive for us as teachers to defuse this sense of threat, since it sacrifices critical thinking to the need for equilibrium, there's a strong reason to do just this; otherwise students may lose a sense of our class as a "safe space." While this need for safety is problematic, as facilitators we can't afford to ignore it since we all need some sense that where we are is safe in order to trust and risk. The pressure is on. People want to appear open-minded to preserve trust in the classroom community, but this story, which hits so close to home for many students, is anything but safe. How can you endure the college admission process and be open-minded about it? Their desire to appear open-minded gets in the way of hard and potentially rich, deep discussion of meritocracy.

Consider another example relating to younger learners with whom our students are working in their field placements. About halfway through a course on urban education, a White, middle-class, male student comments, during a discussion about college access for urban students, "My [placement] teacher asked me to tell the ninth graders about College X [our college]. So I did. But none of these students are going to College X; they can barely sit still during their music class." Following his comment there is a moment of silence. Then several students of color from working-class or poor backgrounds note that *they* are at College X; others argue for high expectations for the urban high schoolers; still others come to the speaker's defense. We try to facilitate a conversation in which we don't vilify the speaker but in which we do critically examine the implications of his claim. Exposing this claim as a "wrong answer" does not help students investigate the myth of meritocracy. Rather, it may leave students with the impression that a classmate who did not act "open-mindedly" is being "corrected."

This moment may have provoked insight for some students. But if it is not understood through more reflexive lenses, it might be interpreted simply as a warning to individuals not to "slip up," rather than as an opportunity to examine complex issues of merit and privilege.

For social justice education to work, we, as facilitators, need to create a low-fear, high-inquiry environment, especially when working with high-stakes issues. We suggest treating the teachable moment as always just one of many transparencies that, overlaid together, renders a rich text for understanding meritocracy.

"Overlaying" to Deepen Learning About Meritocracy

Breaking through the bottleneck caused by students feeling the need to act open-mindedly requires more than pointing out "wrong" thinking. Using an approach we call *overlaying*, we lay distinct, disparate stories and images of personal experience, field experience, and study over one another to catalyze fresh understandings and encourage new analyses of their qualities, gaps, and interconnections. With overlaying, each text is treated like a transparency. Unlike in a traditional biology textbook where the images are somewhat fixed, as we use this approach, each assembly of transparencies can create a new and still revisable text for inquiry.

For us, overlaying is a key facilitation tool. We use it as an ongoing part of our practice. We model and name it as a practice with our classes, coach our students to try it to bolster discussion, and affirm our students' engagement with it in oral or written formats. While our focus in this chapter is on classroom conversation, overlaying is also a useful metamodel for the kind of nuanced, critical writing we ask of our students.

By keeping the qualities and the differences of various texts (including accounts of experience) in play with one another, overlaying helps to expose the unconscious underpinnings of meritocratic ideology and encourage bolder analysis. Overlaying is a longitudinal, relational mode of reading texts, and meritocracy is a concept whose power depends on longitudinal, relational experience. Using one to access the other works because overlaying unsettles fixed ideas about how things are and helps students live with uncertainty as they work to make sense of a more complex picture of the world around them (Baxter Magolda, 2009).

When we are working with overlaying, we are all learners who are re-seeing and revising meanings. In contrast, acting open-mindedly doesn't move us and our students as effectively along in this process. (See chapter 10 for a discussion of how stepping out of the "expert stance" similarly contributes to the effectiveness of literacy educators.) As with a teachable moment, we as teachers might respond to a spontaneous event in the classroom, but an overlaying approach gets us out of crisis response mode because it gives us strategies for valuing all of the material we've got. Not only do we acknowledge all the cards on the table, as it were, but we encourage students to use the full hand in thinking through the issue or challenge. For example, in a discussion about identity, merit, and accomplishment, a White student points out that all of the summer internships she's interested in seek minority students, and a working-class student claims that people's awareness of inequality hasn't brought about change. These comments become more content-rich and useful when stacked and seen in relation to one another, to other comments, and to our readings of McIntosh's (1988/2001) "unpacking" of privilege and Lareau's (2003) analysis of class and success in school.

Let's look at a story likely familiar to other teachers of educational studies, an instance that might have occurred in the class in which the student questioned whether urban high school students could survive, as he has survived, at this liberal arts college. This is a composite rendering of many such discussions we have held in our courses over our combined 30 years of college teaching. We choose here to highlight an instance in which a student initiated the discussion because we are committed to wrapping our practice as closely as we can around students' experiences and concerns, and because we want to show what it means to be prepared as facilitators without controlling classroom discussion.

One day during a class discussion a student shares a story from field work about a teacher in an urban school speaking harshly to a student. We take this, and might even say so explicitly in class, as the first transparency. As facilitators, we note to ourselves an opening for exploring the myth of meritocracy. Although we might not articulate this connection in the moment, the capacity to recognize it is important to social justice facilitation. We do not enter class discussion with a sense that we hold the answers and wait for the moment to share them; we do enter with a kind of savvy sensitivity to openings for critical inquiry. We see this as part of the "pedagogical content knowledge" of social justice education (Shulman, 1987).

A second student asks for a definition of *harsh*, pointing out that people perceive harshness differently, and offers as an example that some adults think it's all right to spank kids (another form of "harshness") and others don't. Taking this as a second transparency means letting it affect how we consider the first statement, but not invalidating either statement. We might advise this approach in class, either at this point or later. These students' comments coexist, now in a more complex relation to one another. If this were being framed as a "teachable moment," we as facilitators might feel pressure to resolve the tension: Are people in authority—teachers, parents— meaner to poor and working-class kids than they are to middle-class or rich kids? If so, is it because they are prejudiced or ignorant or stressed? Is this the way poor and working-class kids are usually spoken to, what they know how to respond to? Maybe "these kids," according to the unspoken meritocratic story, are too "damaged" to handle better treatment (Tuck, 2009).

At this point, we might try to create a contemplative working space within which to juxtapose these difficult ideas. We could begin by describing these comments as transparencies that we can overlay; one way to do this would be to offer a metacommentary on the kind of story we seem to be telling in the class through our movement from anecdote to a call to define and contextualize a key term. For example, in some pictures of the world, these kids only get it so good; acting open-mindedly would mean accepting that or falling back on a guilty, a "survival of the fittest," or a heroic change agent mentality. Because the notion of meritocracy is so prevalent, our students' recognition of its influence on how they see others' lives and options can elicit a frightening sense of isolation and powerlessness.

We also want to consider the role of time—within a class session and over the semester—as a key factor in working with overlaying. Running out of time can actually push us to create other kinds of spaces that lend themselves to using overlays. Recognizing the potency of a given discussion for pushing students' thinking, as a class period ends we might open a Google Document to keep track of highlights of the discussion, and for students to continue working with after the class session. (In a tech-intensive class, we might encourage students to "backchannel" by commenting in real time on the Google Doc from their own laptops.) We might begin the next class by recalling as transparencies several comments from in-class and online exchanges, and invite students to add additional perspectives from readings and field experiences that shed light on the topic.

Rather than being intimidated by intensely expressed ideas, we continue to overlay; to call our students' attention to differences, uncertainties, and conflicts in relation to this "harshness" story; and to seek in all of these previously unavailable understandings. A student connects the discussion of "harshness" with a movie about "inner-city" schools in which teachers and students are rough with each other. As students talk, this transparency—about newspaper reports or a movie that portrays urban students as wild—joins the stack, and a facilitator may ask what it looks like when seen in relation to other texts. When visiting urban schools, how might different people be affected by media representations?

A student then offers that her cherished mentor in an affluent suburban high school was known to be sarcastic but still a strong student advocate. How important, then, is the teacher's tone, she asks? Maybe actions count more and students can be trusted to recognize the difference between what their teachers do and how they speak. As facilitators, we might acknowledge the complex questions raised here: How should we judge efficacy and advocacy? How much should we trust students to know who their allies are? With this transparency, another possibility becomes visible: that harsh speech seems more audible in poor schools.

This might happen next, or could occur later in the semester after a reading of Delpit: a student connects this discussion to Delpit's (1995) argument that people's experience of "harshness" in speech is linked to culturally specific ideas about the expression of relationship and power. Outside of the communal practice of overlaying, this statement might well trigger a debate about the expression of authority as culturally relative. Such a debate could quickly reintroduce the bottleneck of acting open-mindedly, as fear of saying the "wrong thing" mounts: "Maybe poor kids are more used to taking orders . . . better not say that . . ."; or, "Why are these privileged students always acting like urban kids are so fragile and sensitive?" The sense of fear and high stakes around these difficult topics is perennial; its reemergence is part of the learning process. In a class accustomed to overlaying, though, the facilitator and students are practiced at holding a number of ideas in play so that spirited debate is more likely to crystallize fresh understandings instead of driving us into a pretense of agreement or a polarized stalemate.

We've described this overlaying as happening within a single class session as well as over multiple class sessions. In either case, at the conclusion of a class session the facilitator names the process the class is engaging in and clarifies the progress made by the discussion. Sometimes we collect index cards or tweets from students capturing their learning and current questions, or set aside 10 minutes for reflective writing either that day or during the next class session about where their thinking is. Sometimes we have assigned notetakers for each class discussion who post notes with their comments. Or we ask students to continue the discussion in an online forum or to write informally about it as a step toward identifying an area of inquiry for a course paper. The issues we explore using overlays are so deeply embedded that they cannot be resolved once and for all, so we find different avenues for continuing our students' work with them.

In fact, life in and outside of classrooms continually offers up new material for working on these issues as people call on meritocracy to explain why things are as they are. Here we show how overlaying works in a second extended example, this time focusing on a college access program in an urban school. College access, once located mainly at home and in the school counselor's office, has become a broadly networked arena that looks significantly different for urban kids from how it looks for suburban kids. As social justice educators, we have a deep concern with this as an issue of meritocracy. And we recognize both a growing knowledge base and the difficulty and complexity of this work among less-privileged students such as those we work with in the following story.

The Story of S and of Us

Recently, in a course Jody taught on "Identity, Access, and Innovation in Education," most of the students did their field work as classroom assistants in a college access program for seniors in an urban high school. She and her students began by investigating the term *access*. Access is key to understanding the myth of meritocracy, which presumes that anyone who gets to the door can cross the threshold, that opportunity and access are the same. Jody began hearing and framing recurrent questions about access—based in both the field site and course readings—such as who is free to make high-stakes choices (and mistakes) and how young people of different social classes are protected (or not) from risk. Over time the class worked on treating the storylines of individual students as well as educators as transparencies that could be overlaid and reconsidered together rather than ranked.

This is how it looked in one discussion: Jody began class with the instruction, "Write about a dilemma you are experiencing in the field. Be specific about how this is playing out in your practice [as a classroom assistant]. Then share and discuss it in a small group." Voices became louder in one group, in which folks were trying to figure out what happened with a high-school student, S, who missed an appointment with an interviewer from a college. Initially the college students were shocked and offended by S's absence, but at the same time they hesitated to say it plainly because they didn't want to appear close-minded. They had judgments but didn't want to seem judgmental, especially because they understood that the high-school students didn't have the kind of access to college admissions many of them had had coming out of high school. Without recourse to overlaying, this incident might have become a high-stakes "teachable moment" with conditions unripe for deeper, slower investigation.

As this conversation spilled into the class at large, students layered in their own participation in what happened: one had scheduled the interview; another had prepped S; another worked with her on the written forms; another had discussed with S how to dress; and someone knew that S had gone to get her hair done. This created an initial stack of transparencies, suggesting a scenario in which the high-school student messed up. Jody explicitly coached students to treat the various comments and reactions in the room as overlays by keeping them in play and transparent rather than allowing one version to block out others.

As the college students expressed their frustration with S, they began considering other possible factors and interpretations, adding transparencies to the stack. Someone shared an exchange she'd had with S about not really wanting to go to a women's college (which this was); someone else remembered that the interview time was right around senior pictures, and surmised that S may have gone to get her hair done then for that reason. Because we were explicitly looking at and through a number of overlays, we noticed that an initial judgment—the "knowledge" that a hair appointment should never take priority over a college interview—reflected not truth but meritocracy in action: When "they" mess up, they support the idea that they do not know what "we" know or deserve what "we" have.

Jody's treatment of these stories as multiple transparencies helped students begin to see themselves as part of the narrative. Students began to remember and contribute, not only their different experiences with S, but also their own stories about access—their mistakes, chances missed and taken, aspirations and varying degrees of support from families and schools—and points from relevant class readings. A student recalled that when she'd missed an important application deadline, her parents had intervened on her behalf. Another recounted that her parents neither spoke English nor were experienced with bureaucracy and so hadn't been able to help when she had trouble getting SAT results reported to colleges. A third remembered an article we'd discussed earlier in the course about a teacher's struggle to get beneath her own assumptions about her students and their city, and now sympathized with that teacher's struggle (Marinell, 2008). Jody then reminded students of other frameworks about how identity shapes "access," such as Minow's commentary on "the difference that difference makes" (1990) and Markus's (2008) work with young people's identities as students.

Using overlaying made overlaps and gaps across our comments visible, and this prompted new questions that Jody and her students raised, both then and later in the semester: Who gets to decide who has and who deserves "access"? Who gets to make mistakes that are safety-netted? What is our role as mentors (who are also learners)? These kinds of questions helped students make connections and locate new areas for analysis. We captured specific questions generated this way in various formats, such as silent blackboard discussion, informal course posts, and papers. And Jody guided her students to construct course papers and design units for their placements that reached for complexity rather than conclusion. In this sense, a foundational concept for us is Freire's (1998) "unfinishedness," which doesn't mean being lax or imprecise about analysis, but that we aim to yield up greater clarity about better questions.

Over time this process of questioning and overlaying helps students grasp that, while unexamined meritocracy would lead to interpretations and action steps ("motivate" poor youth to attend college; accept "no excuses" from the youth or from their teachers and mentors; "close the achievement gap"), a more nuanced understanding troubled these certainties. Rather than reacting to the threat of judging S by retreating into acting open-mindedly, we collectively held on to those stories and deliberately added others until new pictures and interpretations began to emerge. In this way overlaying can be a strategy for "accessing" a richer, more complex understanding and a stronger platform for action.

Conclusion: Teachers and Students as Social Justice Learners

Teaching for understanding of meritocracy requires dialogue—public inquiry. This kind of dialogue requires much of facilitators. We advocate going beyond "teachable moments" to explore meritocracy in our classrooms through the practice of overlaying. Overlaying is a tool to facilitate discussions in which people risk and withstand disclosure and discomfort. Layering and reading through transparencies reassures students that their stories will neither be left out nor dominate classroom analyses; rather, we can both own and release our diverse perspectives. This alleviates the pressure for students to act open-mindedly and, as a result, frees all of us to grapple with the ways meritocracy disadvantages some and privileges others. It helps us bear the uncertainty of re-seeing/revising stories and imagining new questions, connections, and possibilities. As an analytic form, overlaying runs counter to meritocracy, rooted, as the latter is, in ways of knowing that appear complete and "rigorous."

We want to offer some specific suggestions for people who wish to adapt this idea of overlaying to their own contexts. We remind readers of constructivist teaching strategies, such as asking students to do brief reflective writing or share in pairs, that are focused on guiding students to explore their perspectives and listen actively to others' perspectives. We think the issue at hand is not creating more of these strategies but clarifying the intention we bring to the ones we already have. To that end, we offer these ideas for putting overlaying into practice:

- Suspend the inclination to wrap up an issue and instead use strategies to stay with the process.
- Look to pile up ideas rather than sift, sort, and rank them.
- Name the various and sometimes competing perspectives on the table.
- Ask students to do a group form of active listening, asking each other questions that will help to reveal more of the meaning behind a comment.
- Model ways of responding and encourage students to respond in ways that reveal the sources and implications of the ideas we're exploring.
- Rethink how you position conflict in discussion. Teachable moments often move us into a kind of intimacy, but we can also create space by resisting the tendency for two conflicting ideas to become an opposition that has to be resolved. Instead, invite students to use the differences to ignite more perspectives.
- Ask questions that frame and reframe the issue by using different ideas as lenses, and explicitly recognize and value students' responses when they keep this intellectual work going.

- Bear in mind that conversation of this type is a collective art and experience, regardless of whether the people in the room are conscious of this at any given moment. This can help the facilitator attend to the relationships across perspectives and ideas rather than to any single idea.

Recently a student shared with Jody a frustration. She wanted to teach math because she loved math for its own sake; to her, issues such as understanding students' cultures in the context of "meritocracy" were a distraction. The practice of overlaying is a promising approach because it doesn't ask people to set aside what they see as their core priority, but at the same time it doesn't settle with that priority either. Instead, we stack stories about the challenges that exist for students learning math. So, one transparency might have to do with students as English-language learners; another might concern fears around math, linked to prior experience; still another might be the story of how her own accessing of the topic gives her power to help others, including those who don't arrive at it as she did. We believe this approach offers a pathway for teachers to work *with* learners rather than *correct* them, to legitimize their priorities and remix these with other stories. This makes meritocracy visible because it shows that there isn't just one scale of value, one set of doors and keys. Overlaying helps us expose the meritocratic idea that certain people's experience of education, in this case math learning, is more creditable than others' and should set the bar.

Just this week, a colleague e-mailed Alice to ask for guidance on how to work with his undergraduate students in a course in mathematics pedagogy. Some students had made controversial statements about race and class to which he imagined other students would object. He recognized the potential "messiness," as he said, of the exchange and sought a way to address it. Alice proposed overlaying as a way to work with his students; for teachers not deeply steeped in diversity work and perhaps accustomed to more cut-and-dried teaching techniques, this offers a specific pathway for creating "safe enough" space for dialogue. We hope that sharing this framework and practice of overlaying will help our colleagues and students center, address, and stick with hard topics such as meritocracy, not instead of but in direct relation to content such as mathematics.

We continue to see our own teaching practices/classrooms as potential spaces of evolution within which to step out of meritocratic ways of thinking and feeling and into a place where we can imagine with our students what the world looks like from other angles and, indeed, what other worlds we might create.

Note

1. In classic biology textbooks, a picture of a bodily system, for example, the circulatory system, is inked into one transparent sheet, or page. Next to it in the book would be an inked sketch of another system, say the respiratory system, and so forth. Each transparency, then, depicts a single system and can be looked at independently, or the transparencies can be overlaid and viewed together to represent the interconnections among the systems.

References

Baxter Magolda, M. B. (2009). *Authoring your life: Developing an internal voice to navigate life's challenges.* Sterling, VA: Stylus.

Delpit, L. (1995). *Other people's children.* New York: Teachers College Press.

Freire, P. (1998). *Pedagogy of freedom: Ethics, democracy, and civic courage.* Lanham, MD: Rowman & Littlefield.

Herman, L., & Mandell, A. (2004). *From teaching to mentoring: Principles and practice, dialogue and life in adult education.* London, UK: RoutledgeFalmer.

Howard, G. R. (1999). *We can't teach what we don't know: White teachers, multiracial schools.* New York: Teachers College Press.

Lareau, A. (2003). *Unequal childhoods: Class, race, and family life.* Berkeley: University of California Press.

Marinell, W. H. (2008). Voices inside schools: Capturing authenticity, transforming perception—One teacher's efforts to improve her students' performance by challenging their impressions of self and community. *Harvard Educational Review, 78*(3), 529.

Markus, H. R. (2008). Identity matters: Ethnicity, race, and the American dream. In M. Minow, R. Schweder, & H. R. Markus (Eds.), *Just schools: Pursuing equality of societies of difference* (pp. 63–98). New York: Russell Sage Foundation.

McIntosh, P. (1988/2001). "White privilege: Unpacking the invisible knapsack." In P. Rothenberg (Ed.), *Race, class, and gender in the United States: An integrated study.* New York: Worth.

Minow, M. (1990). *Making all the difference: Inclusion, exclusion, and American law.* Ithaca, NY, and London, UK: Cornell University Press.

Oakes, J., & Lipton, M. (2003). Schooling: Wrestling with history and tradition. In *Teaching to change the world* (2nd ed.) (pp. 2–39). New York: McGraw-Hill.

Pratt, M. L. (1998). Arts of the contact zone. In V. Zamel & R. Spack (Eds.), *Negotiating academic literacies: Teaching and learning across languages and cultures* (pp. 171–185). London, UK: Lawrence Erlbaum Associates.

Shulman, L. (1987). Knowledge and teaching: Foundations of the new reform. *Harvard Educational Review, 57*(1), 1–22.

Thompson-Grove, G. (2004). Foreword. In D. Allen & T. Blythe, *The facilitator's book of questions: Tools for looking together at student and teacher work* (pp. xi–xiii). New York: Teacher's College Press.

Tuck, E. (2009). Suspending damage: A letter to communities. *Harvard Educational Review, 79*(3), 409.

ABOUT THE CONTRIBUTORS

Athene Bell is the district literacy specialist in Manassas City Public Schools, where she works with teachers and students to support literacy initiatives within the school district. For 19 years Athene taught English to adolescents in grades six through eight. Currently, she is a doctoral student specializing in literacy at George Mason University. Her areas of interest include the study of visual and multimodal literacy among adolescents, teacher education, and formative design methodology. Athene's current work uses multi-configured reading interventions within classroom contexts to better understand how high school English-language learners learn to read in English.

Mollie V. Blackburn is an associate professor of teaching and learning at the Ohio State University, where she co-coordinates the sexuality studies program. She has published in journals such as *Reading Research Quarterly*, *Research in the Teaching of English*, and *Teachers College Record*, among others. She is the author of *Interrupting Hate: Homophobia in Schools and What Literacy Can Do About It* and the coeditor of *Acting Out!: Combating Homophobia Through Teacher Activism*, which received the Phillip C. Chinn Book Award, the Richard A. Meade Award, and the American Library Association's CHOICE Book Award. Her scholarship has received the Queer Studies special interest group of the American Educational Research Association's award for a body of work and the Alan C. Purves Award for an RTE article deemed rich with implications for classroom practice.

Warren J. Blumenfeld is an associate professor in the School of Education at Iowa State University in Ames, Iowa, specializing in multicultural and international curriculum studies, and lesbian, gay, bisexual, transgender, and queer studies. He is the author of *Warren's Words: Smart Commentary on Social Justice* and *AIDS and Your Religious Community*; coeditor of *Investigating Christian Privilege and Religious Oppression in the United States*, *Readings for Diversity and Social Justice*, and *Butler Matters: Judith Butler's Impact on Feminist and Queer Studies*; editor of *Homophobia: How We All Pay the Price*;

coauthor of *Looking at Gay and Lesbian Life*; and coresearcher and coauthor of *2010 State of Higher Education for Lesbian, Gay, Bisexual, and Transgender People.*

Paul R. Carr is associate professor in the departments of Sociology and Interdisciplinary Studies at Lakehead University (Orillia), Canada. He is coeditor of several books, including *The Great White North? Exploring Whiteness, Privilege and Identity in Education* (2007), *Doing Democracy: Striving for Political Literacy and Social Justice* (2008), and *The Phenomenon of Obama and the Agenda for Education: Can Hope Audaciously Trump Neo-liberalism?* (2011), and recently authored *Does Your Vote Count? Democracy and Critical Pedagogy* (2010). He is a member of the Executive Board of the Comparative and International Education Society of Canada, codirector of the Global Doing Democracy Research Project, and a member of the editorial board of several journals, including the *Journal of Critical Educational Policy Studies*, the *International Journal of Critical Pedagogy*, and *Canadian and International Education.*

Jody Cohen is a faculty member in the Bryn Mawr/Haverford Education Program whose interests include urban education, multicultural education, and education for ecological literacy, with a focus on linkages among identity, equity, and schooling. She has been deeply involved in the evolution of Bryn Mawr's 360°, a program that involves professors and students in an interdisciplinary cluster of courses focused on a shared theme, and recently she contributed to the 360° "Perspectives on Sustainability." Jody is a long-time teacher of writing, mentor to two Posses at Bryn Mawr (the national Posse Program supports young people selected on a leadership scholarship to attend college), and a cofounder of the Social Justice Partnership Program, a student-driven initiative that supports dialogue about diversity and justice in the college community. Jody was a founding member of Research for Action, an educational research organization based in Philadelphia and committed to doing research and program evaluation seeking to increase equity in education. Her research, presentations, and publications focus on community-based partnerships between colleges and urban schools and on the impact of curricular and cocurricular programming on undergraduates' experiences and conceptions of intellectual community and diversity.

Curt Dudley-Marling teaches courses in language and literacy in the Lynch School of Education at Boston College. He was a special education teacher for seven years before earning his PhD from the University of Wisconsin–Madison. In the early 1990s Curt took a leave from his professorial duties to teach third grade in the North York (Ontario) Public Schools. This experience provided the basis for his book, *Living With Uncertainty: The Messy Reality of Classroom Practice*, which received the James N. Britton Award for Inquiry in the English Language Arts. He has published more than 100 articles, book chapters, and books focusing on struggling readers and students with disabilities. He is also a former chair of the Elementary Section of the National Council of Teachers of English (NCTE) and former coeditor of the NCTE journal *Language Arts*. His current scholarly interests include the social construction of learning failures, the power of "high expectation" curricula, classroom discussion, and disability studies.

Marriam Ewaida is a middle-school literacy coach and a former secondary English/ESOL teacher. She received her BA in English literature and her BEd in English and ESOL from the University of British Columbia in Canada. She later went on to complete her master's in curriculum and instruction with a focus on literacy from George Mason University in Fairfax, Virginia. Marriam is currently a PhD candidate in literacy and educational leadership at George Mason University. She is committed to studying at-risk immigrant youth and their literacy experiences in America, with a focus on social justice and equity. She is also fascinated by multimodal methods of engaging English-language learners in writing and intends to continue her work with Through Students' Eyes.

Paul C. Gorski is an associate professor of integrative studies in New Century College at George Mason University, where he teaches in the social justice concentration and the education concentration. He is the founder of EdChange and the Multicultural Pavilion, a website that has won more than a dozen awards internationally for its contribution to multicultural education scholarship and practice. Paul is the author of *Multicultural Education and the Internet: Intersections and Integrations* (McGraw-Hill, 2004) and coeditor (with Roberta Ahlquist and Theresa Montaño) of *Assault on Kids: How Hyper-Accountability, Corporatization, Deficit Ideologies, and Ruby Payne Are Destroying Our Schools* (Peter Lang, 2011). He has written more than 50 articles and chapters on topics such as economically just schooling, deficit ideology, animal rights, and multicultural teacher education for publications, including *Intercultural Education*, *Teachers College Record*, *Rethinking Schools*, *The Journal of Critical Animal Studies*, *Educational Leadership*, and *Teaching* *and Teacher Education*. He serves on the boards of directors of the International Association for Intercultural Education and the Institute for Humane Education.

James Harmon teaches English in the Euclid City School District just outside Cleveland, Ohio, and is codirector and cofounder of throughstudents eyes.org. He received his BFA in photojournalism from Rochester Institute of Technology and his MEd in computer uses in education at Cleveland State University. Having served as a city schoolteacher for 16 years, he was recognized as an Apple Distinguished Educator in 2007 and became a Google Certified Teacher in 2008. He is also an adjunct teacher educator in educational technology at Baldwin-Wallace College in Berea, Ohio, and has authored and coauthored several literacy-focused articles, presentations, and successful grants in relation to his work with Through Students' Eyes and the impact of iPads on student literacy. Jim serves as editor of *School-University Partnerships*.

Stephanie Jones began doodling as a young girl suffering through boring classes and made her way back to doodling as a researcher trying to produce scholarship that might change the world in some small way. Fortunately, she met James F. Woglom, her artist collaborator, who transforms her doodles into brilliant pieces of art. Stephanie has a lot to doodle about as associate professor at The University of Georgia. She teaches undergraduate and graduate courses on place-based teaching for social change, feminist theory and pedagogy, social class and poverty, early childhood education, and literacy. Stephanie's scholarly interests sit at the intersections of social class, gender, place, bodies, and critical literacies, and her recent publications include "Negotiating Mothering Identities: Ethnographic and Intergenerational Insights to Social Class and Gender in a High-Poverty U.S. Context" in *Gender and Education*; "Making Sense of Injustices in a Classed World: Working-Poor Girls' Discursive Practices and Critical Literacies" in *Pedagogies: An International Journal*; and "Speaking of Bodies in Justice-Oriented, Feminist Teacher Education" (with Hilary Hughes-Decatur) in the *Journal of Teacher Education*. She serves on editorial review boards for *Language Arts*, *English Teaching: Practice and Critique*, *Reading and Writing Quarterly*, and the *Journal of Adolescent and Adult Literacy*.

Alice Lesnick serves as senior lecturer in education and director of the Bryn Mawr/Haverford Education Program, where she received the Rosalyn R.

Schwartz Teaching Award in 2004. A faculty associate of the Institute for Writing and Thinking at Bard College since 1993 and a former preschool, elementary, middle-, and high-school teacher, Alice studies collaborative and dialogic learning, processes of change, and new directions in social justice education, including via partnership with an early learning initiative in northern Ghana. Her most recent publications include "Education Is Life Itself: Biological Evolution as a Model for Human Learning" in *Evolution: Education and Outreach* (with Paul Grobstein, 2011) and "Teaching Intersections: The Surprise of Gift-Giving and -Getting in the Cultural Commons" in the *Journal of Curriculum and Pedagogy* (with Anne Dalke, 2011).

Darren E. Lund is a professor in the Faculty of Education at the University of Calgary, where his research examines social justice activism. His most recent books are *The Great White North? Exploring Whiteness, Privilege, and Identity in Education* and *Doing Democracy: Striving for Political Literacy and Social Justice* (both coedited with P. Carr), and *Duoethnography: Dialogic Methods for Social, Health, and Educational Research* (coedited with J. Norris and R. D. Sawyer). Darren was named a Reader's Digest National Leader in Education and won the 2012 Distinguished Scholar-Activist Award from the *Critical Educators for Social Justice*, American Educational Research Association.

Megan R. Lynch is an English as a Second Language teacher at Osbourn Park High School in Manassas, Virginia. She earned her bachelor's degree in secondary education from Indiana University and her master's degree in instruction and curriculum from the University of Virginia. She is currently a doctoral student at George Mason University and is interested in ESL policy, education leadership, adequacy funding, at-risk youth, and student achievement.

Edward M. Olivos is an associate professor in the Department of Education Studies at the University of Oregon. He received his PhD in education jointly from San Diego State University and Claremont Graduate University. His research interests include Latino/as and education, bicultural parent involvement, immigration and education, policy studies, bilingual education, and critical pedagogy. He is the author of the *The Power of Parents: A Critical Perspective of Bicultural Parent Involvement in Public Schools* (2006) and coeditor of *Bicultural Parent Engagement: Advocacy and Empowerment*

(2011). Prior to joining the University of Oregon, Edward worked at California State University, Dominguez Hills. He is a former San Diego elementary school teacher, where he taught in bilingual education settings for more than 10 years.

Nana Osei-Kofi is associate professor and director of the social justice studies certificate program in the School of Education at Iowa State University. Her scholarship focuses on cultural studies in education, critical and feminist theories of education, the politics of higher education, and arts-based inquiry. Journals in which her work has appeared include *Discourse: Studies of the Cultural Politics of Education, Equity & Excellence in Education,* and *Race, Ethnicity and Education.* She has also served on the editorial board of the *Review of Higher Education* and is currently a member of the editorial board of *Feminist Formations.*

Jeff Sapp is a professor of education at California State University, Dominguez Hills. He has been a frequent contributor to *Teaching Tolerance* magazine and is an associate editor for *Multicultural Perspectives,* the official journal of The National Association of Multicultural Education (NAME). Jeff is a well-known curriculum specialist and writer and has written social justice curriculum for such organizations as the Simon Wiesenthal Center, the Museum of Tolerance, the Southern Poverty Law Center, Teaching Tolerance, the Civil Rights Memorial Center, the Anti-Defamation League, and human relations organizations throughout Southern California. His children's book, *Rhinos & Raspberries: Tolerance Tales for the Early Grades,* published by the Southern Poverty Law Center, won the Golden Lamp Award, the Association of Educational Publishers' highest honor.

David Stovall, author of the foreword, is an associate professor of Educational Policy Studies and African American Studies at the University of Illinois at Chicago. His scholarship investigates four areas: Critical Race Theory, concepts of social justice in education, the relationship between housing and education, and the relationship between schools and community stakeholders. In the attempt to bring theory to action, he has spent the last twelve years working with community organizations and schools to develop curriculum that address issues of social justice. His current work has led him to become a member of the Greater Lawndale/Little Village School of Social Justice High School design team, which opened in the fall of 2005, where he also serves as a volunteer social studies teacher. Furthering his work with communities, students, and teachers, Dr. Stovall works with a collective of college professors in California, Arizona, and New York who teach high school courses in addition to their duties and responsibilities as university faculty. Dr. Stovall received his undergraduate degree and PhD from the University of Illinois at Urbana-Champaign.

James F. Woglom, an artist and educator, received an associate's degree in fine arts from the Fashion Institute of Technology, a bachelor's degree with a double major in studio arts and art history and criticism from the State University of New York at Stony Brook, and a master's degree in art education from the University of Georgia. He is currently working toward completing a PhD in art education at the University of Georgia.

Kristien Zenkov is associate professor of literacy education at George Mason University, having previously served on the faculty of Cleveland State University after earning his PhD from the University of Wisconsin–Madison. He is the author of more than 70 articles and book chapters and books focusing on diverse youths' perspective on school, teacher education, literacy and language arts pedagogy and curricula, and professional development schools. Kristien is the codirector of Through Students' Eyes, an international photo elicitation project that asks youth to document with photographs and writing what they believe are the purposes of school. He is the former codirector of the Master of Urban Secondary Teaching (MUST) Program—an award-winning urban and social justice–focused master's licensure option. He also chairs the AERA Professional Development Schools Research SIG, is senior editor of *School-University Partnerships*, and is a member of the editorial boards of the *Journal of Teacher Education*, *Urban Education*, and *Equity and Excellence in Education*. His areas of teaching, research, and activism expertise include literacy education, teacher education in intensified settings, visual sociology and research methods, social justice education, portfolio assessment, and conflict resolution in education.